T0294101

THE DIALECTICAL DANCER

THE DIALECTICAL DANCER

a simple tale

LARRY ZOLF

Introduction by
PETER C. NEWMAN

Exile Editions

*Publishers of singular
Fiction, Poetry, Translation, Drama, and Nonfiction*

2010

Library and Archives Canada Cataloguing in Publication

Zolf, Larry
  The dialectical dancer : a simple tale / Larry Zolf ;
Peter C. Newman, introduction.

ISBN 978-1-55096-134-8

1. Zolf, Larry. 2. Journalists--Canada--Biography. 3. Authors, Canadian
English)--20th century--Biography. 4. Canadian Broadcasting Corporation
--Biography. I. Title.

PN4913.Z64A3 2010   070.92   C2010-905107-6

Text and Cover Design and Composition by Digital ReproSet
Typeset in Book Antiqua and Optima fonts at the Moons of Jupiter Studios

The publisher would like to acknowledge the financial assistance of
the Canada Council for the Arts and the Ontario Arts Council.

 Conseil des Arts   Canada Council
du Canada   for the Arts

 ONTARIO ARTS COUNCIL
CONSEIL DES ARTS DE L'ONTARIO

The publisher would also like to acknowledge the support of
The Peter Paul Foundation, Murray Frum, and Dennis Mills.

Published in Canada in 2010 by Exile Editions Ltd.
144483 Southgate Road 14 – Gen Del
Holstein, Ontario, N0G 2A0
info@exileeditions.com ~ www.ExileEditions.com
Printed in Canada at Friesens

Canadian Sales Distribution:
McArthur & Company, c/o Harper Collins, 1995 Markham Road
Toronto, ON, M1B 5M8 ~ toll free: 1 800 387 0117

U.S. Sales Distribution:
Independent Publishers Group, 814 North Franklin Street, Chicago, IL, 60610
www.ipgbook.com ~ toll free: 1 800 888 4741

Once again, to my "lovely Greek lady"
Barbara Diakopolou, I dedicate this book,
with all my love.

My thanks
to Barry Callaghan,
my friend at the beginning,
and my very good friend, at the end.

Contents

INTRODUCTION

Larry Zolf has been Canada's most compelling Court Jester –
not in any way a clown but the Court Jester as in its Shake-
spearean version, one of those street-wise minor players who
were the most sophisticated of stage actors, subtly delivering
uncomfortable truths disguised as quips and fables. One
example occurred in 1340 when the French fleet was destroyed
in the Battle of Sluys by the English. The official Jester to King
Phillip VI of France informed His Majesty of this catastrophe
by doing a little victory dance, then mischievously telling the
monarch that "the English sailors didn't even have the
courage to jump into the water, like our brave French!"

Larry Zolf has played that demanding role for most of his
highly productive life, on television, in person and in his
books, and now most particularly in this memoir that so eloquently chronicles his childhood, his youth, and his forma-
tive adult years as a *wunderkind*, a declaimer, a voyeur, a tribal
strategist, a militarist in short pants, a high school dummy, a
burgeoning college genius, a young adult aficionado of cun-
nilingus, a television journalist who refused to suck up to anyone, who delighted in ideologues he disdained, who taught
power how to be comedic and taught comics how to play with
power. Some small minds in power feared him. Men of real
force and presence invited him into their private worlds.
Want to know who was the only journalist that Pierre Trudeau
took seriously, or who Conrad Black regularly met with and
with whom he most enjoyed matching wits and witticisms?
It was Zolf, the self-declared Jaded Observer, the only political

civilian who ever mounted a public campaign to become a member of the Canadian Senate. He was not only after the lucre but felt (rightly) that he alone could have livened up that House of wasted oxygen.

As it was, he often brought news of the troubled world to Ottawa's regal Court, at the same time as he was conveying the inside stories of the Court's intrigues and machinations to those beyond its battlements who had to deal with the discomforts of being cast in the daily reality programs that took place outside the television box.

Larry was in the Court, but not of it.

Any reigning monarch with a pinch of *chutzpah* realized that he had little to lose by allowing at least one Court Jester into his orbit. The Jester's professional ambivalence and daily tightrope act could be exploited, his cunning and pretend obsequiousness turned to useful pursuits. But Zolf knew exactly what he was doing, being the always pleasant but in everybody's-face House Jew, his Cyranoesque *schnozz* marching before him. His charm disarmed his critics; his wisdom kept them enthralled.

If you knew anything about the roots of the man, he could only have been a product of North Winnipeg. That mid-Canadian metropolis, known mainly for having two seasons – winter and August – is in reality a highly forgiving place, holding down the territory between East and West that hardcore Torontonians are pleased to call "fly-over country" – since it is situated roughly halfway between Toronto's Courtyard Café and LA's Polo Lounge, that at one time, it was alleged, seated neither Blacks nor brunettes.

Larry grew up performing all the rites of passage demanded of a North Winnipeg Jewish teenager, including a school where he collided with Anglo-Saxon teachers who were two-fisted in their furies, a madcap rabbi of equal fury, a sojourn at a Zionist summer camp where he played at being a British operative in Palestine and several children of the concentration camps who played poker with their "numbers," all presided over by the local Jewish patriarchs – including the ex-bootlegger Sam Bronfman – most of whom got rich during the war.

As Canada's Vienna – an empire city that lost its empire – Winnipeg once boasted more millionaires per capita than Toronto and during the booming grain trade supplied the West with its goods. The opening of the Panama Canal in 1920 terminated that function and the Manitoba metropolis became a lively ghost town, featuring abandoned yet still magnificent bank branches erected to finance that trade. Growing up in this bypassed metropolis, which practiced more than its share of anti-Semitism, Larry persevered, but eventually joined its Diaspora in Toronto, becoming one of the few truly independent voices on the Canadian Broadcasting Corporation, including its one-time flagship public affairs program, *This Hour Has Seven Days*. His most memorable appearance was on the Montreal doorstep of Tory Associate Defence Minister Pierre Sevigny, when he tried to interview him about his affair with Gerda Munsinger, his German paramour. Instead of answering, the politician hit Zolf with his cane and slammed the door. No way to treat an enquiring Court Jester.

This volume is a continuum and completion of his other works – everything Zolf has written is, subconsciously or otherwise, part of his autobiography, and that's particularly true of the current book, but there's a difference. Instead of merely recording witty tales, which he attracts like a magnet, he has gotten down to the real Larry, and how he became his own man. The members of his family are the impressionist water lilies of his life, seen, and seen again, focussed and refocussed as the light changes over the years. He both loves and hates his often maniacal father, he maintains an almost mystical bond with his mother, but what emerges in these pages – of all things – is a Court Jester, a Jaded Observer, who is that rare thing, a self-sustaining personality, a man who in his singularity has been and remains a national treasure. Enjoy.

Peter C. Newman

A PREFATORY NOTE

On Behalf of Lxxxx Zxxx, Gent.

From *The Life and Opinions of Tristram Shandy, Gentleman, 1759-1767*

THE INFANT *IN UTERO*

It was demonstrated however very satisfactorily, that such a ponderous mass of heterogeneous matter could not be congested and conglomerated to the nose, whilst the infant was *in utero*, without destroying the statical balance of the *foetus*, and throwing it plump upon its head *[eds. note: aborted]* nine months before the time—

—The opponents granted the theory—they denied the consequences.

The logicians stuck closer to the point more than any of the classes of the *literati*;—they began and ended with the word *Nose*; and had it not been for a *petitio principii*, which one of the ablest of them ran his head against in the beginning of the combat, the whole controversy had been settled at once.

A nose, argued the logician, cannot bleed without blood—and not only blood—but blood circulating in it to supply the phenomenon with a succession of drops— (a stream being but a quicker succession of drops, that is included, said he)—Now death, continued the logician, being nothing but the stagnation of the blood—

I deny the definition—Death is the separation of the soul from the body, said his antagonist. Then we don't agree about our weapons, said the logician—Then there is an end of the dispute, replied the antagonist.

If the dispute proved anything, it proved the nose was neither true nor false.

— *STERNE*

The quotations interspersed as a running commentary throughout my story are taken from that great experimental English novel from the eighteenth century, *The Life and Opinions of Tristram Shandy, Gentleman, 1759-1767*, by the Irish-born Laurence Sterne. It is a novel in which time has been shuffled, upended, aborted... and space has been extended or deleted in a seemingly arbitrary way. The same habit of mind may be reflected in my story because over the years, I have grown into a kinship with Mr. Shandy, who, in his dedication to that august political personage of his time, the Right Honourable Mr. Pitt, Prime Minister, said, "I live in a constant endeavour to fence against the infirmities of ill-health, and other evils of life, by mirth; being firmly persuaded that every time a man smiles, — but much more so, when he laughs, it adds something to this fragment of life."

I might say, that in Sterne-like spirit, I recommended mirth as a fence against the infirmities of ill health in politics, that is to say loss of office, to the Right Honourable Pierre Elliott Trudeau, Prime Minister. A telling moment, a fragment of my life, as the reader shall discover.

Larry Zolf

THE ZHOLFS OF ZASTAVIA

In the late 1880s, Joshua Falek Zholf, my father, lived in Russia in Zastavia, a ghetto village just inside the Polish border, a village under the writ of Czar Nicholas II. It was a *shtetl* of *schnorrers* and *shadchans*, peddlers and small tradesmen, men who were known to quote from the Holy Book, "*Tov shem meshemon tov*" ("We were better off without the trains"), poor village people of plain tastes who were loyal to their cultural traditions, the *tfillin*, the *T'hilim*, and particularly the craft of *melamed*, the teaching of the Bible to their children.

Joshua Leib, father to Joshua Falek, had wanted to be a dirt farmer, he had wanted to reach down and take hold of the earth in his hands. "Blessed is he who has earth in his fist." He had even owned a saddle and ridden a horse, and he had almost managed to qualify as a peasant worker, but czarist law, if it was strictly imposed, and in Zastavia it was, forbade Jews from engaging in serious farming, and so – as an ultra-Orthodox Jew – he had eked out a meagre living by teaching the young *shtetl* children Hebrew and the proper practice of their rituals, their religion. "Blessed is he who has the thorn of the word in his heart." As such a teacher, he and his wife, a woman with a club foot, had led a hard-scrabble life, barely able to feed their four sons.

Since he was not only ultra-Orthodox but a rigorous believer, he thought of socialism and Zionism as Jewish heresies, abominations, and so he had sent Joshua Falek, his son and my father, to a place removed from such insidious influences, a big rabbinical seminary in the city of Brest-Litovsk. This *cheder*, this seminary school, had under its roof a rabbi of renown, and Joshua Leib believed that this rabbi would make my father into a scholar, a decoder of conundrums, and, eventually, a rabbi, too. Appropriately, Joshua Falek, the student, wore a caftan, the fringes of his *tallis-kot'n* sticking out, side curls, and the beard of the Chassidim. Though restless by temperament, he sat down and easily and effortlessly mastered the lessons of the *yeshiva* seminary, he mastered the kind of dialogue with God that is sealed in candle wax. He did this during a troubling pre-1917 period when candles were being burnt at both ends, a profoundly revolutionary time, when he often smelled flesh burning in the ditches and barns. History had gone cross-eyed, clocks were wound down, clocks were adjusted, Karl Marx nursing his boils here, and Theodor Hertzl boiling with resentment there, promised a future founded – independent of each other – on an inevitable and acceptable increment of deaths. Lenin was moving inexorably east towards St. Petersburg's Finland Railway Station. At the same time, Czar Nicholas' fierce horsemen, his Black Hundreds, were looting and pillaging the *shtetls*, slaughtering Jews. As well, doltish Polish and Ukrainian peasants had grown churlish, and were turning on their Jewish neighbours. And there – there – saying his Orthodox prayers, looming over them all, a spectral figure for his time, the czarina's crazy bedkick and spiritual advisor, Rasputin.

Joshua Falek Zholf was no supporter of such a czar. He wanted to be rid of him. He had rejoiced at Japan's victory over Russia in 1905. He was sure the czar would soon be toppled. Being of a restless mind, he would sneak late at night into his Orthodox seminary, and then into his *yeshiva* cell where he would read by candlelight all the forbidden socialist (Prud'homme) and Zionist (Ze'ev Jabotinsky) pamphlets.

Socialism, a young man's dream of one for all and all for one in a dialectically driven proletariat, became part of my father's commitment to Russia, his motherland. No matter the Jew-haters and Jew-baiters, Russia was his motherland. Loyalty. To something deep. Roots, he had roots. Maybe not a farmer's roots but his family had been in Zastavia for generations. He felt he owed the fulfillment of his proletarian dream as a debt to Russia, but certainly not to the czar, not to that Jew-baiting autocratic regime. And if his motherland were to fail him, to betray him by disintegrating, by succumbing to brute power at the end of a gun, he believed he then owed a dream to himself, the dream of going to Palestine or America. This dream made the frustration and misery of his life, the humiliations of being a Jew, bearable.

Then came the outbreak of World War I (1914-1918). Czarist Russia entered this mechanised war on horseback, as an ally of Britain and France. Great military fronts, East and West, were formed. Trenches were dug in the earth, and also in the mind and spirit. Men who lived by the sword died by the machine gun. Russia now needed more and more manpower and wasn't purse-mouthed or fussy about where she got her foot soldiers. Even Jews became eligible cannon fodder.

Maybe they were suddenly eligible, but Jews did not support the war of the hated czar. Young Jewish men chopped off fingers and toes to avoid being drafted. Still, no matter their missing digits, thousands of Orthodox Chassidic Jews were drafted into the czarist army.

Joshua Falek Zholf, the son who was of draft age in the family, declined to fight in defence of Czar Nicholas II. He shaved his beard, and dressed himself in peasant's garb. He stared at himself in a small mirror of polished tin, and said, "How could I ever fail such a nose?"

"Nihil me paenitet hujus nasi,"—that is, "My nose has been the making of me."

"Nec est cur paeniteat,"—that is, "How the deuce should such a nose fail?"

— S<small>TERNE</small>

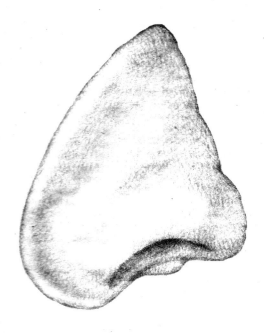

SOLDIER Z

For almost two years, my father lived in hiding in the dense local woods, scrounging for food and shelter. Months passed. The seasons unwound. Sometimes he worked with a hand scythe in the fields and, on occasion, he ventured into town to work in small factories. Though he had our family nose, the *schnozz*, he somehow kept his Jewish identity hidden. Gangs of czarist police were roaming the country roads, punishing Jews who had refused to lay down their bodies in support of the czarist war. Once again, the czar's horsemen, the Black Hundreds, were on the gallop, raiding villages and *shtetls*, raping, looting and killing as if they were living amidst a moment of reckless czarist triumph – even as the czar's armies were collapsing, his foot soldiers dying, even as the German cavalry, cannons, and mechanised infantry advanced.

Zastavia, in 1916, fell into German hands, as did a great swath of czarist Russia, a Russia in upheaval.

In St. Petersburg, Rasputin had been shot several times and then thrown into the icy canal and told to swim for home, while in Moscow, social democracy had reared its unruly head under Alexander Kerensky, forcing the czar, to bring the *Duma* – the parliament – together at a time when the Bolsheviks said that they planned to take Russia out of the war.

In his draft-dodging days, Joshua Falek Zholf had easily run into the Bolsheviks. Activist Jews, men and women, were at the very forefront of the revolution. He was impressed by these Jews, men like Leon Trotsky. Jews were shaping the new history. Joshua Falek Zholf was tempted to join the Trotskyites, but, committed as he was to the preservation of Jewish conventions and Jewish cultural life, he had less confidence in the Bolsheviks... they were not the answer to his or the Jewish people's distress. Dreamer he might be, but he knew that no one had an immediate answer to the Jewish people's social and political problems. Except maybe Kerensky. Kerensky was different. Kerensky intended to amputate the czar, and then continue the war against Germany.

Joshua Falek Zholf consulted his conscience; his conscience told him what to do.

Kerensky represented new prospects for Russia's Jewry: he stood openly for the equality and freedom of the Jewish people. No more would my father be a hapless draft-dodger, playing hippity-hop from house to house, outwitting the local Jew baiters and snitches, the czarist police. Kerensky was going to make Joshua Falek Zholf a free man. Russia was going to be a country where my father could live and raise a family, be a proud Jew and a proud Russian at the same time. At least, that was his belief. In February 1917, after the Revolution, Joshua Falek Zholf came out of hiding and went to one of Alexander Kerensky's wartime recruiting offices. Not only that, he had, inside his peasant blouse, a personal handwritten manifesto. It read:

To the Russian Revolutionary Army
Dear sirs:

Whereas I, Joshua Falek Zholf, have hitherto refused to shed my blood for the bloody Czar Nikolas II, enemy of my people, and whereas, the Great Revolution has freed my people and all

other peoples that inhabit Mother Russia, I today present
myself in payment of my holy debt of loyalty to the Fatherland.

As soon as the Kerensky *apparatchiks* found out he could read and write Russian, Joshua Falek Zholf was sent to an "instant" officer training school. Within a month, he could click his heels, fire pistols with both hands, and bark out commands. He was transported, this scholar in officer's clothing, to the trenches in the Eastern Front to face a German behemoth that was commanded by Paul von Hindenburg and Erich Ludendorff. During his time with the Kerensky-led army, my father saw real action many times, some of it fierce, even hand-to-hand, but there were even longer periods spent in silence and stagnation, living like a mole in the trenches. A dank stillness. A stasis that intimated death. And always, there was the mud, the rats, the dampness in the bones, the cold, the lack of proper food and dry clothing, the boots that wore out, the puttees that shredded.

"One day," my father once told me, "our trenches were visited by a young bearded Jewish revolutionary. He urged us to lay down our arms and walk away from the front – toward the peace, bread and freedom that he and his fellow Bolsheviks were promising.

"Some of my men wanted to do just that. I ordered them to stay put. 'A democratic Russia had to be fought for,' I said. We had to be on the same side as America – the promised land of democracy and therefore the promised land of the Jews. That Bolshevik was wrong, my son. He was a disgrace to the Jewish people. That Bolshevik was Leon Trotsky!" [A name I was to hear again and again, particularly from my father, who found Trotsky's later exploits as commander-in-chief of the Red Army truly heroic, and his assassination by Joseph Stalin pure barbarism.]

Then my father was captured by the Germans. He became a POW.

"The Germans were kind to us," my father said. "They found out I had some rabbinical training and put me in charge of seeing to it that the Jewish prisoners-of-war got proper kosher food. It was crazy. Like a *shochet*, I was. Out there in a landscape blighted by barrages, among fields of charred tree stumps, I slaughtered cattle and checked the insides of chickens for disease. I acted like a proper ritual slaughterer, and the German prison camp commandant gave me an 'A' for a grade."

Then, as a battle tactic, the Germans released their Russian prisoners-of-war, letting them spill by the wandering, starving thousands back into the East, especially into the Polish borderlands, which clogged up Kerensky's – given the civil war that was raging – tenuous lines of communication. This tactic also played into the hands of Vladimir Lenin – who, by then, had passed through St. Petersburg's Finland Station – and the Bolsheviks he and Joseph Stalin were leading; they were manoeuvring for power in Moscow. The chaos that ensued among the ranks of Kerensky's front line soldiers was matched by the anarchy in Russia's cities, towns and villages. The pits of hell had broken open, erupted. And Lenin had emerged stroking his beard, Stalin at his side.

The power and influence of the Bolsheviks ricocheted across the land. By October 1917, they had seized power in St. Petersburg. My father had made his way to Moscow and he was there when the Bolsheviks unfurled their red flag. He stood in Red Square and listened to the impassioned oratory of Stalin, the communist chief who was now in command of

Moscow. By toppling the Kerensky government, the Bolsheviks had cut my father loose from his commitments.

Meanwhile, in the Ukraine, *Hetman*, Symon Petliura, fighting the Reds for the Whites of Ukraine, was massacring hundreds of thousands of Jews. Even as dead bodies abounded, my father returned to the Zastavia *shtetl*.

By 1920, the village was occupied by the Reds, which caused Jewish self-defence vigilantes to form into groups, and my father became one of them. The tension, suspicion, small betrayals and bitterness caused by rapidly shifting loyalties and ethnic and religious animosities did not soon go away. Hunger and starvation ravaged the village. The Reds, fierce in their idealism, brought their own scrupulous sense of socialist and dialectical political correctness to every aspect of the villagers' lives, particularly my father's, because at that time he was very active in Herbert Hoover's American Famine Relief program for that border area of Russia. By supporting Hoover – the ultimate capitalist – he fell afoul of the Red Communist functionaries, who branded him a counter-revolutionary. Once again, he had to go into hiding.

And then, Zastavia fell to the Poles, to a new quasi-fascist government none too friendly to socialists or Jews. My father, a natural born contrarian, always at odds with himself and his destiny, kept his *schnozz*, his Jewishness, close to the ground – but like his father, he took up the role of educating Jewish children, teaching them Jewish cultural values. In no time at all, however, the Poles met him nose-to-nose and arrested him. They thought it might be mildly amusing as well as publicly instructive to execute my father, but as he was being led to the place of execution, the pleas of a young Polish girl, a Catholic neighbour – on a whim, in a burst of goodwill – persuaded the Polish authorities to let my father go.

"It was then that I knew I had to emigrate," my father has since said. "Europe was no longer a home for Jews. My life had come down to a little girl's whim. An afterthought. In Europe we had always been second class, short of breath. But now we were forbidden to breathe, to live."

As it so happened, however, Joshua Falek, reluctant but stand-up revolutionary, reluctant but able officer, reluctant but forceful vigilante – in other words, a man who still, in this life, left himself room to dream – had in that moment, met the love of his life, Freda Rachel Pasternak.

MOTHER

In his memoir, *On Foreign Soil: Tales of a Wandering Jew*, published in 1945, my father wrote: "Beautiful and slim was the youngest of Reb Meier Pasternak's four daughters, Freda Rachel. She was very tall, slender and curvaceous, like a young tree, a veritable sapling. Her black eyes were always smiling; they burned with a fire that lit up the hearts of all those around her.

"Freda Rachel was the embodiment of impish energy. She exuded love of life and a sun-filled happiness. Her laughter was the purest silver. It appeared that life itself had bestowed on her all the intuitions of youthful good looks.

"She was wonderful with children. She would gather them all together and tell them tales, read them beautiful Yiddish and Russian stories. She would then pick up the dolls and play with them. She was really a child at heart. She was the darling of all the Jews and Christians in Zastavia. She would write beautiful letters for them to send off to their children, those who had grown up and moved abroad.

"She also had a great sense of humour. She could mimic all the town's characters. Those who watched her were convulsed with laughter. She knew her Russian and Jewish literature. She loved Sholem Aleichem and his famous little town of Kasrilevka, which was to her like Zastavia.

"And she, Freda Rachel, was an expert swimmer. She was the best swimmer in town.

"Her dark burning eyes and her contagious laughter had my blood boiling. She piqued all my romantic fantasies.

"I would stand outside her window to get a peek of her beautiful aristocratic face, her long, swan-like neck. She would talk endlessly to me, teaching me to see life from all sides: the ugly side, the sunny side, the big and small sides, the dark, sinister side, and the pale, illuminated side.

"When I was with her, my soul brimmed with quiet peace. When she was away, I felt empty and depressed; I missed her terribly. It became clear to me that without Freda Rachel, my life would have no purpose.

"I was luckier than my older brother, Aireh Leib. When he'd asked for her hand, she had let it hang in the air, limp, lifeless. But Freda Rachel, confronted as she was by my own outstretched hand, clutched me to her bosom. Eye to eye, she recognized all of me."

That was the summer of 1920.

FALEK AND FREDA

When I was a boy, my father took me on long walks through the North End of Winnipeg. We visited Jewish chess clubs and legion halls, Jewish schools and fraternal lodges, and the homes of Jewish friends. On many of these walks, my father would cite his manifesto, the one he had presented to Kerensky. "Loyalty is everything," my father would say. "But loyalty must never be blind. The loyalty I gave Kerensky was paid back in Bolshevik coins – the Stalinist murder of our poets, the suppression of our culture, Czar Nicholas II all over again, this time cloaked in the dictatorship of the proletariat." And then he would extrapolate: "I love Canada and you must, too, because Canada loves us – why else would they let us in? For every anti-Semite here, there are nine decent Anglo-Saxons. We have a real King and Queen; they love their people and listen to our wishes. Here, there are no czars. Make sure, my son," he would say, waving his manifesto, "make sure you do all in your power to see that Canada never has czars."

In fact, this manifesto had played a large role in the wooing of Freda Rachel Pasternak. Freda Rachel's father, the small but burly Reb Pasternak, had started out in Zastavia as a journeyman blacksmith. But a primitive capitalism had taken hold in clustered parts of czarist Russia in the last days of the empire. Reb Pasternak had displayed a hearty business hand and a shrewd business sense. Soon, his blacksmith shop had become a booming foundry, and he built a sensible, fairly large brick home for his wife and four daughters.

Joshua Falek's elder brother, Aireh Leib, had come upon my dark-eyed, bountifully bosomed mother while she was swimming on her back in a nearby pond. Her luminous eyes and shy, diffident manner, had hit him immediately and hard. Concluding he was in love, Uncle Aireh had decided to seize the day, to do something about it. He paid a visit to the Pasternak house and inquired if Freda Rachel was at home.

Reb Pasternak, the town *nogid*, the nascent capitalist, was also a bit of a modernist and feminist. He did not approve of arranged marriages. His daughters, he always said, would marry whom they wished.

Freda Rachel did not "like" the looks of my uncle, and she was frightened by his boldness. She had no desire to go out with him, but more than anything, she did not want to embarrass her father – so she hid in her room under her bed. Reb Pasternak announced to anyone listening in the house, that he could not find her, and he told Aireh Leib so.

Uncle Aireh interpreted Freda Rachel's behaviour as a mean-spirited rejection of his obvious charms and talents. He went to Joshua Falek, his brother – who, then a junior officer in Kerensky's tattered army, happened to be home on leave – and told him what had happened. Joshua Falek was outraged. The Zholf men swore retribution, if not vengeance, on Freda Rachel Pasternak. After serious head-to-head consultation, it was decided that Joshua Falek would call on the Pasternak house in the guise of a suitor. Having called on Freda Rachel, he would woo and win her with his easygoing charm, and then, at a ripe moment of romance, he would unceremoniously jilt her. This would pay back Freda Rachel for what she had done to Aireh Leib.

Joshua Falek went to the Pasternak's home by the pond with a bouquet of field flowers in one hand and a handwritten copy of his manifesto (it was always with him) in the other. This time, Freda Rachel did not hide under the bed. Within minutes, they were linked arm-in-arm, she happily walking through the *shtetl* lanes with a junior officer in Kerensky's revolutionary army.

On the banks of the Dnieper River, my father read Freda Rachel Pasternak his manifesto. "I knew then," she told me years later, "that I would soon be in love with this man. Who wouldn't? Such a wizard of words! I loved his manifesto. If they would have let me, I'd have put on a uniform and fought beside him! I hate wars, but sometimes they're necessary. And your father was the most wonderful, handsome soldier I had ever seen. He wore his uniform on our first date. He took off his hat, he bowed to me. I was a sucker for uniforms. And I just loved his smooth-talking talk. He was a real talker."

The Zholf brothers' ludicrous if not totally stupid exercise in retribution had backfired. Aireh Leib felt betrayed. Mortified. Humiliated. With a great throwing up of hands and the calling of names, he left for the United States where he joined the Merchant Marine. Later, he settled in Miami. For thirty years, Uncle Aireh Leib, ensconced in Miami, did not talk to Freda Rachel and Joshua Falek Zholf – who, shortly after their instant coupling (indeed the most handsome coupling in 1920s Zastavia) fell deeply in love and were married; a union which yielded, in rapid succession, three Zholf children.

The Zholfs were not happy in Zastavia. Racist Catholic Poland was no place to put a *schnozz* into the wind, to raise a Jewish family. Reisele Rose, the eldest child, was five;

Meyer, then the only Zholf boy, was two years younger; and Judith was still an infant. So the Zholfs decided to cut their losses and sail away, to emigrate. My father had wanted to go to Palestine, but not only were truculent Polish officials busy obstructing the immigration of Jewish families to the Holy Land, family inclinations had led Zholfs elsewhere – three of Falek's brothers had already established themselves as American citizens. The oldest and most ambitious, Nathan, had gone to Washington in the early 1900s, and become a multimillionaire, and companion of congressmen and senators. Nathan, with one hand open, the other deep in his pockets, lobbied his political confrères, hoping to sponsor the Falek family and secure them status as landed immigrants. But in the 1920s, America was in a xenophobic phase. The Emergency Quota Act had been passed in 1920 and under it, Jews – no matter their worldly goods or well-placed sponsors – were no longer welcome in the land of the Liberty Bell. Though the clang of the bell could be heard throughout the land. Nathan's efforts came to naught.

Then, my intrepid mother remembered that she had a first cousin, albeit distantly known, in Niagara Falls, Canada. Meyer Salit, a former junk and rag-and-bones peddler, a *sheeny* (as locals called such wagon men with their worn-out horses), was well on his way to becoming a tycoon in the border city – and in fact would eventually build, in his own honour and the honour of immigrant Jews, Niagara Falls' first synagogue.

Freda Rachel wrote Meyer Salit a long, heartfelt letter. Canada, Meyer Salit replied, would accept Falek Zholf, Freda Rachel and their three children. He would see to it. Falek, however, would have to come over first, and work as a farm labourer near a tiny crossroads village in Western Canada called Dominion City. Joshua Falek, reluctant world traveller, said goodbye to his family and the Zastavia *shtetl*, and went by wagon and by train to Warsaw, then Danzig, where he boarded a ship bound for Montreal.

IN THE CORNFIELDS
OF HIS MIND

In his memoirs, my father describes his trepidation as he stood in Warsaw facing the brusque, incurious Canadian consul. Joshua Falek Zholf, a Jew, was dressed in the loose blouse, jacket and felt boots of a labouring peasant. He was sure, however, that his soft lily-white hands, the hands of a *yeshiva* scholar, scarred only by candle wax, would give him away as a man of the book, not of the soil, a man unfit for the building of *boordays* on untilled farmland in Canada's far west. And he was sure that his nose would give him away as a Jew.

But the consul, without fluster or flap, gave him a stamped and initialled visa and handwritten directions to a farm in a place called Manitoba, a place that was a blank on Joshua Falek's official map.

After a very rough sea voyage in steerage across the Atlantic, Falek disembarked in Montreal and then went by CPR to Winnipeg. Exhausted, unable to speak English, unbowed but bewildered, he arrived by cart at the Dominion City farm where he was supposed to work. The farmer took one discourteous look at him and said he had no work for Falek Zholf. And so Falek drifted into Winnipeg, a small city of Anglo-Saxon pooh-bahs, parvenus, and provincial mercantile princes, demobbed British soldiers, remittance men, Ukrainian and Polish sodbusters, Métis, and swarms of mosquitoes. Street violence, homelessness, were immediate possibilities, but he weaselled a little work for a few weeks in a porcelain plant that made cheap plates. Then, he put his *schnozz* in at the local Jewish paper. The editor read Falek's manifesto, as well as his recollections and reflections, his little stories, and agreed to print a piece, but of course, paid him nothing. The editor, however, did introduce Falek to a woman who wanted a teacher for her children in that village called Dominion City, total population: twelve. My father took hold of the moment by the throat.

In Dominion City, he received his first letter from his beloved Freda Rachel:

My loved one, how are you? How do you feel? Have you already found yourself a bridge, a purpose in life? Have you at least found for yourself a little corner? Have you bumped into friendly people who are helping you cultivate your resting spot in the new foreign land?

My dear one, I beg you, don't worry. The time of our estrangement will quickly end. Our torn-apart souls will soon be back together again. You will be able to hold your children on your lap and tell them your beautiful stories which they so love, and play with them as you once did. They miss you terribly.

Your departure has had a depressing effect on the whole of Zastavia. Everywhere, people are talking about you. Everyone asks about you. Everyone wants to know if you have found a purposeful pursuit. A lot of people are jealous that you have escaped Poland, the land of Amalek. People now look at me as though I am only a guest in this town.

My heart is ruled by emptiness, unease, and longing for you.

Above all, our children are fatherless. Their young minds cannot understand what has happened. They never stop asking: "Where is Papa? Will he soon be coming back?" The first days after you left, they wouldn't eat, drink or go to sleep.

Maier has been protesting. He keeps crying: "Give me my tata! I want my tata! Why did he leave us! Why?!" One day, I told him, "Our kind tata has gone abroad looking for bread for all of us." Maier cried even more and said angrily, "You have bread in the house!"

Reisele does not cry and scream. She is a steady, sweet soul, always beside me, always cuddling up to me. She strokes my cheek and says, "Mama, dear one, don't cry. Tata will come back. You'll see. He'll come. Stop crying."

Judith, of course, is happy. She is good, quiet, a saint. She sleeps, eats, and lies in her crib and smiles to herself. Life is good for her. She doesn't know her father has gone away. She doesn't miss him. She doesn't worry.

Thanks to the beloved children, I have bounced back and picked up the rudder of our sinking ship in my hands.

Dear one, don't miss me. Don't worry. Don't lose your grip. Hang on to your mood. Your faith in yourself fans your energy which has always escorted you in all your wanderings.

Write, my loved one, write, my dear one, about everything. Write every day. Tell us all that life is bringing to you. Only our letters can bring a little light and happiness into this lonely, grey penned-in life. So do this now, real quickly now and hopefully God above will help us.

Signed, your wife and children who hope to see you soon,
  Your Freda Rachel.

This letter wrought instant change upon my father. He abandoned the one-horse town, Dominion City, packed his steamer trunk, and set out to secure his fortune in Winnipeg.

There, he once again went to see the editor of the Yiddish newspaper, *Jewish World.* Again, the editor liked a story, this one titled, "The Chinaman and I." He said he'd print it, and that this time he'd pay for it. He also said there was an opening at the Isaac Loeb Peretz Folk School for a Jewish teacher.

Falek Zholf applied for the job and got it. *Huzzah!* In the cornfields of his mind, *dybbuks* danced, and *golem* gambolled.

With a stamped and approved regular job, he now had the right to sponsor his family. He found a narrow shack posing as a house on Redwood Avenue, deep in the squalid immigrant North End. He secured the rental and began to prepare for the arrival of his wife and children. It was 1927.

children, left to right: Meyer, Judith and Rose

Overseas, Freda Rachel of the swan neck, her three children, and two steamer trunks went down to the Zastavia Station platform. Train carriages stood waiting, not yet coupled to the locomotive. Then, the locomotive blew off steam, whistled, and the loud coupling was completed. The carriages swayed, and then off they flew down the tracks – only to stop, uncouple, change carriages, and then fly again – through town, village, town, to Warsaw, child's hand holding child's hand, frightened on the crowded Danzig docks, then huddled, cramped in foetid steerage to cross the ocean...

At long last, many, many months after that first letter, my father, arms wide open, beard palpitating, nose pulsing, greeted my mother and his three children at the Pacific Railway terminal in Winnipeg. The Zholfs, as they stood, were now legitimate North Enders.

CRD

In the middle of the winter of 1934, the worst year of the Depression, Freda Rachel Zholf decided to visit her doctor, the well-known communist, Dr. Victor. Freda Rachel had missed a period. Freda Rachel wanted to know why. She put on her velvet hat with the feather in the band and the netting that veiled her brow. She put on her black gabardine suit, her comfortable black shoes, and her cloth coat with the big round buttons, and she walked out to Dr. Victor's office on Salter Street.

In the anteroom of Dr. Victor's office, she eyed the sombre engravings of Lenin and Stalin that hung on the bare plaster wall. They stared at her. Stern visages. Being superstitious, she feared the portraits might portend harm or radical change.

Dr. Victor's examination was brief but thorough. No harm, no, but change was in the offing. "Congratulations, Comrade Freda Rachel Zholf. You are pregnant."

"But I'm 44," said Freda Rachel Zholf. "I already have three hungry children to feed."

"The class struggle will show you a way out," said Dr. Victor.

"I'm not interested in the strategies of communism, Dr. Victor," said Freda Rachel Zholf, "but I do want this child. He will be the last born in this family but the first born in this country. God will keep an eye out for him. God will let him brazen his way into this world."

> We know not why—But mark, madam, we live amongst riddles and mysteries—the most obvious things, which come in our way, under the moon have dark sides…
>
> — *STERNE*

Shortly after my conception, whilst I was *in utero*, as they say, my father said that an extra mouth to feed was not what he was looking forward to, not on his mere pittance of a salary. Much in love, and very satisfied to be in love, he insisted that it would be more sensible for him – as a socialist, a Zionist, and something of a modernist – to cuddle and caress my mother rather than cuddle and caress a greedy lip-smacking fourth child in the grimmest of Depression poverty.

My mother, however, was more than a little Orthodox – always eagerly blessing our Sabbath candles, salting meat to get out the blood – and, of course, a fervent believer in the Evil Eye. As such, she had secretly, very secretly, become leery of the local socialist and Zionist ladies, especially those Jewish feminists in and around her husband's world; she found them too brash, too freewheeling, too dogmatic. She was cautious, careful, perhaps paranoid. She shuddered when they talked about free love, she grew queasy when they talked about abortion. At school social gatherings, she would often excuse herself and go to the cloakroom. There, she stuck pins into Jewish-looking voodoo dolls, then called Jewdoo dolls, and put the Jewdoo dolls into the pockets of the coats belonging to members of the free-loving Mothers' Union, very wealthy women attached to the school. In the sleeves of these coats, she put cloves of garlic, small vials of chicken fat, and pages from the Jewish Woman's Prayer Book – namely excerpts from the segment in which Moses calls upon the Israelites in the desert to stop sinning and behave themselves.

My father – always at the mercy of his compulsions and contradictions – dreaded the Wicked Witches of the Isaac Loeb Peretz Folk School, but he also secretly envied them. He envied their sophistication, their ruthless pragmatism, their modernism. These women told my father how – as a man set free by socialist ideals – to cope with my mother's pregnancy.

And so my father had suggested to my mother that I, the foetus, be drowned before birth, in a rapid series of very hot baths.

In response to this hot-bath diktat, my mother did not flinch. She looked straight into the eyes of her husband, the abortionist, and said nothing. She went into the kitchen and stopped the clock that sat atop the icebox; she spat in her hands twice; she spread chicken fat all over her face; and she threw a whole salt shaker over her left shoulder to ward off the works of the Evil One. But she offered no active form of resistance to my father, her lover, the abortionist – to be sure, she had always loved her Long Nose and still loved her Long Nose.

Apparently, as far as my father knew, my mother was taking several hot baths a day. The family had heard the taps running upstairs and had seen my mother carefully and demonstrably drying her hair downstairs shortly thereafter. Weeks and months passed. Soon, my mother began to itch and scratch herself. And sometimes, after she'd leave a room, an odd smell was left behind.

Even as a foetus, I consciously absorbed my mother's lifesaving body odour, I loved her madly. I loved the gossip and the secret plans that she whispered into my tiny foetus ears. I, the foetus, had been told by my mother that she was so determined to have me, she wasn't taking baths of any kind, not a one, so as to make sure that my father, the abortionist, would be thwarted. And so there I was, already the confidante of my gorgeous, voluptuous mother. Could any foetus ask for anything more? When my mother talked to me about duping my father, I would give her a playful kick in her tummy or pass a little foetal wind to convey my approval of her latest connivances to keep me alive. Without my fully understanding it, my natural nose for politics – in this case, the politics of abortion – had already won me my life in my mother's womb.

When I was finally delivered into this world by Dr. Victor – our neighbourhood Dr. Bethune – I cried long and ferociously. I cried *huzzah*. I was safe at last. My father, the abortionist, could no longer drown me.

Naturally, this highly personal experience made me leery of abortionists, their feminist socialist allies, and in particular, my father for years to come. I howled like a banshee when he tried to pick me up from my hospital crib to give me a cuddle. When he leaned into my baby carriage and tried to rub his *schnozz* against my *schnozz*, father to son, my tiny hands shot up, grabbed his nose and refused to let go. For a long time I responded in complete terror to the eerie, life-denying sounds of the hot bath my mother would run for my father – my father, my very own spitting image, whose nose, like mine, was enormous, nine pounds, dotted with carbuncles, warts, pimples, moles, and other fleshy appurtenances.

Is it not, said she, is it not a noble nose?"

'Tis an imposter, my dear, said the master of the inn, 'tis a false nose.

'Tis a true nose, said his wife.

'Tis made of fir-tree, said he, I smell the turpentine.

There is a pimple on it, said she.

'Tis a dead nose, replied the inn-keeper.

'Tis a live nose, and if I am alive myself, said the inn-keeper's wife, I will touch it.

— *STERNE*

THE NINE-POUND HONKER

I had known long before my birth that I had a nose for politics. Indeed, much of my actual birth consisted of Freda Rachel Pasternak Zholf's long and sideways contractions, all intended to free my nose from its foetal containment.

My nose, as if it were the legendary *dybbuk*, had been outed on July 19, 1934, in the general maternity ward of St. Joseph's Polish Roman Catholic Hospital on Salter Street near Selkirk, very deep in the ghetto of ghettos, the North End of Winnipeg, the spiritual home of the Winnipeg General Strike and Canadian socialism.

The wimpled nuns in attendance had *oohed* and *aahed* and crossed themselves at the sight of my tiny, tiny frame attached to such a huge honker: a nine-pound-eight-ounce baby boy – his nose *alone*, in fighting trim, weighing in at *nine* of those pounds.

My father named me Yehuda Leib after his grandfather. Quickly, I came to be called Leibele. The *Word*, the local Yiddish newspaper, said that I had come third in their 1934 Baby of the Year contest. At my mother's ample breast, precocious lad that I was, I joyfully counted my blessings: *ein, zwei,* three, four… Immediately I was at home in two languages, and immediately, somewhere, the nuns lost an *h* – a sign of my impending independent manhood – and I became Leibele Zolf, natural born and joyful citizen.

Equally joyful was my mother. She was certain that her *mezinik*, her youngest son, was in possession of a nose that would always be handy, perhaps in the Rabbinate, or as a *Truth or Consequences* radio quiz show champion representing our people, or as an eye, ear, nose specialist. With such a proboscis, she was sure her youngest would nose the truth out of the most subtle of Kabbalah secrets, the most tangled of Talmudic diatribes. With such a nose, her youngest would quickly expose the false and fair-weather friends of Jewry, as well as Jewry's enemies from within. My great baby proboscis would thus make me a Nose *Golem*, a Jewish secret weapon, if not a bit of a redeemer, or so my mother fervidly believed. After all, I was not the first nine-pound Jewish nose in the family (nor was I the only Jewish child who'd had an appendage declared special: born with his penis circumcised, Irving Layton had already in 1912, been declared the Messiah by his mother). In Alexander Kerensky's Russian Revolutionary Army, my father's nose had been recognized as so fleshy, so long, so powerful, that he'd not only dug his own trench with it – but sometimes the trenches of the crazed and wounded around him.

My mother, having married this Long Nose she loved wildly, had dreamed of giving him a Long Nose child, one who he might take for walks or on picnics, and perhaps rub noses before the fire. Her first three children, however, all had button noses. My mother's disappointment in them had been palpable. She had gone into semi-mourning after the birth of each of her perfectly snub-nosed children. But now, at long last, a Second Long Nose in imitation of the First had not only appeared, but was fully ensconced in the house.

A trumpeter and a trumpeter's wife, who were just then coming up, had stopped to see the stranger pass by.

Benedicity!—What a nose! 'tis as long, said the trumpeter's wife, as a trumpet.

And of the same metal, said the trumpeter, as you hear by its sneezing.

'Tis soft as a flute, said she.

'Tis brass, said the trumpeter.

'Tis a pudding's end, said his wife.

I tell thee again, said the trumpeter, 'tis a brazen nose.

I'll know the bottom of it, said the trumpeter's wife, for I will touch it with my finger before I sleep.

— *STERNE*

MY DARKEST HOUR

By accident, I found a way for my father to partially atone for his Original Sin, his sin of trying to abort my life. When I was three or four, my father was asleep on the couch, snoring loudly and rhythmically. Having nothing to do at the time, and being a very restless child, I decided to act out one of my favourite childhood fantasies, the one where the little Jewish socialist shoemaker is tapping away at the shoes on his workbench.

I took a small hammer from the kitchen and a wooden matchstick. I placed the matchstick in my father's left ear and, pretending it was a nail and my father's ear a shoe, I drove the matchstick very slowly right through his eardrum, puncturing the eardrum completely. It nearly killed my father and ultimately cost him all hearing in his left ear.

When my father came out of the anaesthetic at the hospital, he did something I didn't expect. He forgave me completely. Perhaps he did so because he was soon to discover that he could now hear better out of his one good ear. Perhaps he forgave me because I could, even at my early age, already speak English and Yiddish fluently, read and write Hebrew completely, and play child parts in Yiddish plays that came on tour to Winnipeg from New York.

Perhaps my father forgave me because in those Depression days, it was assumed that a three- or four-year-old child who drove a matchstick through his father's eardrum had to be too young to know what he was doing and certainly too young to feel any guilt. It was this assumption that led my parents to keep this episode a secret from me until my *bar mitzvah* at age thirteen, when they then considered me man enough to know about My Darkest Hour.

After the matchstick-in-the-eardrum episode, my father and I became the closest of companions. Day in and day out, he couldn't help showing how glad he was that I was alive, even though I was a fourth mouth to feed. Sometimes I paused and wondered when I caught his baleful look as I consumed huge globs of borscht, blintzes, *kreplach* and kasha as if it were all Gerber Baby Jewish soul food.

In my childhood, I became the apple of my father's eye, the sound of music in my father's one functioning ear. I went everywhere he went. I stood beside him and together we devoured pastrami sandwiches, played chess, went to the Yiddish theatre, and made Yiddish political speeches in Peanut, St. John's and Stella parks. I was to be my father's Boswell, his little prodigy who would – he said – soon deliver the Jews of North Winnipeg from their poverty, their sorrows, their pinched and narrow lives.

My father went on as follows,

* * * * * * *
* * * * * * *
* * * * * * *
* * —Very well,—said my father, *
* * * * * * *
* * * * * * *
* * * * * * *
* * * and so without stopping a
moment to settle it first in his mind, whether the Jews
had it from the Egyptians, or the Egyptians from the
Jews,—he rose up, and rubbing his forehead two or
three times across with the palm of his hand—he
walked down stairs.—How my father went on, in my
opinion, deserves a chapter to itself.—

— *STERNE*

FALEK THE FICTIONER

Diligent and witty, my father became a renowned teacher of Jewish literature, poetry and history at the Isaac Loeb Peretz Folk School in the heart of the North End. He was a scrapper by spirit, a fighter – for Jewish identity, Jewish pride, and for those Jewish rights that he felt were his natural due as a citizen of British North America. To him, British imperialism was no abstract spillage of pink on the map of the world, but a concrete reality. He believed that, relatively speaking, the empire was a benign force, something neither Anglo-Saxons nor Jews needed to be ashamed of. In my father's eyes, British North America – that is, Canada – had become the real, the functioning, American Dream. It was Canada, he said, that steadfastly allowed Jews to be both Jews and British North Americans at one and the same time. In the mid-1930s, he had become a fervid monarchist and maniacal defender of British institutions, even as the English closed one imperial eye and counselled with Hitler, and even after they closed the other eye when the Nazis entered the Sudetenland. No matter. To anyone who would listen, he predicted that his hero, the Zionist Tory, Winston Churchill, would not only one day be made Prime Minister of Britain but would lead the world in the struggle against fascism. Britain, my father prophesied, not the United States, would stand on principle and immediately go to war against Nazism and fascism.

My father, though he was a British Firster, a sort of weird rabbinical socialist Tory, was not – like so many of his fellow citizens – anti-American. After all, along with the Washington-based Nathan, two of my father's brothers were gung-ho salute-snapping Amuricuns. Aireh Leib, a veteran of the First World War – having served in the American Merchant Marine, he had faced, on more than one occasion, the dreaded U-boats of Admiral Tirpitz – was now a Miami Beach tavern keeper, as well as elected president of the Miami Beach American Legion and head of the Miami Beach Masonic Lodge.

Uncle Lazar, younger than Nathan but like Nathan, too old for the Great War, was a union organizer in New York's garment district. His wife, Bella, was a union organizer, too. In the 1920s, the Jewish garment manufacturers, given to a love of *gelt* even more than *gefilte* fish, had brought in Mafia goons – criminals – to smash the International Ladies' Garment Workers' Union. Lazar had been badly beaten by these goons; his beautiful wife, Bella, had been disfigured by the acid thrown in her face. Their two sons were about to become prominent New York city communists, notably, cousin Jerry, the chief proofreader for the *New York Times* who was personally attacked in a Senate committee hearing headed by none other than that drunken Irish lout and bully, Senator Joseph McCarthy.

But it was not only my father's deep sense of blood-brotherhood that prevented him from indulging in an easy anti-Americanism north of the border; it was his fervent and passionate love for President Franklin Delano Roosevelt. "Here is a man," my father would say to me, "who surrounds himself with Jews – Frankfurter, Hillman, Brandeis – and cares for

Jews. Sure, he has an anti-Semite like Joe Kennedy around, but that's strictly because Roosevelt wants the Irish vote. Who can blame him! Do you know how many Irishers there are in America? Millions, millions! But don't worry, my son, an Irisher will never be president. There will be a Jewish president long before there will be an Irisher!" (About that, Pop was obviously wrong, but he was right about Churchill, and one out of two ain't bad.)

What had secured my father's affection and admiration was the speech Roosevelt had given at Queen's University in Kingston during convocation in the spring of 1938. "My son," my father explained to me, "Roosevelt said to the Nazis – fire one torpedo at Canadian soil, sink one Canadian ship, land one platoon on Canada's Atlantic coast – and America will be at war with Adolf in less than twenty-four hours. It was a great speech; Roosevelt is a great fighter against fascism – and he sure gave Hitler food for thought!"

To my father, fighting anti-Semitism and saving Jews was the key to fighting fascism. "Hitler," he would tell his audiences at the Isaac Loeb Peretz Folk School auditorium or in Peanut, St. John's and Stella Parks, "made us – Jews – the centre of his ideology. Our destruction is Hitler's victory. Killing Jews is Hitler's business. Killing Nazis is our business – and the business of all who cherish freedom and liberty."

In the public parks of Winnipeg, I would watch my father debate crypto fascists and crypto Nazis who all too often proclaimed that Hitler had every right to dismantle the Jewish world as he saw fit. Why, these dangerous boneheads argued under the spreading elms, should Canada fight a war for the Jews? In Yiddish-tempered English, my father, his beard bristling, would retort: "The Jews of Europe are innocent, innocent of all crimes. The Jews of Europe are decent, hardworking and intelligent people. If Canada should allow the slaughter of our innocents in Europe, why should such a slaughter stop there? The fascists are the enemy of the Jews. Period. Put there a *Punet*. But the fascists are also the enemy of decency, fairness, honesty, compassion – qualities that have made Britain the just and decent empire that it is. The Jewish cause is the cause of decency. The cause of decency is, and will always be, the British way of life."

◎◎

Joshua Falek Zholf also continued with his writing and ultimately became a fully-fledged author, one of the better-known Yiddish writers in Canada as well as the United States. A good deal of his writing was done for *Der Yiddishe Vort*, or *The Jewish Word*, the weekly Yiddish newspaper that had published him back when he'd first arrived in Winnipeg. For this newspaper, he wrote features, essays, vignettes, editorials, lampoons – whatever the paper would print, which led, in 1945, to his memoir, *On Foreign Soil: Tales of a Wandering Jew*.

In the late 1930s, in one short lampoon he wrote for *Jewish Word*, Joshua Falek Zholf asked: "If the character of Fagin had been just another Scotsman or Yorkshireman, who would want to read such a boring book? If Shylock had just been a Venetian butcher, would his request for a pound of flesh have been the stuff of which classic drama is made? Had Shylock uttered these lines – 'Hath not a Yorkshireman eyes? Hands? Organs? Dimensions? Senses? Affections? Passions? If you prick a Yorkshireman does not all Britain bleed?' – would a whole world gone *meshugana* have been moved to compassion?" Finally, he asked: "Would anybody have ever paid good money to see a play called, *The Scotsman of Malta*?

His lampooning eye, his acerbic spirit, however, often got him into dire trouble. A short story he wrote in 1940 called, "Is a Clothed Doukhobor Woman Good Enough for a Nice Jewish Boy?" was a thinly disguised portrait of a Plum Coulee Jewish tavern keeper whose eldest son had run off to marry a fully clothed Doukhobor woman.

There was a flash-fire local uproar. In those days, Jews were, of course, too poor to sue or litigate, but not too poor to organize a boycott of *Jewish Word*. Threats were sufficient to cause the paper to react and (appear) to retract; the editor ran this front page apology: "The editorial staff of *Jewish Word* wishes to assure Mrs. Dvorke Dubnov, whose eldest son, Herschel, married Titanya Grobshanski, on Assumption Sunday, at Winnipeg's Holy Ghost Polish Roman Catholic Cathedral three months and four days ago, this very day, that Herschel is in no way related to, or indicative of, the completely fictitious Feivel Flinker of the tavern-keeping family from the completely fictitious Manitoba hamlet of University City, who ran off with a totally fictitious and fully clothed Doukhobor woman, Svetlana Svarkov, Svetlana and Feivel being the purely fantastic creations of *Jewish Word* writer, Falek Zolf, who assures us, as we assure you, Mrs. Dvorke Dubnov, that he and *Jewish Word* have nothing but the highest regard for the Dubnov family."

Then, one day, the doorbell rang. Even though I was only six, I could speak English fluently and could cope with the police or other English-speaking authorities, which my parents – unnerved by all non-Jewish authority – could not do. Answering the doorbell was one of my duties.

Standing just outside the front door was a solid through-the-shoulders, tough-looking Jewish woman in her early fifties. She had an umbrella in her hand. She smiled beneath knitted brows and asked in Yiddish, "Is your father, *the writer*, home?"

"Papa," I shouted, "it's one of your fans!"

Papa, of course, dropped everything. He very much admired those who admired him. At the front door, however, he was greeted by ebullient umbrella blows about his head and over his body. "You gossip, you yellow journalist, you ruined my life!" the woman shouted. Falek Zholf became a fast-afoot Harry Greb with a beard: he bobbed, slipping blows, he weaved and ducked. All the while, from within his crouch, he tried to mollify the woman: "You don't understand, Mrs. Dubnov. My Doukhobor piece is pure fiction, pure fantasy. It's all in my mind. It never happened."

The woman's arm finally tired; two *whumps* became one *whump*, and she then stopped swinging her umbrella and growling, and took her leave.

I was shaken, a bit frightened, at having seen my father beaten about his bearded head by a woman.

He calmed me down. "My son, the woman is mistaken. It was only a story, a piece of fiction. Any resemblance between my story and real life is purely coincidental." Having convinced himself, and having done so rather easily, he added: "My son, writing fiction is a dangerous profession, like soldiering in a war. Fiction, too, can kill you!"

He went on risking his life.

In another fantasy, "Wrapped in the Old Red Flag," he sardonically described the delicious social dilemmas caused by a Jewish worker who, having enjoyed life at the sewing bench of an uncle-by-marriage, happened to fall in love with Uncle Joe, Joseph Stalin, embracing communism and giving up his job, real uncle, wife and family for the good of the cause.

Again, an uproar ensued. *Jewish Word*'s apology, this time, was even more acerbically wry: "Falek Zholf and *Jewish Word* apologize profusely for suggesting that communism in general, and admiration for Josef Stalin in particular, is now – or has ever been – a laughing matter!"

Falek Zholf again put his beard on the line with his piece, "The Car With No Driver." In this story, a car with no driver starts moving slowly down Portage Avenue towards the southern end of the city. This car with no driver is suddenly seen as a kind of miracle; people, sidewalk acolytes of the car, begin to follow it. As the car turns along Main Street, the crowds grow. Passions inflame. Taverns and pool halls empty out. Brothels disgorge customers. *Holy holy holy* is heard in the land. The miracle car with no driver attracts even bigger crowds. Finally, at Selkirk and Main, in the heart of the North End, a police officer stops the car, opens the door and, in Lea-cockian fashion, finds a four-foot-six-inch man holding on to the bottom of the wheel.

In real life, the four-foot-six-inch driver, who had indeed been stopped by just such a police officer at just such a corner, was Sholom Miller, a board member at both Jewish *Word* and the Isaac Loeb Peretz Folk School; and it was, not surprisingly, to both boards that Sholom exposed his wound and aired his grievances.

Again, Joshua Falek, fictioneer, survived. "I have nothing against short people," he argued. "My story is an allegory about the hopes and dreams of the little people of this world for a new and better life."

Naturally, his pen being his mightiest sword, he, like the great Bandersnatch – snicker-snack, snicker-snack – cut a broad swath on behalf of the causes he believed in. And, with his dark, flashing eyes, his oratorical gifts and his facility

upon the page, he had, unwittingly, been readying himself –
in fact, rarely has any man been so well prepared and made
ripe – for Armageddon, should it come.

Amen: said my mother, *piano*.

Amen: cried my father, *fortissimo*.

Amen: said my mother again—with such a sighing cadence of personal pity at the end of it, as discomfited every fibre about my father—

— *Sterne*

MY MOTHER AND ME

Freda Rachel's love for, and coquettish romancing of, my father, was the constant talk of North Winnipeg. When they were in their sixties, they would walk arm-in-arm, hand-in-hand, down Selkirk Avenue and Main Street, a rebuke to all those in the neighbourhood who had devolved into nattering, battering couples.

Freda Rachel's respectful love for my father was nonetheless tempered by a shrewd awareness of his excesses. He would, for example, never settle for a single cutting insult when a dozen razor-sharp rapid-fire epithets would do. He would never voluntarily give up the joys of a harangue. And his harangues could go on for a long tedious time. But my mother's call *"genug schoen!"* – "enough already!" – always restored him to a sense of equilibrium. She was the real force in the house, but as for the overt wielding of power, she, of course, never laid a punishing hand on members of the family. Her hands were clean. His hands were dirty.

While she did differ sharply with my father on certain issues, like abortion, she shared his view that I should be exposed early on to East European Jewish life and learning. When, at the age of four, I was enrolled in the Isaac Loeb Peretz Folk School kindergarten program, my mother was happy to know that for two years, I would be working with clay and finger-painting while listening to the stories of great

Jewish men and women, the same stories that she had heard as a child: Samson, Bar Kokhba, Queen Esther, mothers Leah, Rachel and Rebecca, and Jewish assassins such as Hirsh Lekert and Simon Schwartzbard.

My enrolment in grade one at the Isaac Loeb Peretz Folk School, however, was, for her, a different matter. My father and mother solemnly escorted me down Salter Avenue, past the Burrows Court home of our CCF (Socialist) MP, A.A. Heaps, past the Alfred Block where the widow, Levson, her husband having been killed in the Spanish Civil War, supported two growing boys in one room on a relief stipend, a true pittance, and then on to Aberdeen Avenue, where the Isaac Loeb Peretz Folk School loomed large, a pile of bricks taking up at least a third of the block.

My father, being a teacher at the school, of course entered first. He waved goodbye to us, turning towards his own classroom while my mother hauled me by the hand to the grade one classroom.

Suddenly, tears were coursing down my mother's face.

I was frightened. I asked her what was wrong.

"For six years, my son," she said, "I and I alone have protected you from the real world, from all its burdens and all its terrors. From now on, my son, you're on your own. You're in the real world and you and you alone can make something of it, make it fit with your life, your hopes, your dreams."

"But why are you crying, Mama? What is there to cry about? I'm ready for the world," I said.

Immediately, she knew how little I knew. I ran into my classroom; I was running into life.

I learned to read from a Yiddish *Dick and Jane — Max and Molly* primer. And it was in Yiddish that I first read *Huckleberry Finn, Tom Sawyer, Rip Van Winkle* and *Moby Dick*.

Upping the political awareness ante, my father threw in the *Jewish Children's History of the Life and Times of Eugene V. Debs*, as well as *The Life and Times of Samuel Gompers*, and *The Life and Times of Emma Goldman*. By the tender age of nine, I knew that Franklin D. Roosevelt was God the Father, David Dubinsky of the International Ladies' Garment Workers' Union was God the Son, and Sidney Hillman of the Amalgamated Clothing Workers of America was God the Holy Ghost.

I had, in fact, been touched by the spirit, the spirit of inquiry.

I was eager to be seen for who I was and who I intended to be. Whenever a teacher asked a question, I had my hand up before all the other children. If no one else, I had my mother to please, and pleased she was. She watched with approval as her growing child was invited to recite Yiddish poetry in some of the finest Jewish socialist homes in the city, and she applauded loudly when I was given the lead in the grade one play – a skit I'd written myself. My mother beamed with pride.

Still, my life as an emerging *wunderkind* grew complicated. Though my father continued to make his living by teaching in a progressive socialist school, secretly, in his heart of hearts, he had turned back on the tribe, and was becoming more and more Orthodox. When I, as a six-year-old "hambone" (funny, how so many Jewish comedians are born hambones), was showboating in grade school and socialist circles, I simultaneously had to adjust to the ludicrous that is inherent in all of life: I discovered that my father was planning for me to attend a theological seminary in the United States. He believed that by age fourteen or fifteen, I could be a full-fledged rabbi, which meant that he, my father, would be able to tell himself that he had fulfilled, in spite of his socialist sins, the pledges he had made to the Almighty Pawnbroker. As for an example of how such forward thinking might work, Rabbi Staten's son – who was my age – was already in a theological seminary in Chicago, preparing for the rabbinate.

Even as a six-year-old, I was not keen on being a rabbi. If anything, I was a peregrinating socialist who had conservative inclinations and liberal street smarts. I had no innate religious awareness and I could just as easily, in my *wunderkind* way, have memorized and performed that minor Anglo-Saxon epic, *The Dream of the Rood* (Anonymous), as I did memorize and perform that Jewish epic, *In The City of Slaughter* (Haim Nahman Bialik, Israel's first national poet).

My mother, a religious but pragmatic woman, found herself caught between the two men in her life – the child she had saved from a hot-bath abortion, and the man she deeply loved. For me, her love was profound and constant, no matter my emotional highs or my emotional slumps, both swings in disposition caused by my appearances week after week, as my father's talking seal. In my short pants and knee socks, I performed in theatres, school auditoriums, the Royal Canadian Legion Hall – where, astonishingly, so listeners said – I gave one nighttime audience a detailed strategical history of the El Alamein campaign in the desert, and another a carefully crafted war exhortation on behalf of Buy War Bonds. Sometimes, I made up to twenty appearances in a week – until my mother, no matter her pride, would intervene, saying, "*Genug schoen*" – and get me a two-week reprieve. I would then spend happy time in her company.

During one of these breaks – on Saturday, September 2, 1939 – Mama deemed me old enough to attend adult movies. I was five. We walked down Aikins Avenue and headed east on Selkirk towards Main Street, passing the General Monash Branch of the Royal Canadian Legion, where every day Jewish veterans of the Great War gathered out front to discuss *blitzkriegs*. Hand-in-hand, my mother and I walked by the market where the bounty of the Ukrainian and Mennonite farmers was laid out: milk, cheese, vegetables, nuts, honey, and various fruits, pomegranates, dates, tangerines and apples. We passed the Oasis Delicatessen (great *gefilte* fish), the communist bookstore (polemics and pamphlets direct from Moscow, pulp paper and cheap boards), and not one but two British fish-and-chip shops, fish frying in the storefront windows. My mother, always suspicious, and convinced that fried cod or halibut was never as advertised, said, "See, my son, that's pork they're frying there. If you listen hard, you'll hear gurgling, sizzling sounds, quite unlike those made by frying kosher meat. Maybe it's the soul of the pig protesting his maltreatment. A pig's *dybbuk*, so to speak. Never eat pork, my son. It will corrode your intestines." We went on to pass the Bell Hotel – a fleabag dive frequented by Métis, Poles, Ukrainians, pimps and hookers – owned, if not operated, by none other than Samuel Bronfman, our very own scion of Zion and bootleg booze. And at last, we stood in front of the North End's Palace Theatre, the Starland. We bought tickets and took our seats. She liked popcorn and she liked being with me, so she put up with the sour body odour emanating from so many of the immigrant patrons – in particular, the single men who lived in rooming houses – present at the Saturday matinee double feature.

My first movie, on its second run, was called *Four Sons*. It was, of course, black and white. Stark. Like the times. It was directed by John Ford and starred Margaret Mann. She was a widowed Bavarian. Three of her sons had gone to the trenches for the Kaiser in the First World War, but her fourth had settled in America. As the United States entered the Second World War, the fourth brother enlisted to fight against the Germans. In Bavaria, Mother Bernle was accused of raising a traitor.

Moved and perplexed by the story, I said to my mother, "I'm the fourth child of the family and the youngest. Will I ever turn against my family like young Joseph did?"

My mother laughed and said, "You're a Jew, my son, not a Nazi. How could you turn against your family? Turn against the enemies of your people and you will be okay."

Then, the newsreels came on. They were wonderful. Dramatic. Charged with the emotion of disaster. The world turning. I had not really seen Nazis before. There they were, all apple-polish and razor smiles, heads poking out of svelte tanks, trucks and armoured cars driving through pastoral Poland, soldiers marching, *stomp stomp stomp*, and singing and laughing, their thunder gods with them, stride for stride, boot for boot, their blond hair and sharp cheekbones exuding exaltation and happiness. I, too, felt excited. I didn't know why. I just did. That rush of exhilaration vanished, however, when I saw the tears in my mother's eyes. She knew what the newsreel meant.

Though she knew, and though she wept, my mother enjoyed hunching down in her seat to watch these war movies with me at the Starland Theatre every Saturday afternoon, the huge screen full to brimming with bombs exploding, machine guns firing. She liked the intrigue, the double-dealing, the comeuppances, she liked seeing sinister Nazis in their death agonies. Over the years, we saw many movies, including *In Which We Serve (1941)*, *Hitler's Children (1943)*, and *Commandos Strike at Dawn (1942)* – good movies, all of them, but I still remember that her number-one war picture was a Sherlock Holmes story starring Basil Rathbone: *Sherlock Holmes Faces Death (1943)*.

Holmes, active in the World War II effort, was trying to expose a Nazi spy ring. In the garden patio of a wonderfully stuffy British aristocrat's country estate, he had lined up five suspects under a bower of white roses, but he was getting nowhere. Being an outstanding detective, Holmes pulled a sly one. He whipped out his handkerchief and blew his nose while uttering a loud, "Achoo!" One of the five suspects, a gentlemanly well-bred fellow, said, "Gesundheit!"

"Holmes has got the Nazi now, God bless him," cried my mother, as she roared with laughter. So did I, crying, "Gesundheit, gesundheit," and so did the ladies of her local Jewish group, her Home circle, when she told them the Gesundheit story, after serving them black tea with heavy almond cookies.

My mother would also take me to the State Theatre on Selkirk Avenue where we would watch Yiddish movies. The roles of theatre manager, projectionist, usher and janitor were filled by the State Theatre's sole employee, Don Haig.

Don was a gentile. Constant contact with the Jews who flocked to the State Theatre, however, had enabled Don to speak first-class Yiddish. (Haig went on to become a legend in the Canadian film industry, not just as a producer of films such as *I've Heard the Mermaids Singing*, but the owner of Film Arts, the outstanding Toronto documentary film-editing house on Jarvis Street.) Don liked my mother and her shrimp of a side-kick; he always gave us the best seats in the house.

Language, not storyline, was the strength of the Yiddish movies. The plots of all these movies, especially my favourite, *A Brivele der Mama – A Little to Mama* – were the same.

Each film opened with music in B-flat, with a Sabbath banquet, the whole Melamet family, one hundred and twenty strong, gathered around the dining table. Guitars and balalaikas were played. Songs were sung and toasts were made. Toasts to life. At this point, everyone in the audience knew that by the end of the film, only one Melamet would survive.

Approximately ten of the Melamet clan would die in a pogrom; twenty more would die of typhus; twenty more would be trapped behind enemy lines; twenty more would die from open-heart, open-liver, or open-kidney surgeries performed without anaesthetic; thirty would try to commit suicide; and twenty would convert to Christianity and become violent anti-Semites who would then turn in yet another twenty Melamets to the czarist police.

One day, after a second-run screening of *A Brivele der Mama*, I asked, "Why do Jews make movies where so many Jews die?"

My mother was a logician. "Jews die or are killed everywhere, my son. Why should it be so different in the movies? Why shouldn't they die or be killed in their own movies?"

My mother had at least one more reason for being a fan of Yiddish movies: *"A Brivele der Mama,"* she said, "is a movie that's good for Jewish mothers. It's done in good taste. It reminds me of my hometown in the old country. Besides, in all Yiddish movies there is a little boy and he is always spared. Like you, he will do great things for the Jewish people in the future."

"But he'll be so lonely, Mama. No father, no mother, no brothers, no sisters," I said.

"Don't worry, my son. Like you, he will meet a nice Jewish girl, and he will settle down."

My mother's stern assurance that I would meet a Jewish girl who would not only be beautiful, intelligent, and a queen of *kreplach* cuisine, but "nice" was certainly welcome, but at the tender age of ten, I was already casting a lascivious eye upon the pretty little snub-nosed Polish, Ukrainian and German girls who strolled, in their pinafores and tunics, along Selkirk Avenue. I knew, even then, that my mother was my best friend – it was she who not only loved me but wished me love. She was also my protector – it was she who could and did stiff-arm my father whenever he became too controlling, too demanding of his little magic boy-child. And, it was she who turned me loose into my soul-saving career of comedic gab.

In fact, she reminded me many years later, that when I was just two years old I delivered my first stand-up one-liner. I had been naughty and my mother was angry at me. "Where is your *tushie*? I want to spank it," my mother had said. Like a coquette, I had replied, "It's gone to a meeting."

In fairness, in the interest of allowing us equal stage time, I should report my mother's best, though more mordant, one-liner. Towards the end of the war, the *News of the World* newsreel at the Starland Theatre depicted Mussolini and his mistress, Clara Patacci, hanging from their heels in a Milan marketplace. The whole theatre cheered, none louder than me. My mother remained silent. I asked her why. "My son, never wish for the death of a tyrant," my mother said. "The next may be worse!"

☙❧

Freda was very tall, elegant and long-limbed for a Jewish woman. At five-foot-ten, she was four inches taller than my father, and he had to crick up his jaw (and his beard) to look into her oval face with its high cheekbones. Even as a little boy, I noticed that lascivious men tipped their *shtreimels* to my mother and some even tried to bribe me with candy so that I would play somewhere else for a while. My mother, of course, was flattered – who wouldn't be – but she remained, if coquettish, a one-man woman all her life.

A one-man woman and never a socialist. She disliked her modern "liberated" contemporaries: "These socialist women, they get divorces on a whim – so fast, it's like plucking tissues from a tissue box," she said. "These socialist women," she whispered in my ear, "are they married to their husbands? No. They live trapped in free love. They change partners like we change streetcars. Their children look like everybody else's children which means they look like nobody's children."

As a four-year-old boy, I had been told, in the most chilling terms of the rapine and violence visited upon my people by Ukrainian Cossacks and Polish ultranationalists. My father had done the telling, and he strongly suggested that we not be naïve about our old country neighbours newfound on the block. Not that he ever said we shouldn't play with Ukrainian and Polish children. But we had been warned.

As it happened, at six years of age, my best friend was Teddy Warga. He was Polish. His father was the janitor at the Isaac Loeb Peretz Folk School. Mr. Warga, a Polish Catholic, spoke flawless Yiddish. Sometimes, a boil would burst in Mr. Warga and in Yiddish, he would say: "You Jews are the scum of the earth, and now, here in Canada, in this country, you run everything, you hike our prices to kike heaven. Hitler is after you like a mad dog, and all of Europe is hoping to surrender their Jews to him. When Hitler comes to Canada, I'll be first in line to do the same."

Mr. Warga, however, was the best janitor the school had ever had. He was a natural fixer. He had a kindly mien, a soothing air, a gentle hand that, like a paw, he'd lay upon a shoulder. Things that broke or went bust in the night were repaired by the morning.

Upon our first meeting, Mr. Warga's son, Teddy, beat me up on the street. Four more pummellings followed. *Hook hook hook kick hook smash.* Then, Teddy decided that beating me up was boring. He adopted me, and we became the best of friends. So, whenever I, as a big-mouthed, and big-nosed teenager, got into any kind of rumble or scuffle Teddy would appear out of the mists of his ancestral forest and beat my would-be assailant about the ears.

Teddy, seldom if ever at school, seemed to roam the streets to no purpose at all. Then, he suddenly found a profession, something he could do, something he liked doing, something that, if done well, would prove real profit. Teddy became a bank robber. In his mind, he became Baby Face Nelson. Unfortunately for Teddy, he was caught every time he tried to heist a bank. He was caught so many times that he was sent down as a habitual criminal.

What I remember best about life with Teddy and Mr. and Mrs. Warga, however, was my very first Christmas. I was six years of age. Curious, and given a crazy kind of nighttime freedom by my mother, I went with the Warga family on Christmas Eve to the Church of the Holy Ghost, the big Polish Catholic church across the road from where they lived on Selkirk Avenue. Father Sikorsky's stirring sermon was translated for me by Mr. Warga: "The enemies of Poland – the Nazi scourge, the Bolshevik menace, and the Jewish World

Conspiracy – will, in Christ, soon be subsumed and Poland will rise to its old glory."

I elbowed in on the sacramental act; I lined up alongside the centre aisle pews with the family and took a wafer on my tongue, sipped wine. Why not?

Afterwards, we walked in our galoshes to the Warga home for Christmas dinner. On a small table, they served up a huge ham. I'd never eaten ham before. It was delicious. Then the Wargas carried in plates of *kapusta*: sauerkraut that had been soaked in brine for decades. I ate huge mouthfuls of *kapusta*. A nice lard sandwich went down well. So did pig's feet and pig's knuckles.

Fully stuffed, bloated, I hurried the two blocks home.

My mother was wildly agitated. "Where have you been?" she cried.

"I've been at Christmas dinner with the Wargas," I answered.

My mother threw her hands up in horror. "What did you eat?"

As I named each dish, she rolled her eyes (I left out the communion caper). She then dragged me to the all-night grocery store which had the only telephone in the area, so that she could call Dr. Victor. She told him in as much detail as she could muster, about my first Christmas supper. She was adamant. My stomach had to be pumped. Dr. Victor was adamant, too. He insisted that I was young, healthy, and would survive my first Polish Christmas supper.

My mother tried to calm down. But she kept applying compresses to my stomach and my rear end. Each fart, each burp was greeted by, "*Oi vey*! My poor child!" Wrapped in shawls, she sat in a chair beside my bed and kept a keen eye on me all night long.

The next day, I leapt out of bed. "I'd like to go and play with Teddy," I announced majestically.

"Not today, my son," said my mother. "Not tomorrow, but maybe soon. Maybe."

◎◦◎

My mother was terrified of inventions and contrivances.

The one time she entered an automated elevator, she panicked as the door closed – there was no elevator operator. She lay in a corner of the elevator in a foetal position for half an hour.

She thought a pressure cooker was a mini nuclear weapon, unnatural in a Jewish home. She feared that a vacuum cleaner might not only suck up dust, but suck wallpaper off walls and carpets off floors.

As a little boy, I would go with Mama to Eaton's, a six-storey edifice on Portage Avenue where we always used the operator-run elevators or the stairs, never the escalator. I once asked my mother why.

"That's easy, my son," she said. "Do you remember Mrs. Greenberg who lived down the street, the widow with forty cats?"

"Yes, I do, Ma."

"Mrs. Greenberg," said my mother, "went up the Eaton's escalator once – and never came back!"

Yet this superstitious *shtetl*-reared mother of mine would think nothing of walking alone down the streets of North Winnipeg. With the aplomb of a champion swimmer she would weave through the homeless, the bereft of reason, the pickpockets and second-storey men, the bully boys and the odd rapist, never blinking an eye.

Nor was she frightened by the largest tomcat in the North End, a sixty-pound tabby with fierce teeth who, having snuck into our summer kitchen one evening, opened the icebox and sunk its teeth into the large porterhouse steak that was to be our supper. My mother wrestled the cat to the ground, pried open its jaws, retrieved the steak, and then kicked the cat monster out the door.

We'd then eaten the steak.

Nor did she suffer from a fear of mice and rats. In our house, they usually came out of a hole below the sink in the kitchen. I watched with awe and admiration wherever Mama, usually in the middle of doing the dishes, would spot one of these rodents; with a large snowshoe, she'd whack it over the head until it was dead – leaving me to wonder where she'd gotten the snowshoe and how she'd come to think of it as a rat-killing weapon.

Love being blind, my father was blind to the excesses and limitations of Freda's cooking, and always had two or three helpings of everything she put on the table. And all the Yiddish teachers, writers, actors, poets and playwrights who clustered around our table, of course enlivened and enchanted by Freda's presence, licked their chops because, true to the tradition of Jewish cooking, she never removed the fat from anything, and often served up platefuls of *grieben* – deepfried chicken skin – as if it were candy. Fat that went straight to the heart!

She was also terribly absentminded and would put anything and everything into the pot – to the point of barbarity. One day, while daydreaming of the old country as she chopped carp for *gefilte* fish, she chopped off the very tip of her thumb. The severed portion fell in with the fish. A sliced carrot was laid atop the fish as it cooled, and then the dish was served to my father who ate the entire concoction, tiny thumb tip and all; he chewed with joy and fervour.

My sister Judith and I (as a family, we were not always at the table at the same time) appalled at this act of semi-cannibalism, were confirmed in our determination to avoid Freda's cooking at all costs, a food avoidance we'd come to share early in our lives simply because we'd been forced to eat one of her so-called culinary delights, *kontleten*. To make these Jewish hamburgers, Freda had combined ground meat, breadcrumbs, and egg yolk, then shaped the mixture into small discus-like patties which she put in the oven. I was six and Judith was fourteen; we were in the middle of a heated suppertime argument at the kitchen table. I reached for one of my mother's *kontleten* and sailed it, backhanded, at my sister. A toss that had a certain grace. The *kontleten* hit her flush on the brow and opened up a wound that required several stitches at the local hospital.

Crust and Crumb
Inside and out
Top and bottom—I detest it, I hate it, repudiate it—
I'm sick at the sight of it—
'Tis all pepper,
   garlick,
   staragen,
   salt, and
   devil's dung—by the great arch-cook of cooks, who
does nothing, I think, from morning to night, but sit down
by the fire-side and invent inflammatory dishes for us, I
would not touch it for the world—
—"Not touch it for the world," did I say—
Lord, how I have heated my imagination with this Metaphor!

— STERNE

MY OLDER SISTER, ROSE ZHOLF BORODKIN

My sister Rose, thirteen years older than I, was bright and practical, a very pert, blonde, blue-eyed woman who made every North End Jew wonder whether she was really Jewish, whether she was actually one of Falek Zholf's children, or whether she had been secretly dropped on the Zholf doorstep by an unwed Polish mother.

She had been born with a nose that was not a *schnozz*, yet – still and all – she had a superior nose for gossip, in lockstep with a first-class sense of humour. When it came to all folks Jewish who drew breathe (or ceased to breathe) in Winnipeg, Rose not only knew about it, but had all the inside dope – on the breathing, the decline thereof, and especially, the dying. Sometimes, her body count of the local Yiddish-speaking dead rivalled that of those in the Yiddish movies. During our regular phone conversations over the decades, Rose would knock off father's contemporaries, and for good measure, throw in a sudden passing from my own North Winnipeg generation.

She was not so much morbid as an archivist, and so, in a way, it was not surprising that over the years, she became my own living scrapbook of sorts – my personal archivist – collecting not just the dead but every press clipping that ever mentioned me, as if I were about to die. In fact, Rose eventually refurbished the basement of her home to create a kind of suburban rec room of Zolf records. Though I knew it was crazy, as we got older, I grew to dread calling Rose on the phone lest I find myself truly on her Drum Roll of Death.

◎◎

Rose was my mother's best friend. They kept constant company, not unlike two women still living in the *shtetl*, because Rose, who had only known Zastavia as a very small child, had somehow internalized the whole town, and it was this map she'd made – a kind of reverse pioneering – that secured her world. And so, she sometimes shared with my mother an intense longing for certain Zastavia shops, the lanes between the shops, the wood houses with the broken fence slats, and the reed-heavy lake at the edge of town, going swimming with my mother.

Their yearning bewildered and perplexed my father. Of course, Rose understood better than my father that the highlight of my mother's life, no matter her freedom in Winnipeg, remained her girlhood in the comfortable Pasternak house beside the lake, the hours she'd spent drifting, floating in that lake with her sisters and her Polish, Lithuanian and Jewish girlfriends. Rose understood that even though the death camps had taken all my mother's immediate family – her parents and three sisters – Freda still longed for the old days: the family closeness, the intimate familiarities, the sepia lighting, and Yiddish, her *shtetl* tongue.

◎◎

My mother was always somewhat fearful of Canada, and so she had learned English slowly. Despite her deep longing for

61

Zastavia, *deportazia* – deportation – was the scariest word in her vocabulary. For years, she had refused to take out citizenship, fearful that obscure Canadian authorities would, upon the "discovery" of her presence, initiate *deportazia*. It was Rose who patiently and persistently talked my mother out of her fears; it was Rose who tutored my mother, telling her about Canada and Canadians; and it was Rose who, at last, took my mother to write the citizenship test. Quiet and ever-dignified, my mother wore her black gabardine suit, black oxfords and black cloche hat with the feather in the band. She was the most beautiful new citizen of 1947 – only twenty-one years after she'd bravely crossed the seas and entered the country.

In the 1930s, the years of the Great Depression, money was tight in the Zholf household. There was no university offer on the table for Rose, no suggestion that she might easily meet a nice Jewish internist and settle into a Donna Reed lifestyle. Rose, born with an unfailing, cheerful disposition within which to shelter her obsessions, her morbidity, enrolled in several commercial courses at St. John's Technical High School; she learned to take rapid dictation, type up a storm, and file for hours. Always at the top of her commercial classes and always self-sustaining, Rose found jobs for herself, never needing or counting on my father's allegedly impeccable contacts.

Her first job saw her as confidential secretary to Mr. Andrew Schwartz, a modestly successful pharmacist who had, with all the illogic that is life, become a hugely successful auto wrecker. Mr. Schwartz was married to Lillian, one of the beautiful Arkin girls, the *crème de la crème* of Winnipeg Jewish society (it seems that there was such a thing). The Schwartzes fell in love with Rose. She filled some gap in their lives. They cultivated her. They confided in her. They took her in their boat and cruised down the Assiniboine River. They advised her, admired her, and served her high tea in their Wellington Crescent mansion.

The matriarch of this family was Mrs. Anne Arkin. (Her grandson is Gerry Schwartz, presently president of Onex Corporation. Not only is Gerry one of Canada's wealthiest entrepreneurs but a former president of the Liberal Party of Canada. In his presidential capacity, I've come to know Gerry very well. Once, during a telephone conversation with Gerry I was praising Mrs. Arkin, and I said: "Mrs. Arkin had this very beautiful daughter, Lillian, and a son-in-law who looked like Lew Ayres, the actor." An exasperated Gerry Schwartz interrupted me: "For God's sakes, Larry – you're talking about my mother and father!")

It was not long after meeting Rose that Mrs. Arkin steered the chauffeur to our home, our *chalupa*, our down-and-out dump deep in the North End of Winnipeg.

Mrs. Arkin loved to speak Yiddish, and my father, always poised to please the rich, was a perfect companion for her. When she heard that my father was writing a book in Yiddish, she bought him a Yiddish typewriter. For my mother, Mrs. Arkin brought cast-off dresses. I got britches with leather kneepads to items that her children or grandchildren had worn out.

These unusual gifts caused problems in the Zholf household.

Since my mother had been bred into a reasonably well-off continental family, she was insulted by the second-hand dresses and the attitude behind them. "We may not be rich," she said to my father, "but we're not *naket un borves*" – naked and barefoot – "either." My sister, Judith, felt much the same way; she threw the hand-me-downs from Mrs. Arkin straight into the garbage. And I complained that my threadbare britches made me "look like Sabu the Elephant Boy."

My father, however, insisted that Mrs. Arkin represented an opportunity for the Zholf family. After all, she had already set up Jewish lessons to be taught by my father to Jewish kids on Wellington Crescent. "I'll take Leibele with me to these lessons," said my father, "and he'll see the better life. He'll see that what I have planned for him is good, is perfect."

In his eyes, I had already become a street urchin. He was certain Mrs. Arkin would make a gentleman of me.

The first time my father took me to Wellington Crescent, we were welcomed into the sprawling mansion by a butler. My father entered an anteroom where his two pupils, show-ing no enthusiasm, were waiting for him. Left alone in the foyer, I wandered outside where I was besieged by ten rich, prissy, Jewish children. I was wearing the Arkin boy's britch-es because my father, who was almost totally devoid of social acumen – or, to put it more bluntly, devoid of street smarts – had decided that seeing the discarded britches on me would please Mrs. Arkin.

"Hey kid," said one little Jewish boy, "have you picked your nose today? One pick a day keeps poverty away!" Everyone laughed. A second mussed my hair. Then he kicked me in the shins and said, "Little *sheeny*" – garbage-picking "boys have to watch their step." Another little boy took my good cloth cap and sent it sailing down the road. Yet another said: "Jewish Pop Quiz! Which of these names is not Jewish: Roosevelt, Mackenzie King, Lawrence of Arabia, Othello?"

"Othello?" I offered. My second try, Lawrence of Arabia, left them sitting on the tailored lawn slapping their knees.

Then, two rich little Jewish girls circled me. "He stinks of garlic! Poor little Jewish boy hasn't got a proper diet," said one. Then the other piped up: "This one would still stink 'em up even if he was living and dining in Buckingham Palace!"

I quickly found my social betters rude and cruel, and their manners and deportment stiff and stupid. What they needed, I concluded, was a real good pogrom to shake them up. But then, before I could reconstruct myself as a one-man Cossack wrecking crew, my father arrived, and of course noticed nothing out of the ordinary. He took me to Mrs. Arkin.

"Ah, Leibele, I love your britches!" said Mrs. Arkin. "My son Morris looked like a tank commander in them. Keep wearing these britches, Leibele, and you'll be a tank commander one day yourself!"

Mrs. Arkin ordered tea from the maid. She then taught me how to hold a teacup and teaspoon, how to stir the sugar, how to pour the cream, how to avoid slurps, the smacking of lips, and burps, and how to pat-pat-pitter-pat the lips with a napkin afterwards. Slowly, but surely, Mrs. Arkin made me one of the North End's rarest breeds in britches – a Little Lord Fauntleroy of the Hebrew persuasion.

—I'll put him, however, into breeches, said my father,—let the world say what it will.

— STERNE

We should begin, said my father, turning himself half round in bed, and shifting his pillow a little towards my mother's— We should begin to think… of putting this boy into breeches.—

Not but the child looks extremely well, said my father, in his vests and tunics.—

He does look very well in them,—replied my mother.—

— STERNE

OF RINGS AND THINGS

Rose announced there was a man in her life. He was Harry Borodkin, a jeweller who worked for his father in a shop kitty-corner to United College on Portage Avenue.

Harry was a beached flounder among the Zholfs – he was neither argumentative nor overly opinionated. He was quiet, he was considerate. Still, if asked his opinion, he gave it clearly and boldly, and above all, briefly, and so he was liked by the Zholfs.

As Harry was in his late thirties and still working for his father, Joshua Falek (my domineering if not totally overbearing father who was devoid of any sense of irony about himself) expressed the opinion that, upon marriage, it would surely be time for Harry to become his own man – as any man should be his own man – and move into business for himself.

(Essentially, my father was hoping to secure a style of living for Rose that he had been unable to provide for his own family, a shortcoming that cut his vanity to the quick.)

It was 1942; I was eight years old. Rose asked me to be the ring bearer for her wedding. I said yes. Mrs. Arkin had inculcated in me a confidence about matters of etiquette and social decorum, and it was Mrs. Arkin who actually helped my mother buy a blue puff satin pillow on which to lay the wedding ring.

Just five years earlier, Joshua Falek, public defender of socialism and the secular life, public responsibility and the common man, had refused to give my older brother a *bar mitzvah*, and he had raised Rose, as one might expect, to be a good socialist. But now, he was nibbling at Orthodoxy – at the *yeshiva* days of his youth – seeking respect from men of good standing and reputation. And so he asked the Chief Rabbi of Western Canada and Environs, Rabbi Kahanovitch, to conduct the matrimonial ceremony under a *chupa*. That Rose's best friends were the daughters of the local Rabbi Herson, and that she wanted Rabbi Herson to marry her, didn't matter a hoot to Papa.

The Chief Rabbi had a very impressive presence; he was a born performer. He had the build of a stevedore, a huge black beard, and an enormous head, and he was sporting full Chassidic gear – long black coat and *shtriemel*. He was so fierce-looking, he scared me half to death.

Still, I was the Little Prince of the Ghetto, and being strictly show biz myself, I got over my fear of the barrel-chested, thickset, Chief Rabbi of Western Canada and Environs. With the gold ring perched atop my little blue satin pillow, I waited for my cue. The congregation was in tears. Decidely weepish. But I was tearless. I was a ring bearer. A professional. When the good rabbi asked for the gold band, I passed it to Harry without emotion. Not a flicker. After all, I'd learned how to drink tea without slurping; I'd learned how to button my lip and my britches; above all, I'd learned that I could do for my beloved sister, Rose, what needed to be done. Fauntleroy could flaunt his stuff with nary a glitch.

Life was markedly different without Rose in the house. My father, though he'd never have admitted it, was happier after she was gone. After all, Rose had often slept with my mother, and so my father had spent many restless years sharing a bed with my brother, Meyer, and myself. With Rose gone, my father finally had my beautiful mother all to himself in the matrimonial bed. There was a lithe spring to his step. A lasciviousness in the lilt of his Yiddish. And yet, my mother and father were now so out of practice in the bed – not sex, but the intimate quiet talk that can take place in the bed – that long pauses, long silences, all too often fell between their pillows.

Now she had a way that was never to refuse her assent and consent to any proposition my father laid before her— She contented herself with doing all that her god-fathers and god-mothers promised for her—and so would go on using a hard word twenty years together—and replying to it, too, if it was a verb, in all its moods and tenses, without giving herself any trouble to enquire about it.

This broke the neck, at the first setting out, of more good dialogues between them, than could have done the most petulant contradiction—:

—But indeed he is growing a very tall lad,—said my father.

—He is very tall for his age, indeed, said my mother—

—I can not (making two syllables of it) imagine, quoth my father, who the deuce he takes after.—

—I can not conceive, for my life,—said my mother—

—Humph!—said my father.

(The dialogue ceased for a moment.)

—I am very short myself,—continued my father gravely.

—You are very short,—said my mother.

—Humph! quoth my father to himself, a second time: in muttering which, he plucked his pillow a little further from my mother's,—and turning about again, there was a pause in the debate (for three minutes and a half).

—When he gets these breeches made, cried my father in a higher tone, he'll look like a beast in 'em.

—He will be very awkward in them at first, replied my mother.—

—And 'twill be lucky, if that's the worst on't, added my father.

—It will be very lucky, answered my mother.

—I suppose, replied my father,—making some pause first,—he'll be exactly like other people's children.—

—Exactly, said my mother.—

—Though I shall be sorry for that, added my father: and so the debate stopped again.

— STERNE

MEYER, MEYER, PANTS ON FIRE

During his eleventh grade in high school, my older brother, Meyer, lithe and robust, contracted rheumatic fever. His bout with the fever confined him to bed for almost twelve months. After he recovered, because he had missed so many classes, he – and his pal, Ruben "Beansy" Bider, who was in fact, a little slow-witted – were told to take seats in the "dummy" class at St. John's Technical High School. My father had always been proud of Meyer at the Isaac Loeb Peretz Folk School. After all, at the age of eleven, Meyer had written and published a Yiddish poem in *Der Tag*, the New York-based national Jewish daily. But now, Meyer had been demoted to the "dummy" class" where, as a complete goof-off, he'd been keeping intellectual company with his best friend.

My father was not amused.

Nor was Rose amused. She would whack "Beansy" with a broom and chase him out of the house, blaming him for Meyer's propensity to hang out in pool halls, dance parlours and bootleg joints.

Meyer quit school and went to work hauling 150-pound console radios on his back for Gotliebs' Empire Radio Store on Portage Avenue.

By 1939, Meyer had become not only muscle-bound but a fair shot at pool, a dandy on the tango floor, and an imbiber of smooth-as-silk white lightning – homemade vodka laced with coke.

He got in serious fist fights.

I worshipped the ground he walked on.

And, when I was the tender age of nine, after he got his nose broken, he was even more ruggedly handsome. His English, German, Ukrainian and Polish girlfriends were all beautiful. I loved the dingy pool halls and squalid bootleg joints my brother took me to. I thought my brother the perfect modern Canadian. He knew all about Marvel coloured comics and he could run all the reds on the green baize.

Often, on a Sunday, when Rose and my mother and father were out of the house attending a Dr. Zhitlovsky lecture or a Mani Leib poetry reading, Meyer would call together Beansy Bider, Larry Brooker, and Nathan Coop for a card game. And at Meyer's request, I would stand guard at the window, keeping an eye peeled for my father.

There was never any money on the table; they used matchsticks instead. My brother always had the most matchsticks, Beansy the least. Curious and guileless as to why Meyer and his friends would fuss and fight, curse and blaspheme, and count and recount matchsticks – only to sell them outside Smith's Groceteria for five cents a box – I asked my most trusted friend to tell me what was what.

My father's raid on Meyer's illicit poker game was worthy of Elliott Ness and the Untouchables. Meyer was grounded for six weeks and his friends were barred indefinitely from the Zholf household.

Still, a good older brother understands that a child's curiosity is not malevolent. Meyer had a warm, friendly chat with me; from this chat I learned the meaning of new words and concepts: stool pigeon, canary, rat, fink and quisling.

I swore undying fealty; he, not my father, was now my best friend. As such, Meyer taught me how to shine his shoes, press his shirts and pants, and shovel winter's frequent ten-foot Winnipeg snowfalls off the walk that fronted our house.

Above all, my older brother taught me lessons of love.

Meyer refused to limit himself to one woman, preferring to please many. Conflicting dates, two different women in two different places – these problems were not moral but logistical. And so, I became Mister-In-Between.

SALLY

I walked thirty to thirty-five blocks through a freezing, thirty-degrees-below zero Winnipeg blizzard – past dingy beer parlours, malodorous fish-and-chip emporiums – to Child's Restaurant at Portage and Main. I easily identified Sally from the Kodak snapshot my brother had shown me. She was waiting, not for Meyer but for Michael, as he liked to call himself when dating *shiksas*. Even if I was only nine I knew that Sally was as beautiful as any stars I'd seen in the movies. I could only conjure up, therefore, the beauty of Wanda – for Meyer-Michael was standing up Sally to be with Wanda.

"Sally," I began, "I know you will be overjoyed to hear that my brother has been drafted by the New York Rangers. His stay in training camp will only be a month! However, he has already left, so he won't be able to come and pick you up tonight."

"He won't be able to pick me up tonight," replied Sally, "because he is with Wanda. Besides, you may not know it but your brother can't skate!"

I was crestfallen.

"Don't let it get you down, kid," said Sally. "What are ya doing right now?"

"Nothing," I said.

"Okay, I'll take you to the movies!"

OLGA

"The Jews," said Olga, Meyer-Michael's very pretty Ukrainian girlfriend, "can't farm for shit and are scared shit-less of swords, umbrellas and gunpowder. When you pull their beards their balls fall off.

"The Jews only bet on horses, they never ride 'em. But once in a long, long while along comes a really good Jew, good in bed. Get me? A real somebody, a handsome devil, a goddamn *zhid* but a he-man with heft nevertheless – that's your brother Michael."

I told Olga that Meyer had gotten a bit part in yet another remake of *The Prisoner of Zenda*. "He's in Hollywood," I said, "taking fencing and riding lessons."

"Bullshit," said Olga, as she passed me another clove of garlic to nibble on, "and bullshit don't baffle brains."

Because they were *shiksas*, Meyer-Michael's beautiful women couldn't phone him, but they could phone and ask for me – and they did, at all hours. I would speak to them in a cryptic code. "Oh, the symphony at eight will be just fine," I would say. (That stood for: "Yes, he'll meet you at the Aragon Ballroom at eight.")

My father didn't understand. He was forever asking my mother, "Why does he get so many phones calls?"

"I don't know," my mother would say, winding the moon-faced clock that sat atop the icebox, the clock that bore the same type of bell often affixed to bicycle handlebars.

"Pray, my Dear," quoth my mother, "have you not for-got to wind up the clock?"

—"Good G—!" cried my father, making an exclama-tion, but taking care to moderate his voice at the same time,—"Did ever woman, since the creation of the world, interrupt a man with such a silly question?"

Pray, what was your father saying?—Nothing

– *STERNE*

PILLOW TALK

At the age of eight days, I'd lain upon a small pillow, naked and screaming, as a tall man with a tall hat and a broad beard that fell low, almost to his knees, took out a short knife, said the apparently appropriate blessings, and without *once* consulting me, pared off my foreskin like you'd pare an apple. To this day, when I contemplate my private parts in private, I'm convinced Baruch Moishe, the *mohel*, took off too much, leaving me at a competitive disadvantage.

In any event, the *mohel* officially made me a Jew. And the world I stepped into was no Jewish heaven. One year later, in 1935, Hitler's Nuremburg Laws were proclaimed. In my child's bed, I took them personally. We heard in our hearts the breaking of Berlin shop windows, glass and crystal tinkling in the night. The Jew-hating Hun had trapped my father's cousins and mother's families in Zastavia.

Feverishly, Joshua Falek besieged the Mackenzie King government, requesting that he be allowed to sponsor his Polish and Lithuanian relatives, sponsor them for landed immigrant status and ultimately Canadian citizenship. He got *zilch*. His good friend, the North Winnipeg socialist MP, A.A. Heaps, was also a good friend of Prime Minister Mackenzie King. Heaps personally intervened on behalf of the Zholfs. He, too, got *zilch*. Mackenzie King was politically aquiver; he feared an anti-Semitic Québécois response to

Jewish refugees in Canada. King stalled Heaps for months before delivering his final answer, an unequivocal *no*. Joshua Falek's desperation, the suffocating sense of doom that he felt at his family's entrapment in the old country, turned him into one of the North End's fiercest fascist fighters, a real gunslinger.

One morning – in 1938, almost a year before the war broke out – my father alone, save for four-year-old me at his side, stood at the corner of Mountain and Arlington, at the heart of North Winnipeg's German community. Rabbinical in his presence, he had shaken his fist at a flag, the Swastika of Nazi Germany that was fluttering over the Royal Canadian Legion's German-Canadian Hall.

"Murderers! Butchers!" my father had shouted. "You have no place in Canada. You have no loyalty to this country. Today, you fly the Swastika, the banner of butchery, tomorrow, we will crush fascism and all you stand for!"

This Legion Hall was the meeting place for German-Canadian veterans of the First World War, old soldiers who, together, drank beer and played darts, like legionnaires everywhere. These men, however, had fought in the trenches for Canada, King and country; they'd fought against their motherland, lost brothers in that battle against their motherland. Now, hearts torn and dreading the worst, they tried to believe that their motherland and Canada could be brought together in some kind of accommodation.

So, they'd flown the Swastika. Beside the Red Ensign.

My father was unforgiving.

He was dead certain that when war broke out, German-Canadians would have to choose which side they were on, and many, he believed, would select the Swastika, and – as Hitler now called it – their motherland. My father further believed that those who did make such a choice should, without recourse to compassion, be placed by the army and/ or the police in internment camps.

He was adamant.

By the fall of 1938, Joshua Falek Zholf and the whole Zholf family were ready for total war.

Ruth (standing), Judith (seated, left), Meyer (middle) and Larry

—The act of killing and destroying a man, said my father, raising his voice—you see, is glorious—and the weapons by which we do it are honourable—We march with them upon our shoulders—We strut with them by our sides—We gild them—We carve them— We in-lay them—We enrich them—Nay, if it be but a scoundrel cannon, we cast an ornament upon the breach of it.—

– S<small>TERNE</small>

EXTRA, EXTRA,
AND A RIM SHOT

At midnight on September 3, 1939, I was awakened by shouting outside our home on Aikins Street. I got out of bed in my bare feet. I shivered in my pyjamas. The upstairs floor was ice cold. The wood stove in the kitchen was responsible for heating the whole house; its fire was dead.

I heard my brother. Meyer was out in the street, yelling: "EXTRA! EXTRA! HITLER INVADES POLAND. BRITAIN DECLARES WAR. MACKENZIE KING TO FACE A SPECIAL SESSION IN PARLIAMENT. EXTRA! EXTRA! READ ALL ABOUT IT IN THE *WINNIPEG TRIBUNE: WAR EDITION.* EXTRA! EXTRA!"

He gave me a copy of the *Tribune.*

"Go wake Papa. He'll want to know all about this."

The Zholfs gathered in the dank, ice-cold living room and huddled on the couch. While my mother stacked kindling in the wood stove, my father tuned the radio to CBS where H.V. Kaltenborn was broadcasting war updates. He said the *blitzkrieg* by the Nazis in Poland had been so rapid that the Nazis had already captured Danzig and were only a few miles from Brest-Litovsk. This was the city in which my father had studied for his rabbinate; and Zastavia was not far away. Soon, my father's father, the Pasternak sisters, and Aunt Peshe and her family would be trapped by the *blitz* behind

Nazi lines, hollow-eyed and hollow-cheeked with hunger. My father had seen that look. Behind battle lines. He was furious that Canada had not immediately declared war on the Nazis.

My mother brought us cake and jam.

My father ate very little, full of foreboding – in particular for his old father. Old men should not die on the run. They should not die abandoned to wild dogs. My father had heard the howling of dogs. Then he perked himself up. Churchill was in charge of Britain, he said, and that old bulldog would grab Hitler by the neck and choke him to death. "Let's not be sad. We Zholfs have a war to fight. Meyer will be a soldier. Rose will be a military secretary. Judith will knit sweaters for the troops."

"What about me, Papa?" I asked.

He laughed. "Maybe we'll find German toys for you to destroy. Or somebody's piano. You will run messages and help our soldiers. You will do your part."

Meyer was excited at the thought of being a soldier. He wanted to kill Nazis immediately.

"You'll get your chance, Meyer," my father said. "Now, let us all go back to bed. We have a lot of work to do. For us, the war starts now!"

> …as the knowledge or arms tends so apparently to the good and quiet of the world—and particularly that branch of it which we have practised together in our bowling-green, has no object but to shorten the strides of Ambition, and intrench the lives and fortunes of the few, from the plunderings of the many—whenever that drum beats in our ears, I trust, corporal, we shall neither of us want so much humanity and fellow-feeling, as to

face about and march… and the faithful corporal, shouldering his stick, and striking his hand upon his coat-skirt as he took his first step—marched close behind him down the avenue.

— STERNE

For my father, World War II had in fact begun on August 23, 1939: a day of evil connivance and complicity. On that day, Hitler and Stalin signed a non-aggression pact. These gangster governments agreed that Latvia, Lithuania, and Estonia would be turned over by the Great Aryan, Adolf Hitler, to the Great Soviet Beast, Josef Stalin. As well, Poland was to be divided into two parts: one Soviet, one Nazi.

Back in March 1939, Britain – once again confirming my father's faith in the imperial power's basic principles – had guaranteed the existence of an independent Poland: any nation tampering with Polish independence would find itself at war with Britain. *Huzzah!* Now that Hitler and Stalin had carved up Poland, my father knew that the war was on. Horrifically, however, he also knew that his family, trapped in Zastavia, would probably be killed.

He waited the authoritative word on Soviet intentions from the Yiddish newspapers from New York. *Der Tag*, and *Der Forvertz*, *The Day* and *The Forward*, confirmed my father's worst fears, fears that ran counter to an ache he held in his heart for the Jewish communists back home who, like him – as a condition of their loyalty to the Soviet Union – had extolled the virtues of Yiddish as the official language of the Jewish masses. Jewish communists – now being betrayed by the Nazi-Soviet Pact – were much like those who would come to be known as Mapamniks – Left Labour Zionists who wanted

Yiddish to be an official language in the promised Jewish homeland, Palestine.

In 1939, my father was an enthusiastic supporter of the man who would found Israel's Mapam party, and the Jewish fighting force there, the Palmach. He was Zarubavel, a landsman, a fellow dweller in the town of Zastavia. On one occasion, Zarubavel, being a strongman blacksmith, lifted a horse over his head to attract a crowd for his speeches in revolutionary Russia. His Mapam strategy for a Jewish state in Palestine leaned heavily on Soviet geopolitics and Soviet power, which meant that Mapamniks and Jewish Reds had much in common – both envisioned a Jewish state in Palestine built by Jewish workers. The Mapam people believed that the Soviet Union was destined to deliver a Jewish Palestine. Communism, they believed, would be their safest, truest bulwark against Nazism and fascism.

On the day that Hitler and Stalin confirmed the Molotov-Ribbentrop Pact, my father – taking no notice of the knife sharpener with whom he crossed paths – visited Dr. Victor, his staunchest of communist friends and his most sympathetic of supporters when it came to Jewish cultural affairs.

I went with him.

The doctor was all smiles. He invited us into his office (oh blessed site wherein the Nose had received reprieve from the abortionist's knife; had my father ever troubled himself about this matter as he and I trundled along the speakers' circuit working as Zholf and Zolf?). Dr. Victor locked the door. Tea, cookies and strawberry jam appeared on the coffee table. The Yiddish newspapers from New York lay strewn on the sofa.

And so began the great debate.

"Well, I must say," said Dr. Victor, "I'm pleased to see that the Soviet Union has bought a valuable piece of time it needs with this Molotov Pact – time to rearm and resupply its forces so that it is prepared for the war of the future against the Nazis."

"Bought time, Dr. Victor? Bought time?" my father fumed. "The Soviet Union, the world communist movement and especially the Jewish communists, have squandered their international socialist goodwill for a mess of Polish pottage. Stalin has handed Poland over to Hitler; he has handed its Jews over to Hitler. It's the most cynical act in the history of the world. Stalin, champion of the worker, will now swallow up the Baltic republics. He's a Red fascist; Hitler's a white one."

"You're too emotional, Zholf," said Dr. Victor. "If Stalin had not made this deal, the Brits would have weaselled out of their guarantee of Poland's independence. Then, another Munich on our hands! Hitler would have grabbed Poland anyway and then turned on Russia; Russia would be alone against the Nazi beast. Now, there will be a world war and Russia won't be in it. Russia will have time to rearm and rebuild. A rearmed Russia can then save the Jews of Europe!"

"By the time Russia gets around to helping the Jews, they'll all be dead," said my father scornfully. Then: "Say, anyone here heard anything of Mandelstam, Gebertig – our great Jewish-Soviet poets? Look at that fine socialist Mayakovsky. Most poets write about love, sex, ingrown toenails, acne, psoriasis, shingles, madness, an eye tic, an eye sore. Mayakovsky, however, writes a whole book about Lenin – such puckering up, such ass-kissing the world has never seen. And what did Mayakovsky get for his buss upon the behind of the great beast? A bullet in the left ear! Stalin is probably working out a little deal right now: Gebertig and Mandelstam, wherever he is, for a carton of German binoculars. No, for two poets, two cartons. Stalin drives a hard bargain. Communism is not Jewish, Dr. Victor, communism is stupid!"

The debate went on, sometimes acrimonious but never insulting. Both knew that Canada would soon be at war with Germany. And both knew that the Molotov-Ribbentrop Pact would lead the Mounties to identify all communists as political undesirables, and then, with impunity, lock them up in internment camps along with Canadian Nazis and fascists.

Dr. Victor wanted my father to help him persuade key Jewish communists to go underground to escape detention. Joshua Falek, embittered by the Molotov Pact, felt that the Jewish communists could not be trusted in regards to the Palestine question or loyalty to the British-Canadian Empire. But then, engaging the logic of his own contradictions, he reasoned, the communists could still be good Jews and good Nazi-haters – and therefore good people, and good citizens.

Joshua Falek did not want to see Jews hunted by anybody – not even by the Royal Canadian Mounted Police. Knowing that he was about to break the law, to fly, in effect, two flags over the heads of his family, he agreed to help facilitate Dr. Victor's underground operations.

❦

On September 10, 1939, Canada ceased being a neutral country; war was officially declared on the Nazi Third Reich.

Mr. Glazer, a revered World War I veteran who owned Smitnik's on Aikins Street, asked to see me at Smith's Groceteria, where he was a hot-stove regular.

I, at five years old, was also a regular, and Mr. Glazer loved my stories of Jewish heroes and Jewish athletes, stories

I had moulded and fashioned as Zolf specials after hearing them at the Isaac Loeb Peretz Folk School.

"Wear something appropriate. I have a job for you."

From my closet, I retrieved the outfit my mother had bought me from the Bay earlier that year in honour of the 1939 Royal Tour; I'd worn it in May, the day we welcomed the King and Queen on their tour of North Winnipeg. The outfit was spectacular: a Union Jack cap and shirt, along with matching Union Jack short pants, socks, shoes.

When the Royal Tour passed us as we stood at the curb of Magnus and Main streets that day, my father sang "God Save the King" in Polish, so that his Polish neighbours would know where his loyalty lay. And to the applause of all the Zholfs gathered, I banged the toy tin drum that my brother had bought for me in honour of the royal visit; its skin bore a picture of the King and Queen and its drumsticks were printed with the Union Jack.

Now, on this day in September, I put on my Royal Tour suit and took up my toy tin drum to meet the revered Mr. Glazer at Smith's Groceteria. Mr. Glazer was smartly dressed in his brown-belted World War I uniform, complete with puttees and polished boots. On the sleeve of his jacket were the three stripes of a sergeant, stripes that had been hard-earned.

Mr. Glazer was so thrilled by my outfit that his wattles shook. His elbows joggled as he tried to contain his excitement. He asked me to come with him to the General Monash Branch of the Canadian Legion on Selkirk near Main. The General Monash Branch represented all those Winnipeg Jews who were veterans of the Canadian army and had fought in the Great War, 1914-1918. Ten members of the Monash branch – also dressed in their World War I uniforms – were waiting for Mr. Glazer and waiting for I.

Mr. Glazer was to lead a parade of the Jewish veterans. I was to walk beside him.

He carried the Union Jack in one hand and the flag of Jewish Palestine in the other. We marched down Main Street. As we passed City Hall, the Monash legionnaires dipped their flags and sang "O Canada" and "God Save the King." I played my toy drum. We then passed the Grain Exchange and headed up Portage Avenue, crossing in front of Child's Restaurant, the Capitol Theatre, Eaton's and the Hudson's Bay Company. All the while, Mr. Glazer stomped his feet to the beat of my tiny tin drum.

At last, we stood before the sobering silence of the grey stone Cenotaph on Memorial Boulevard.

With verbal snap, Mr. Glazer called out: "Men, halt. Men at ease." He saluted the dead and then delivered a eulogy: "Here is a plaque for Ben Himmelfarb, shot down by German machine-gun fire in the trenches at Ypres. Here is a plaque for Maxie Goldbloom, blown up in the trenches at the Battle of the Somme. And know this – as veterans and Jews, we survived the hellfire of the Germans in the Great War so that we would be alive today, to say to the Nazis: we, the Jews of North End Winnipeg and the General Monash Branch of the Canadian Legion, will fight you from here to hell and back. A roll of your drum, Leibele, *mein kind*."

I obliged with a rap of my sticks and a rim shot.

On day one of the Second World War, I, a little corporal with my drum, was already a Nazi fighter – the first Nazi fighter in the Zholf family.

—Ars Longa,—and Vita brevis.—Life is short, cried my father,—and the art of healing tedious! And who are we to thank for both the one and the other, but the quacks themselves,—who have first flattered the world, and at last deceived it?

– *STERNE*

As happy as sprung jailbirds, Beansy and my brother, Meyer, marched off in lockstep to Fort Osborne Barracks. They were singing a popular song set to the tune of the "Colonel Bogey March":

> *"Hitler has only got one ball,*
> *Goring has two but very small.*
> *Himmler is somewhat similar,*
> *But poor Goebbels has no balls at all!"*

Two hours later, Meyer, ashen-faced and desolate, was home. He sat on the sofa and held his head in his hands.

My father asked Meyer what had happened.

In a bare whisper, Meyer said that he had been rejected by the army. They'd told him that because he had a heart murmur, he was not acceptable. "I can lift 150-pound radios all day long but I'm not strong enough to kill Nazis! Not acceptable!"

My father took my brother in his arms and said, "Meyer, what is, is. What is, can't be undone. You want to fight Nazis? Work in the cordite plant. They need workers. Cordite goes into bombs. Bombs are dropped on Nazi heads. You're a brave man; you have nothing to be ashamed of!"

They rocked back and forth on the sofa, entwined in embrace. Mama and I watched; we said nothing. For the first time in my life, I understood consolation – the power of it, the need for it.

Mama prepared a platter of tea and cookies and placed it on the coffee table. She was in turmoil: relieved that my brother would not have to face the muzzles and cannons of war as my father had during the Great War, but also, aware that had my brother been healthy, she would have been a proud, if frightened, mother. About the Germans, she was ambivalent. Those that she'd known back in Zastavia, she had admired and liked.

"In those old days," said my mother, "German soldiers wore a helmet with a kind of spike sticking up from the top. They were very courteous to all the women in the village, especially the prettier ones. I always liked the way they took off their helmets, bowed from their waists and clicked their heels when they saw me coming down the street.

"But now, these Germans come to the doorsteps of our families in tanks and armoured cars. They line our friends and relatives up against the walls and shoot them. They burn synagogues, tug rabbis by their beards like they are silly horses, rob and loot and murder. There's a hate in them now," my mother said, "a hate for us Jews. If the British can't stop them, no one can. Still, we'll all do our part: Meyer at the cordite plant, Papa at the school, and you, my son, in every way you can. We are at war, all of us." She glanced at Meyer and my father. "Look, Meyer is having his tea. Your father seems contented. Things will be all right!"

Helping to make things right was the lapel pin that the enlistment board had given my brother. The pin had a cross on it, and wording that said that Meyer was an honourable volunteer for duty overseas and an honourable rejectee.

My brother always wore that pin: on his pyjamas before he retired to bed; on his undershirt when he exercised before the mirror in the bathroom; on the sweaters, sports jackets and suits he wore to movies and dances; on the overcoat he donned in stormy weather; on the uniform he wore into work each day at the cordite plant, where he churned out bomb after bomb.

There were, of course, consolations: Helga and Ingrid and Olive and Hazel and Susan, Madeleine, Popsy, Cuddles and Coo. My brother was easily one of the best-looking men in town; maybe he couldn't kill Nazis but he sure could slay women.

Not all of Meyer's girls, however, were as tolerant and affable as Sally had been.

One winter night when I was sixteen, I was woken from my sound sleep in the bunk bed that Meyer and I shared. *Plink, plink.* Pebbles were being thrown against the bedroom window. It was 5 a.m. Meyer was not in his bed. I went downstairs to the front door. Standing in the yard in the deep snow was Meyer, his hands covering his cheeks. He was frightened and very upset. I got him into the house. He lifted his hands from his face. Someone had gouged chunks of flesh out of his cheeks.

"What the fuck happened?!!" I asked.

"Monique. I was shooting pool at One-Eye Louis' when Monique showed up and insisted we go dancing. I was having such a good run at the coloured balls that I told her she should fuck off. She screamed and then she played Catwoman all over my face!!"

I was taken aback. Monique Pelletier was a pretty young woman, very well-endowed. She was a secretary at the cordite plant, a Franco-Manitoban from St. Boniface who loved to sing, dance and party.

Meyer and Monique had been a couple. But after a time at the cordite plant, Meyer enrolled in a chartered accountancy course and moved up in the business community – at which point, he suggested that Monique disappear. Monique had refused to oblige. In the emergency ward at the Winnipeg General Hospital, my brother's facial wounds were cleansed and stitches were applied.

Meyer, ensconced in the world of chartered accountancy, was very near the top of his class, his emerging specialty being tax avoidance. He had given up *shiksas* and was only dating rich Jewish girls from the emergent South End, girls whose last names evoked the great financial capitals (London, Berlin, Paris, Frankfurt) and romantic duchies (Luxembourg, Lichtenstein, Breslau). Their first names suggested great poets and places: Elizabeth, Victoria, Regina, Savannah, Laura, Florence. Their faces seemed to have absorbed, by osmosis, the ambiance of the Anglo-Saxon upper classes. They wore Edwardian tweeds, Byronic velvet pantaloons, Punjabi polo shirts, Holt Renfrew cashmeres, and the conical brassieres that Jane Russell would soon popularize. Their shoes were Oxfords, flat and comfortable; their necklaces cultured pearls. More often than not, their noses were seriously bobbed. Sometimes their taut little *tushies* were encased in Jantzen swimsuits or Spalding tennis shorts. Their armpits were always Arrid, and Modess, not the plebeian Kotex, gave them monthly comfort. Bars of Lux bobbed in their sunken bathtubs, Ipana made their capped teeth sparkle, and their breath was Sen-Sen pleasant. Above all, they – like well-brought up girls – chewed no gum.

Meyer was already dating one Gladstone and one Savannah. Frankly, I preferred his *shiksas* to the snobby, aloof, high-class Jewish girls of the South End. And I liked Monique, but she had become a veritable menace to my older brother and the whole Zholf family.

"Meyer," I said, counting the stitches in his cheek, "Papa must *never* see you like this! He's a heavy sleeper. I'll set the alarm for six in the morning every day. You'll get dressed and sneak out of the house. At breakfast, I'll tell Papa that you're taking two extra courses – fiduciary trusts and debenture management – and that you have to be at school by seven. Papa will love that. If you need anything, just call me and I'll deliver it. Nobody will ever know that you were once our very own Scarface of the North!"

The whole family had a compound interest in Meyer's future – a chartered accountancy degree, an opulent wedding, a blue-chip wife – it was all written on the Big Board in the sky.

Meanwhile, I was sure Monique would strike again.

A month passed. Meyer's wounds healed and the stitches were removed. Then the phone calls began.

"Hi, is Meyer there?"

"Sorry, Monique, Meyer is in Berne, Switzerland. He's doing the books for the International Zionist Conspiracy Headquarters."

Meyer, who was lying on the sofa, loved that line.

"When will he be back?"

"Oh, six weeks. Then he's off to Ethiopia to do Haile Selassie's books!"

Monique hung up.

"She'll be back," I said. "She'll do you damage, Meyer."

"Relax, kid," he said.

Returning from high school one day, I saw two police cruisers parked in front of our house. My heart broke as I saw the look of terror on my mother's face, and the anger and confusion on my father's face. They still hated and feared the police.

I stepped inside, nose aquiver. Immediately I intervened and asked the officer what the trouble was.

"Monique Pelletier of 1244 Vanier Crescent says one Meyer Zholf stole a cigarette case and a wristwatch that belong to her. Miss Pelletier says that one Meyer Zholf has also been making improper advances towards her."

His cold, impersonal tone made my mother shake but it didn't intimidate me. "Sergeant," I said, trying my best to adopt his manner, "Miss Pelletier is one very miserable and unhappy woman. The proof of the falsity of her charges as stated is easy. Wait a moment." I ran upstairs, ransacked a secret bureau drawer, and returned, exculpating evidence in hand. I handed the officer the cigarette case.

"Would you read the inscription please?" I asked.

"'Meyer, I love you madly. Monique.'"

"Thank you, Officer. Now for the inscription on the watch."

"'Meyer, love and kisses as always, Monique.'"

"Now, sir, you don't think that my brother actually stole these items and then quickly had them engraved, do you? Miss Pelletier always gave him gifts. My brother is very handsome. My brother doesn't pursue women. They pursue him. We are the Zholfs, Sergeant. Ladykillers, maybe. But we don't steal, and we don't beset women."

The police departed.

Two hours later, a buoyant Meyer strode into the house brandishing his exam results: third in his class. The pallor of police gloom, the pallor of dread lifted. Tea with lemon was served along with fruits and juices. Meyer, the Zholf family's Muse of Security and Substantial Bank Accounts smiled. Blessed forgetfulness settled over the Zholf home.

Monique, however, was not finished. Phone call after phone call after phone call. My answers got wackier and wackier.

"Meyer is doing the books for the Billy Graham Crusade."

"Meyer is doing the taxes of the Shah of Iran!"

Monique's last call was different. "I want to speak to Meyer. Please, Larry. I know he's there. Just once, please. If you don't let me talk to him, I'll kill myself."

I was neither moved nor shocked by what Monique said. It was an old ploy and one I had heard often from Meyer's cast-offs. My response to Monique was as cutting as ever: "You're so beautiful, Monique. You have everything to live for. Live for me. I'm only sixteen now, but in two years time, I'll be eighteen and I'll be coming after you. You won't regret the wait!

"As for Meyer, he's in Ottawa meeting with Prime Minister St. Laurent and the cabinet. There are a few glitches in the Family Allowance scheme that they need Meyer to straighten out."

Monique hung up.

The last Monique phone call was from the police: "Mr. Zholf, tell your brother that late this afternoon, one Monique Pelletier set herself and her house on fire. We think she may have mailed your brother a note. After he gets it, the note has to come to us."

The note arrived two days later.

"I love you, Meyer: the way your body moves in bed, the way you laugh, the way you listen and the way you talk. Without you, life is shit, so fuck it. See you upstairs. Monique."

Meyer responded with appropriate relief and moderate guilt.

He continued to date only Jewish girls, and he became a chartered accountant for Edwards, Morgan and Halliday; shortly after his employ he was sent to represent the firm in Edmonton.

—And lastly—for all the choice anecdotes which history can produce of this matter, continued my father,—
this, like the gilded dome—crowns all.—

– Sterne

BEANSY BIDER –
BEAUTIFUL LOSER

Ruben "Beansy" Bider: many of his friends said he had got the nickname because he was always full of energy, full of beans; many of his enemies said it was because he was always farting.

Beansy farted in the synagogue and in elevators; he farted while climbing his neighbours' stairs, and while riding the escalator at Eaton's department store; he farted in the Jewish Old Folks' Home, and the "dummies" class at St. John's Technical High School; he farted during the school's annual Christmas play, which was always called, *Gone With Beansy's Wind*.

A short young man who looked like a cross between a raccoon and Oscar Levant, the Hollywood concert wit, Beansy was unlucky in love, unlucky at cards, unlucky at all and everything. My father would often practice his Yiddish and English by listing qualities that, in his opinion, best described unlucky old Beansy: "*Auswurf*: booted out of the house for debauchery. *Ligner*: liar. *Shicker*: drunk. *Momser*: bastard. *Shiksa schlepper*: skirt chaser among the gentiles.

But Beansy was lucky at war. He had passed the physical test and successfully enlisted with the recruitment board at Fort Osborne Barracks.

My brother and I saw Beansy off at the CPR station at Higgins and Main. Beansy was going to Camp Shilo for military training. My brother looked pensive.

Beansy, however, was all smiles. He boarded the train and gave us a stiff military salute. Then he winked and said, "Take care of all my girls," as the train pulled out of the station.

"What girls?" my brother asked rhetorically.

Then, my brother told me a dark secret. "Beansy was with me when we were jumped by those Jew-hating Polacks who broke my nose and ribs. I was doing good; I was giving as good as I got. But when I turned around, there was no Beansy – nowhere, no fuckin' where. I hope Beansy remembers, 'cause the Nazis will always be there."

Months passed. There was no word of Beansy. But then D-Day came and the bloody battles for Allied supremacy in Normandy began, and Beansy was there – especially at the 1944 Battle for Caen. Alexander McKee, a British war correspondent, filed Beansy's story in London's *Daily Telegraph*. The McKee story also ran in the *Winnipeg Free Press*:

There had been a delay in attacking Verrières, which was on the ridge west of Bourguébus; the 7th Armoured Division was late in moving out and letting the Canadians in; there was time for the Germans to bring up reinforcements. The 272nd SS Infantry Division was up there along with some seventy tanks of the 1st SS Panzer Division, and a battle group from a Vienna-based panzer division which had been hurriedly transferred to help block 'Goodwood.' It was not until early afternoon that a Canadian division went forward to the attack.

The South Saskatchewan Regiment was going into its first real action, and with them went Private Ruben Bider from Winnipeg. On the right, the attack made progress slowly, but the German-armoured counterattack from Verrières hit the SSR and hurled them back down the slope. The last step was to evacuate the wounded in the carriers, before the infantry's rifle companies caved in, and Bider helped with this. There was no one left to give him orders any more. His company commander was dead, his platoon officer was wounded, his section leader was dead. It was rough, for a first battle.

"I just stayed around and found some fellows who had been wounded. Among the last was Pte. V.A. Aston; he was hit in the leg and had lost a lot of blood. I gave him a smoke. I was told to stay there by a Major, and I did, till another Eastern outfit came to re-take our position, four hours later.

"I was alone till then, cut off from our own lines. I got myself a Bren, two Stens and two rifles. Some Germans were advancing. I shot at them with the Bren and saw some fall. I then saw a German tank move up, and their soldiers pull back. I crawled to another position so that I could see our own tanks advancing. Some troops from Ontario came along, and I joined up with them and stayed there that night. I didn't get back to my unit till two days later. I got put in for the Distinguished Conduct Medal, but I didn't get it. I guess if my name had been James M. Smith, I would have got a ribbon."

Montreal's Samuel Bronfman, head of the Canadian Jewish Congress, was impressed. "This guy Beansy is fucking something," said Bronfman. "We'll give the kid a fucking welcome at the station, a big fucking parade and a big fucking banquet."

Prime Minister Mackenzie King made it known that he wanted this young Beansy boy plucked from the battle lines of the South Saskatchewan Regiment; he wanted him brought home to sell Victory Bonds, to give Jews a hero, and to help King hold the Jewish vote.

The platform at the CPR Station in the North End was jammed with well-wishers. The mayor and the premier were there, and so was Samuel Bronfman. Platoons from the Cameron Highlanders, the Manitoba Dragoons and the Winnipeg Light Infantry were assembled. There were four Highland military bands; they were led by a big drum major waving a staff twined in dried, tanned rabbit skin.

When the Beansy parade reached Portage and Main, the city's prettiest girls waved, cheered and lifted their skirts just a little. At the Cenotaph on Memorial Boulevard, Beansy laid a wreath in memory of his fallen comrades. "Taps" was played and tears were shed.

The banquet was scheduled for that night. My father had not been invited. It was a Bronfman enterprise and my father was no friend of the bootlegging Bronfmans. Meyer had not been invited either; he was out with Melba Maugham, a lithe, five-foot-nine-inch Jewish beauty from the south end of town.

"What do you think of Ruben?" my father asked me.

"He's a hero, Pop. He's a Jewish hero! What's to ask?" I said.

"Well, before the war, Beansy was a bum."

The doorbell rang. There was Beansy, tipsy, dishevelled and haggard, there was a little spittle at the corner of his mouth. He asked for Meyer. My father did not know where Meyer was. "Thank you, Ruben," my father said, "for all the Nazis you have killed." He offered Beansy a drink, and then left the room to retrieve some of Bronfman's best Crown Royal. Beansy wandered into the kitchen. Sharp female screams erupted. My father and I rushed into the room and found Judith in tears, her blouse ripped.

My father was enraged. "War hero, my ass! A bum is a bum! Get out of my house!" He fetched his World War I pistol.

Beansy left quietly and Judith calmed down. But something in me had died: hero worship. Never again would I entirely trust a Jewish hero – not even Sandy Koufax.

As it turned out, Beansy had gotten drunk at the banquet and made a pass at an attractive Winnipeg matron who was Sam Bronfman's cousin. Bronfman and Beansy had come to blows; Bronfman delivered an uppercut and Beansy fell headfirst into his soup. After he was revived, Beansy had teetered out of the hotel and taken a cab to the Zholf home.

He was returned to his regiment. He re-crossed the ocean once again and continued to kill Nazis. He was demobilized in 1945.

After the war, Beansy became a member of Calgary's distinguished gambling and bookmaking fraternity. He did well; most of the time, he stayed flush.

Poetically, death came to Ruben "Beansy" Bider between horse bets in the late 1950s. The Royal Canadian Legion gave him a military funeral.

Jack Nocholson, a South Saskatchewan Regiment and Caen veteran who credited his life to Beansy's bravery, said – getting the hierarchical value of military medals nicely reversed – over the grave: "Ruben Bider deserves a Military Cross but I'll settle for a Distinguished Conduct Medal for his widow, Janet."

Then, Nocholson read mourners a poem that he had written. It was called "The Ballad of Ruben Bider:"

Normandy, July 1944, Hill 72, Caen
We had just taken
Up our position,
When the first heavy
Shelling began:

A barrage beyond
All comprehension.
Now my outfit's wiped out
To one man, me.

My situation's become
Quite confusing,
I'm ducking
Each .88 shell.
I find this
Dilemma amusing
Though I haven't
Got one hope
In hell.
And the build-up
All day
Has been steady.
There's Tigers and Panthers
Galore.
The SS Division is
Dug in and camouflaged
At the ready.
And they have anti-tank guns
By the score.

But even if death should
Befall me,
I'll stand here and fight
All alone.
The name's Ruben Bider,
'Beansy' they call me.
A young Jewish kid

On his own.
I'll fight like a fiend
To the finish,
I'll never go down in disgrace.
For no act of mine
Will diminish
The proud heritage of my
Race.

I've gathered the guns off
My dead mates all around me,
A grim aftermath of our rout.
And I by chance the Nazis
Should surround me,
I sure hope my ammo holds out.
There was a spot where
The Nazis didn't detect me:
The hedgerow behind
That stone fence.

That gave me a
Wide range of vision
As the enemy troops
Advanced.

I cover the wounded,
Alone in battle all day,
And pray that
Someone will find me,
Else there's no way
I'll get through this day.

JUDITH,
PRINCESS OF THE JEWS

Though he taught sixty hours every week at the Isaac Loeb Peretz Folk School and gave another thirty hours each week to private tutoring, Joshua Falek's larder was often close to empty – it was the Great Depression. Still, he somehow found ways to please his youngest daughter, Judith – his Princess of the Winnipeg Ghetto. Svelte, she had a full closet of her own in the ramshackle, enlarged shed, the *chalupa* we called home: plaid skirts, ruffled blouses, dresses, pinafores, slacks, and sweaters of cashmere, angora, and lamb's wool…

Joshua Falek envisaged his Judith, then fourteen, as a figure skater on a sheet of pristine ice, spotlights bouncing off her black hair and hazel eyes, her white leggings, her gossamer skirt: "The new world champion, Judith Zholf, daughter of North Winnipeg's renowned Jewish teacher and Yiddish writer, Falek Zholf, now takes her place among Canada's skating immortals." All too often, he heard this oracular voice in his one good ear.

His dream ended up stillborn. Judith never put on her expensive figure skates, nor did she ever take a skating lesson. Her ice costume hung from a nail on the wall opposite the staircase leading to the cellar. Below the stairs, her rusted blades gleamed dully.

My mother sat *shiva* for the outfit and the figure skates. "She never even used them once," she moaned. "This is a sin before God and man. With the money we spent, we could have taken Leibele, my sweet darling, to the movies and the zoo a hundred times. Our daughter thinks this is a palace and that she is a princess. This house is a dump and our daughter is a Raggedy Ann doll."

No silver blades were bought for me. I never learned to skate. Road hockey was my sport. Dreams of getting out of the Winnipeg ghetto and standing under the rippling marquee lights of major league hockey arenas in Montreal, Toronto, New York and Boston disappeared among the steaming dung "balls" dropped on the road by delivery-wagon horses. When my sister and I quarrelled, which we did often, my only cutting line was: "I could have been an NHL candidate, if not for you!"

When Judith was eighteen, however, a real NHL contender, so to speak, entered her life. He was a burly, camel-nosed Jew, aged twenty-eight, with a slight hunch. "I'm Max Labovitch," the apparition said to me, the first time he knocked on our door. "Is your sister Judy in?"

"I'll see," I said. Many had knocked – few had been admitted. This one, however, was sporting a New York Rangers jacket.

"Let him in," Judith said.

Being terribly shy, my mother never greeted any of my sister's callers.

And my father would never stop working at his desk unless the visiting beau gave off a whiff of trouble.

This time, however, was different. My father, *schnozz* twitching, beard bobbing, was all over Max Labovitch. "Are you a rabbinical student?" my father asked. "If not, why not? Are you perhaps a medical student? An architect maybe? How about an interior decorator?"

"That's for girls, Pa," said I. "Max here plays NHL hockey."

"Hockey? What's that?" my father demanded at the top of his lungs.

Since I was a mouthy ten-year-old, I volunteered the basics of hockey: "Men chase each other all over an artificial ice rink, Pa," I said, "trying to get a small rubber disk called a puck into the net of the other guys."

"What's a Jew doing playing a *goy* game like that?" my father yelled. Turning to Max Labovitch, he asked: "What do you want from my daughter? She should maybe put on hockey skates and join you in the crazy house?"

"It's only a date, Pa," I said. "Let our Judy go," I whispered into his bad ear, his deaf ear. "Let her go out with Max and nature will take its course."

From Max, I got an official New York Rangers sweater. My father got a New York Rangers lighter and ashtray. My mother got a dozen New York Rangers drinking glasses. My brother got a New York Rangers robe. New York Rangers bracelets and earrings adorned my sister and so did a short-skirted cheerleading outfit. Everybody quickly learned to like Max. His cleaning lady said that he was as neat as a pin. His landlord said that Max never defaulted on rent. The kids outside his apartment block said that Max bought them goalie pads and a net for the pickup games on the street. No one mentioned that Max, for some reason, was not in the army fighting World War II. No one asked whether or not Max was a good a player. No one asked what his record was in the NHL.

A local sportswriter for whom I did delivery favours said that he would look into this Max Labovitch for me. He was back with answers *tout de suite*. "Well, kid," he said, "Max the New York Ranger has zero assists, zero goals and has never seen the opposition net, much less dented it. What did you expect, kid? He's a Jew! Jews and hockey do not go together. Max is only in the NHL because all the good players are in military uniforms." Then he added: "Poor Max, he only makes twenty-five dollars a week with the Rangers."

I passed the information to my father. "Hitler is killing us in Europe," I said, "and Max is chasing a little rubber puck across a patch of ice – for a pittance yet. Max has no future in this house. I'll tell Judith."

Judith didn't care. Forget Max! She had met a soldier. She told Max, and Max never stood on our stoop or darkened our door again. The soldier turned out to be a whim and he was sent packing. The next upstart to appear as a serious suitor in my sister's life was a Jewish Adonis. He was an extremely charming and muscular boy, a nifty tango dancer, a pool shark, a quirky young businessman, a close friend of my brother Meyer, who called himself Alex L.

My father did not approve of Alex L. After all, Alex's parents not only cleaned our house and washed our floors, they dabbled in the black market and had connections in the underworld. In fact, the first time Meyer brought Alex to our house, my father and Meyer had words; Meyer stopped bringing Alex home.

But I liked Alex. He mussed my hair, slipped me money, and treated me like the adult I thought I was.

Judith also had gone nuts over Alex. They became a secret couple, wandering around the various night spots and dancehalls in town.

Alex, however, had a reputation, and there was talk that the law would soon be on him. So Alex said goodbye to Judith and moved his business operations to the more tolerant climes of Alberta.

Judith was heartbroken, as I have since learned. It is a universally acknowledged truth, however, that the hearts of dark-haired, hazel-eyed, long-legged, dusky beauties like my sister, Judith, do not stay broken for long. What's more, she knew it. Even in her sorrow, there was an air of self-assurance about her. After all, she had all the social graces, and she was a good dancer – from ballroom to rumba to jitterbug. In fact, Judith was so popular at dances that she was often double-booked.

Those who were to be sloughed aside, left alone on the dance floor, had to be told – and since I had been well-trained by Meyer, this became my appointed task on behalf of my beloved Judith. And so, some Harvey, some Nathan, some Max or Merv, was told that Judith had been afflicted by none other than the Virgin Mary, indeed a personal appearance, and not only had she converted to Catholicism, but she was on her way to a nunnery in Rhode Island. If I was feeling really mischievous, I would whisper that Judith's option had been picked up by the Edmonton Grads, then the women's world champion basketball team, and that she was, at that very moment, bouncing a ball on a gymnasium floor somewhere in the Alberta foothills.

She was a fully developed woman – wearing a one-piece bathing suit, she was a knockout – a woman who cherry-picked her favourites, and light-footed it through politics and history. She told a date who was a Jewish Young Liberal that she thought Mackenzie King was the monarch of Scotland.

As a Jew, her interest in tribal affairs was confined to an unthinking Zionism and a knee-jerk aversion to inter-marriage. Nonetheless, since contradiction was in the warp and woof of the Zholfs, she liked being with gentile boys.

I remember looking out the back window of a Selkirk Avenue streetcar and seeing my sister lift her lips to those of a Canadian soldier who was as Jewish as haggis. Shortly thereafter, I saw her strolling down Main Street arm-in-arm with the same soldier. I was only eight, but I was as patriotic as any other Canadian; I concluded that my sister was simply keeping up the morale of the gentile soldiers so that those soldiers could go overseas and kill those devil enemies of the Jewish people, the Nazis. On the night of Judith's sixteenth birthday, our parents went out and left me in the hands of Sweet Sixteen Judy, who was having a party. Whenever I was forced with such circumstances, I played my favourite game: detective.

Lying beneath my parents' bed, I watched as Luba Pepesko's panties were slowly removed by Asher Fleishman, the optometrist's son. In the living room, I saw my sister dancing cheek to cheek. I saw Manny Cooperman's hands running like rivulets all over Claire Zamick's ripe and ready mammaries. I also noticed a very handsome, elegant gentile boy of about eighteen sitting by himself on the Zholf sofa. The boy's calmness and equanimity attracted the sleuth in me.

Sitting down opposite him, I said: "You're not Jewish, are you?"

"No, I'm not," he said.

"Are you Ukrainian?" I asked.

"No!"

"Polish?"

"No!"

"German?"

"No!"

"English?"

"No!"

I had gone through the whole of my North Winnipeg Ethnic Hall of Fame.

"Kid, I'm Danish," he said.

Joy shot through the veins of my heart. Nobody cherished Danes more than my father.

"The Danes," I gushed, "are a great people. My father says the Danes wear the hated yellow Star of David on their arms in sympathy with the Jews. The Danes saved their Jews by smuggling them into Sweden. My father says the Danes are the Just People who keep the world going." By this time, there were tears in my eyes.

My sister, however, didn't like my speech. "How dare you pester my guests!" she said forcefully. "In the morning, I'll tell Papa about your appalling lack of manners, your complete boorishness!" Then she burst into tears and ran to her bed.

I didn't sleep that night, and in the morning, I was too tense to eat my breakfast. My father was on his second helping of pancakes when Judith joined the table.

She wasted no time. In precise detail, she told him how I had waylaid an innocent gentile high-school mate of hers, that I'd asked him questions about his race and talked about the Danes, the Jews and the Nazis.

My father listened intensely. He turned to me: "Did you talk to the boy about the Danes wearing the yellow Star of David in sympathy with the Jews?"

"Yes, Papa, I did."

"Did you say that I told you the Danes were a Just People who keep the universe going?"

"Yes, Papa, I did."

"Good boy, Leibele. You're a good boy. I'm proud of you!!"

He asked Judith to step forward and he slapped both her cheeks, hard. "How many times do I have to tell you, I don't want *shkotzim* (young gentile boys) in my house unless I'm around to keep an eye on them?"

⊙⊛⊙

Judith was bored with school. She took a job at a garment factory, where she worked as both a secretary and a model. She spent all of her money on clothes and thought that if she was well-dressed and well-coiffed, successful Jewish boys would fall into her lap like little green apples.

Cut off from the university crowd, however, she found her social life crimped. She suffered long periods between dates. In a strange way, I became the young Jewish man in her life. I went with her to movies and plays. I escorted her to weddings and funerals. We did the dishes together, and had playful pillow fights, and fierce, half-erotic wrestling matches.

Then, one day, when I was sixteen, a Jewish gentleman stepped into my sister's life after parking his Cadillac outside our front door. He wore a blue blazer, grey flannels and white shoes. On his head was a jaunty yachting cap. His English was slightly accented, not unlike the cinematic representations of characters in London's Saville Row. He had a bouquet of flowers in his right hand, and a box of chocolates in his left hand.

"Is your sister home?" the Jewish squire asked.

"Whom should I say is calling?"

"Tell her it's the Prince of Pleasure. She'll know."

"Judy," I yelled behind me, "it's the Prince of Pleasure calling."

111

My sister chortled at the flowers and chocolates. Her cocktail dress was dazzling, her French cloche hat was sauciness itself, and her gold earrings jangled in the stiff prairie wind.

"Larry, this is Allen Teitelbaum. Allen, this is my kid brother, Larry."

After that, my sister was engaged in a mad whirl of dances, cotillions, bazaars, movies and museums, as well as cruises down the Assiniboine River in *The Cupid*, Allen's boat.

People stopped my father on the street to ask if the wedding had been scheduled. Others suggested he might retire from teaching now that a rich son-in-law – owner of Milady Chocolates and a downtown restaurant also called The Cupid – was in the offing.

"He never lays a hand on me. He's always so polite," Judith told my mother with great pride.

My mother cocked a quizzical eye.

Then, a small item appeared in the *Winnipeg Tribune*.

"Allen Teitelbaum – restaurateur, chief executive officer of Milady Chocolates and man-about-town – and pastry chef, missing." The article said that thirty-sex-year-old Allen was last seen giving Juan a ride home from the restaurant in Allen's Cadillac. Both had been missing for more than a week.

Meyer, who'd only been there a few months, flew in from Edmonton and a family council was held. Meyer was delegated to tell Judith the truth.

"The reason Allen has never laid a hand on you, Judy, is that he doesn't like laying hands on women," Meyer said.

My sister broke into violent sobbing.

"He likes me better than he likes you. That's where he feels free. He wants my body, not yours – get what I mean?"

Judith did, and wept copious tears.

—a tear of sentimental bashfulness—another of gratitude—and a tear of sorrow for her misfortunes, started
into his eye, and ran sweetly down his cheek together;
—he stood silent for a minute and a half; at the end of
which he took his hand away, and making a bow,
went on with his story of his and the Jew's widow.

— STERNE

OUR BLOCK

Our first home had been one in a row of four semi-detached houses, wood-framed firetraps, often bedbug infested, that had interlocking cellars. Fires were endemic.

Of our immediate neighbours, Mr. Barsky – who made his living by painting the exterior of CPR boxcars – was Winnipeg's chess champion. My father would take me to Louis' Delicatessen on North Main Street. The Winnipeg Jewish chess club met in the back of the deli; the noise here was deafening. My father knew very little about chess yet, full of male strut, he said to me: "Chess is a Jewish game, my son. Jews are the world's best chess players. Look at Mr. Barsky. Jews use their brains. Jews do not commit pogroms."

Next to the Barskys lived an old Jewish widow, Mrs. Shecwitz. One day, when I was four, I went to visit Mrs. Shecwitz. As usual, she was sitting alone in her rocking chair. Her face, however, was wrapped in spider webs, and caught in the webbing were little flies. I tried to shake her, to wake her.

I breathed upon her with my mighty nose.

Nothing.

Beside Mrs. Shecwitz were the Rosenbergs, famed for their tomcat who was the size of a small panther. He gleefully and publicly molested lady cats. He bit the throats out of male cats. Somehow, through the Rosenberg cat, I understood – without anyone having to say it – that there is a deep violence in all sexuality.

In the fourth house lived the Kleinmans. There was some-thing very sad about the Kleinmans. The patriarch, with his straggly grey beard, had been in World War I. He was still shell-shocked. He did not have a job; he hadn't in years. Every afternoon at 2 p.m., Mr. Kleinman would leave his house and walk the length of the four semi-detached houses. Then, he'd cross the street to Manitoba Avenue and, ever so slowly return home, his head bowed as if he were a no one from nowhere.

Our house, with its tiny veranda, was very small. Our sti-fling little dining room was used only on Jewish holidays. The kitchen was our living room. It held an icebox (one of my earliest jobs – as a four- or five-year-old – was to take my little red wagon to the ice works on Salter Street and bring back a huge block of ice), a huge pot-bellied woodstove with four hot plates, a small table, and a cluster of kitchen chairs not just for the family but for the Jewish writers, actors and poets my father would bring home.

Down the street, at the corner of Selkirk and Aikins, was the Holy Ghost, Church Dom Polski – Western Canada's largest Polish Catholic cathedral. Holy Ghost nuns and priests were everywhere on our streets, along with Galicians ("hunkies") in fur hats and Cossack boots. There was the State Theatre of Yiddish movie fame. There was Mitchell's Kosher Meat Market, where the city's socialist mayor, John Queen, a leader of the Winnipeg General Strike, liked to entertain Jewish matrons with stories about the glorious 1919 strike. There was Mac's Bowling Alley.

And then there was Oretski's, where my mother took me whenever I needed new shoes. Oretski's had a new-fangled, so-called fluorescent x-ray machine that showed how fast a child's feet had grown. During one visit, Mr. Oretski said my feet had grown by four inches. My mother, however, said nothing.

"They're only ten dollars, Mrs. Zholf. These new shoes will let Leibele run around and have more fun. His toes won't hurt him anymore."

My mother stood tall and silent.

"Well, perhaps ten dollars is a bit too high a price, Mrs. Zholf. Seven dollars and fifty cents should be about right!"

Still, my mother said nothing.

"Okay, Mrs. Zholf, you win. Five dollars, not a penny less."

My mother gave Mr. Oretski a five-dollar bill, put the new shoes on me, and said: "Let's walk down Selkirk Avenue. We'll stop and buy some cakes and buns at Gunn's Bakery. We will eat to celebrate the price of your new shoes."

Rubenius threw him down upon the counter all kinds of shoes which had been in fashion with the Romans.—

There was,
The open shoe.
The close shoe.
The slip shoe.
The wooden shoe.
The soc.
The bushkin.
And
The military shoe with hobnails in it, which Juvenal takes notice of.

— *STERNE*

THE LITTLE DECLAMATIONIST

At the Isaac Loeb Peretz Folk School, I was a prodigy; I was a "declamationist."

In 1904, international Jewry's number-one poet in Yiddish and Hebrew, Chaim Nahman Bialik, had written *In the City of Slaughter*, an epic poem about the Kishinev pogrom of 1903. Jewish men, women and children were massacred and hundreds more wounded during the three-day anti-Jewish riot.

Amazingly, when I was six years old, I memorized the poem. Not only did I know the words but where to show sentiment, where to show anger, and where to cry out to the skies: "O God, why have you abandoned us!!"

My father arranged for me to appear of an evening in the sumptuous home of Clara Selchin, chairperson of the Mothers' Union of the Isaac Loeb Peretz Folk School. There, I declaimed before Mrs. Selchin and the rest of my father's female bosses: Mrs. Mayman, Mrs. Keller, and Mrs. Cherniak.

In full boyish voice, I described how the Cossacks had raped and murdered innocent Jewish women and children. I spoke of Jewish women trying to keep their modesty as the brutal Cossacks ran amok, and I bemoaned the plundering and pillaging, the barbarity.

My audience was rapt. My father, hunched forward on the couch, beamed with love and approval. I finished in a flood of tears on behalf of the pogrom's victims.

Clara Selchin, almost giddy, pressed me to her ample bosom. "You wonderful darling, Leibele. Your declamation reminds us all, alas, of the Slaughter Cities in Poland, what the Nazis are now carrying out against our people. Leibele, you are what the Peretz School is all about. You are your father's son. You are the future of the Jewish people. It's a pleasure for me to be able to hold you, to know you!!"

Bless us!— what the noble work we should make!—
how should I tickle it off!—'tis too much—I am sick—
I faint away deliciously at the thoughts of it—'tis more
than nature can bear!—lay hold of me—I am giddy—I
am stone blind—I'm dying—I am gone —Help! Help!
Help!—But hold—I grow something better again, for I
am beginning to foresee, when this is over, that as we
shall all of us continue to be great wits—there would
be so much satire and sarcasm—scoffing and flouting,
with rallying and reparteeing of it—thrusting and par-
tying in one corner or another—Chaste stars!

— STERNE

TAG DAY

Before I became the family *wunderkind*, Meyer – a proud socialist at the age of eleven – had written a poem in Yiddish. In 1935, at the height of the Depression, the poem appeared in *Der Tag* in New York. The poem was titled "The Rich and Poor of New York."

In New York there are millions – of rich and poor.
The rich live in big houses, where the sun always pours in.
The rich have beautiful yards with big gardens.
They spend their time at sumptuous balls, dances and
frequent tea parties.
They have their own yachts, cars, airplanes and other
things.
They have a lot of servants.
They eat nothing but gourmet food and drink from the
fanciest of goblets.
The rich own huge factories; for them the workers toil
ceaselessly.
The rich pay their workers a pittance.
The American government always sides with the rich.
Often the rich control even the president of the United
States.
However, in New York City there are far more poor than
there are rich.

The poor live in old small houses
Somewhere in the back alleys.
They have little to eat,
Except the odd scrap of bread.
The men wander around without work.
Their children peddle newspapers on the street.
The poor of New York sleep on old creaky beds
And wrap themselves in old rags.
Sometimes the poor are so hungry
They even eat the odd scraps of wood and bits
Of coal they find in the streets.
And so dwell the rich in their great satiety
And the poor in their abject poverty.

What is the life of man! Is it not to shift from side to side?—from sorrow to sorrow?—to button up one cause of vexation—and unbutton another?

— STERNE

OF OILS AND FATS

In 1942, Prime Minister Mackenzie King, through his governmental agency, the Wartime Prices and Trade Board, announced that he had a plan for the children of the nation. We were to collect oils and fats in our little red wagons. The oils and fats were to be turned into glycerine, an essential element in the making of bombs.

The Prices and Trade Board was headed by a severely impressive woman, Phyllis Turner, the widowed mother of a small boy about my age, John Turner (who would later become prime minister of Canada). Phyllis Turner – about to become the country's queen of oils and fats – was Canada's first senior female deputy minister.

In North End Winnipeg, I became the Crown Prince of Oils and Fats by turning to the community.

I began with our neighbour, Mr. Goldberg. He had a huge ramshackle chicken coop in his backyard. The coop overlooked our backyard and every day, hundreds of wretched, cooped-up chickens deposited their poop in our yard, fouling up the air.

I went to Mr. Goldberg of the well-worn white undershirt and asked him for *schmaltz* – chicken fat – from his chickens. He gave me five full containers of *schmaltz*.

Then I called upon Basovsky's Kosher Butcher a half-block away. Mr. Basovsky gave me the unkosher parts of chickens and other discarded meats which, when boiled, would produce oil and fat.

Next, I hauled my wagon to Kelekis, a restaurant on Selkirk Avenue. Mr. Kelekis gave me jars of oil that, now stale, had been used to cook french fries. In gratitude, I promised Mr. Kelekis, a Greek, that I would no longer celebrate Chanukah, the Jewish victory over the Greeks.

Then I went to Kugelman's Kosher Salami Factory. In his office, Mr. Kugelman was chomping on a fat hand-rolled cigar. He took me into the factory and gave me a whole rack of spoiled salami. He also threw in meat that had been rejected by the rabbis who worked for him. "Take all this stuff, kid," Kugelman said, "and shove it up Hitler's ass."

Mrs. Warga, a yard wide, gave me four jugs of lard.

It wasn't long before – as Li'l Abner's Mammy Yokum might say – I was the local champeen of oils and fats. I was rewarded by Phyllis Turner at a huge gathering of fellow oils-and-fats enthusiasts at the McGregor Armoury deep in Winnipeg's North End. I was only eight at the time, but I still remember Phyllis Turner vividly. An elegant woman in her double-breasted suit and veiled hat, she stood for over an hour so that she could say a kind word and present a badge to each of the hundred little boys assembled.

Proud of my badge, I headed straight for Smith's Groceteria. Mr. Smith was proud of me; he slipped me a sweet in violation of the Wartime Prices and Trade Board's strict rationing of chocolate.

My personal war against the Nazis was going very well.

Though I am old enough to have told the story so far myself,—and young enough, I hope, to have done it without malignity—'Tis a point settled,—,—and I mention it for the comfort of Confucious, who is apt to get entangled in telling a plain story—that he may go backwards and forwards as he will—'tis still held to be no digression.

This being premised, I take the benefit of the act of going backwards myself.

— *STERNE*

THE *SCHMALTZ* FACTOR

When I was four, my father introduced me to a visiting Yiddish theatre troupe, New York's finest Yids on the boards. As a result, at an early age I met a refined class of nice Jewish girls – in particular, the very beautiful Celia Adler, daughter of the greatest of all Yiddish actors, Jacob P. Adler. Among her siblings were Stella Adler, the legendary acting coach (whose students included James Dean and Marlon Brando and Robert De Niro), and Luther Adler (future star of *Hawaii Five-0*) who, in 1951, would go on to play Hitler twice in *The Desert Fox: The Story of Rommel* and *The Magic Face*.

Celia Adler had a gorgeous figure, a dusky face, and an actress's quirky coquettish temperament. Wisely, at my young age, I did not declare my intentions to her. Her close companion, Jacob Ben-Ami, (she was married to the actor, Nathan Forman), a man with a leonine head of hair and an aristocratic manner, who always appeared in velvet, was the Laurence Olivier of Yiddish theatre – and he was acutely jealous of anyone Celia paid attention to, even of boyish me.

The troupe travelled to Winnipeg every year and during each visit, they employed in their performances local offspring of Hebrew persuasion because Yiddish plays always had parts for small children. These troupes were in search of what they called the "*schmaltz* factor" – the chicken-fat factor – something the local audience would warm up to and love. A young hometown boy, therefore, would be perfect to deliver a Yiddish line or two onstage, milking special applause from the loutish yokels, the peanut-munching working-class crowd of Jews in the upper balconies. The *schmaltz* factor would often cause the performance of the play in question to soar to the rafters, to the skies.

My father knew the troupe, and they had decided I was pure chicken fat. He took me backstage where I watched the lady performers dress and undress. They were magnificent in their bras and half-slips, their lipstick, silk stockings, and hair curlers. I decided that womanly beauty was the future and its future was me – or at least, it should be.

The line given to me by Ben-Ami was: "Rabbi! Rabbi! Alarm! Alarm! Rabbi! They're killing Jews in the market-place!" I had not, however, been given a cue.

Desperately determined to vindicate my father's belief in my talents for *schmaltz*, and desperately eager to please my fellow North Winnipeg Jews in the balconies, I burst onstage during one of Ben-Ami's major soliloquies and shouted: "Alarm! Alarm! Rabbi! Rabbi! They're killing Jews in the marketplace!"

The entire audience in the Pantages Playhouse Theatre stood up and cheered for me, their local *wunderkind*, Prince of the Jewish Winnipeg Ghetto, *schmaltz* in the pre-pubescent flesh. They cheered for five minutes. Sour-faced Ben-Ami was not amused. He waited for the applause to die down and then, returning to character, delivered the rest of his soliloquy, coldly, cuttingly, flawlessly.

After the matinee, I sought out the sandwich my mother had prepared for me. I had put the sandwich in the pocket of my little pinafore jacket, which was hanging in a closet in the men's dressing room backstage. As I reached for the sandwich, someone – presumably from the New York Yiddish theatrical community – locked me in the closet. My screams of terror subsided only after I was let out two hours later.

I was certain that the perpetrator of this cruel deed was the man in the velvet suit, the legendary Yiddish actor, Jacob Ben-Ami; he was punishing me for the *schmaltz* applause I'd received by locking me, a mere child, in the closet.

This was the gist of the story I told my father. My father laughed and said, "Ben-Ami is a very good man. What happened to you, Leibele, is some kind of prank or weird accident."

How could I, a four-year-old, persuade my father that he was dead wrong?

'Tis a pity, that truth can only be on one side,—considering what ingenuity these learned men have all shewn in their solutions of noses.—

—Can noses be dissolved?

—My father thrust back his chair—rose up—put on his hat—took four long strides to the door—jerked it open—thrust his head half way out—shut the door again—took no notice of the bad hinge—returned to the table—plucked my mother's thread-paper out of Slawkenbergius's book—went hastily to his bureau—walked slowly back—twisted my mother's thread-paper about his thumb—unbuttoned his waistcoat—threw my mother's thread-paper into the fire—bit her satin pincushion in two, filled his mouth with bran—confounded it;—but mark!—

'Tis well my father's passions lasted not long; for so long as they did last, they led him a busy life.

This of course requires translation:—it shows what little knowledge is got by mere words—

In order to clear up the mist which hangs upon these pages, I must endeavour to be as clear as possible myself.

Rub your hands thrice across your foreheads—blow your noses—cleanse your emunctories—sneeze, my good people!

—God bless you!

Now give me all the help you can.

— STERNE

THE LITTLE PROPAGANDIST

By 1942, I had become a military expert. I followed the war on the radio and in the movies and, along with my father, I read *Der Tag* and the *Tribune* every day.

I also devoured the book my father gave me written by General Sir John Monash; it discussed World War I military tactics.

The book helped me follow the day-to-day troop and tank movements during the 1942 El Alamein campaign in the desert – in particular, the manoeuvres of Montgomery's Eighth Army as it encircled Rommel's tanks and kept the Afrika Corps from capturing El Alamein, the gateway to Cairo and the Suez Canal.

A year later, my mother and I saw a British documentary, *Desert Victory,* at the Starland Theatre. We watched with glee as British Tommies in knee socks and short pants drove bayonets into the stomachs of Rommel's infantry; we clapped with delight at the sight of thousands of German and Italian soldiers dead in the desert, and the thousands of Germans, their hands on their heads, being marched into prisoner of war camps. Montgomery, seen inspecting his notorious Eighth Army, had driven Rommel out of the war.

In the midst of her joy, my mother began to weep, overwhelmed at the sight of Nazi defeat. She wept also because she still had not received word from Zastavia, she had no idea whether or not her sister, Aunt Pesha, and Pesha's children were safe.

A few weeks later, Mr. Glazer – who loved my impromptu re-enactments of the British bombing Rommel's tanks – had decided to take me to a Royal Canadian Legion Hall in the West End, the Anglo-Saxon enclave in town, so that I could tell my El Alamein story.

At the hall, I acted out *Desert Victory* – in the round, so to speak. I provided the documentary voice, and various sound effects: tanks fighting in the desert, the Royal Air Forces's carpet bombing of the Afrika Corps. "37,000 dead, wounded or captured fascists – all by the British at El Alamein!" I cried.

"As Churchill put it, the war has turned. We have the Hun on the run."

The Anglo Legionnaires cheered.

I stood up on my skinny legs and sang:

Rule Britannia!

Britannia rule the waves.

Britons never, never, never shall be slaves.

The legionnaires put a Legion beret on my head, hoisted me onto their shoulders, and sang, "For He's a Jolly Good Fellow."

Mr. Glazer, proud of his little Leibele, took me to Kelekis for soda and chips.

At the age of eight, I was a strategist, a propagandist, and a morale booster.

We would need all the morale we could get. By the end of the war, all my extended Zastavia relations were dead, the whole family gone.

Joshua Leib Zholf and family

From the first moment I sat down to write my life for the amusement of the world, and my opinions for its instruction, has a cloud insensibly been gathering over my father.—A tide of little evils and distresses has been setting in against him.—And now is the storm thickened and going to break, and pour down full upon his head.

I enter upon this part of my story in the most pensive and melancholy frame of mind that ever sympathetic breast was touched with.—My nerves relax as I tell it.—Every line I write, I feel an abatement of the quickness of my pulse, and of that careless alacrity with it, which every day of my life prompts me to say and write a thousand things I should not—And this moment that I last dipped my pen into my ink, I could not help taking notice what a cautious air of sad composure and solemnity there appeared in my manner of doing it.—Lord! how different from my usual rash jerks and hair-brained squirts—

— STERNE

THE LITTLE PRINCE OF
THE WINNIPEG GHETTO

When I was eight, I read the original Yiddish version of *Jewish Cowboy* by Isaac Raboy, the tale of a Jewish immigrant who earns his status as a permanent U.S. resident by ranching in North Dakota. In my inner eye, I saw this Jewish cowboy played by someone like John Garfield – a nice Hollywood Jewish boy. The title of the movie would have a Yiddish touch, too: *Tallith in the Saddle*," which translates as *Prayer Shawls in the Saddle*. I posted Isaac Raboy a letter about my movie plans and the state of Canadian Jewry. He liked my letter and gave it to the editor of *Der Tag*, who published it. The well-known Yiddish poet and journalist, Daniel Charney, brother of the equally well-known Yiddish critic, Samuel Niger, read my letter in *Der Tag* and decided to respond to it in his own *Der Tag* column. Before my father had any inkling of any of this, I had not only been published in a New York Yiddish newspaper, *Der Tag*, but I was sending regular letters to Charney, who published them and replied to them in print.

Local Yiddish newspapers in Winnipeg, Toronto and Montreal picked up this new feature: *A Briv Fun Aeyn Leibele*, or *A Letter From Little Leibele*. My father's vest buttons popped. Jewish writers from New York who were visiting Winnipeg – Abraham Reisen, H. Leivick, Mani Leib, and the playwright, Peretz Hirschbein, told my father that I was some kind of *eilu*, a child wizard.

Salon doors all over Winnipeg were open to me. My puffy little cheeks were pinched by wizened old socialist Jews who were otherwise at loose ends, out wandering the streets of the North Winnipeg ghetto. More than once, I stood suffocating between the ample bosoms of the members of the Peretz School Mothers' Union. Beautiful young Jewish women, a little more discreet in their mothering sexuality, praised my writing and then bestowed the warmest and sweetest of gentle kisses upon my lips. Infertile Jewish women rubbed my head for luck and allowed me, as they accommodated me, by bending down to do the same.

I was in demand. *Huzzah!* A *wunderkind*. Nose in the air. I was a hit – the toast of Jewry, from Lower Broadway to Selkirk and North Main.

Loved by my mother, worshipped by my father and adored by my neighbourhood, I soon indulged myself in wild, unabashed self-love, my operatic warm-up every morning being *me-me-me-me*.

As a publicly acknowledged prodigy, I told Meyer that he would have to pay me prodigy rates for my role as go-between amongst his beauties. He laughed for a full hour.

I told Judith that, since I was a prodigy, she would do well to introduce all of her potential boyfriends to me for examination and approval. Her hairbrush had my head.

I told my mother that as a prodigy I should be served first at the table – even before Papa. She gave me her best *La Gioconda* smile, and said nothing.

I insisted.

She said: "*Genug iz genug.*"

I went back to being a little boy.

But my writing continued. At the age of eleven, I won the Isaac Loeb Peretz Folk School essay contest in both Yiddish and English.

I wrote my English essay on Master Sergeant Meyer S. Levin, the bombardier on a plane that had actually sunk a Japanese ship – the *Natori* – off Pearl Harbor on December 7, 1941. Later, on January 7, 1943, Meyer Levin's plane, a B-17 Flying Fortress, crashed in flames in the South Seas. Posthumously, he was awarded the Distinguished Flying Cross, a Silver Star with two oak leaf clusters, and a Purple Heart. My essay included one line perfectly suited to Rotarian applause: "Meyer S. Levin was not only a son of America but a son of Israel and of the world."

Inspired by success, by all that head-rubbing, and by my father's Zionism, my *bar mitzvah* speech – which marked my thirteenth year and was declaimed before the host of bearded pious ones at the Orthodox Beth Jacob Synagogue on Schultz Street in the deep slums of North Winnipeg – was a prodigy performance.

"Jewish love of Canadian institutions and the British monarchy knows no bounds," I said. "Still, this should not blind us to the perfidy of the British Labour Party and their wicked policy on Palestine. Attlee, Bevin and their ilk are as vicious a bunch of war criminals as Göring, Goebbels and Hitler."

My father loved my *bar mitzvah* speech, particularly my reference to Winston Churchill: "We Jews have played the game of waiting for Winston Churchill for many many years. We've supported him for years, and waited for Winston Churchill – this great friend of our people, this son of a great friend of our people, to kick out the appeasers and lead the world fight against fascism. The bulldog did not fail us. Now, we wait for Churchill to kick out the nest of socialist traitors to the Balfour Declaration for a Jewish homeland in Palestine. We will not wait in vain."

At this climactic point, the pious ones, their *shtreimels* aquiver, stood up and cheered. They joined arms and danced the *sher*. Shots of Bronfman whisky were poured. My head was petted, my cheeks pinched. Tears ran down the faces of the assembled Chassidim.

My father was in Chagall's seventh heaven. Buoyed, he did not hesitate (what a work of contradiction is man) to also play his social secular hand, ordaining that I participate in a kind of parody of the religious rite – a *bar mitzvah Socialiste* in the Isaac Loeb Peretz Folk School auditorium. There would be no prayers, no rabbis, no Chassidim. There would only be me, the Little Prince of the Ghetto himself, who, in 1947, at thirteen, was already, by Jewish law, a man.

The man!

I repeated my Beth Jacob speech.

I beefed up, however, the Winston Churchill part. I also praised to the skies the great Yiddish writers of America. One of them, Abraham Reisen – then seventy-one years of age – was the guest of honour. Tears welled up in Reisen's eyes.

My father also wept. He was deliriously happy. He could not ask for more.

But he was getting more.

My brother was doing well in accountancy. My father's 1945 memoir, *On Foreign Soil: Tales of a Wandering Jew*, was selling like *latkes* in the hothouse realm of Western Jewry. And his Little Prince of the Ghetto was about to enter the post-*bar mitzvah* world. Papa could hardly wait; he was sure I would be a star there, too.

I, on the other hand, took heed of my mother's message: "Never wish for the end of the old; the new is always worse."

מר. און מרס. פ. זאַלף

האָבן דעם כבוד אײנצולאַדן אײך צו דער

בר-מצוה

פון זײער זון

לײבל

שבת, דעם 25טן אָקטאָבער, 1947

9.30 אינדערפרי

אין בית יעקב שול

וועטשערע : שבת, 7 אזײגער אין אוונט

אין י. ל. פרץ זאַל

וויניפעג, מאַן.

Albeit, gentle reader, I have lusted earnestly, and endeavoured carefully that these little books which I here put into thy hands, might stand instead of many bigger books—yet have I carried myself towards thee in such fanciful guise of careless disport, that right sore am I ashamed now to intreat thy lenity seriously —in beseeching thee to believe it of me, that in the story of my father—in the affairs of the nose—If 'tis wrote against any thing,—'tis wrote against the spleen! in order, by a more frequent and a more convulsive elevation and depression of the diaphragm, and the succussations of the intercostals and abdominal muscles in laughter—

— *STERNE*

THE FUNERAL

As a declaimer of the first order – as a quick-witted boy with a nose for nuance and the nonsensical – and with a talent for performance, and as a boy who was already writing for the New York Yiddish newspapers – it became clear to all and sundry that I was an *eilu*, a magic child blessed by the universe. As such, it was inevitable that I would draw the attention of Samuel "Mr. Whiskey" Bronfman, presiding King of the Jews himself.

In Winnipeg, this master bootlegger in want of respectability had kept his own nose close to the ground, except perhaps for his very public ownership of the Bell Hotel on Main Street. He listed the hotel as one of his main assets which since he was a man of means – didn't make much sense. The place was a dump. It had once been a lavish liquor emporium, but it had fallen into neglect, it looked rundown and dilapidated, and its clientele reflected – if not on its owner – then most certainly on its appearance. Fortune tellers, bedbugs, con-men, boiler room brokers, hookers, hustlers, drunken Slavs and Métis – all the living and half-dead had, at one time or another, spilled out of Bronfman's lobby into paddy wagons.

In the thirties, Bronfman stood tall as Mr. Big among the short-arm fatties of the bootlegging world in Montreal and the United States. In Winnipeg, however, he presented himself as something of a patriarch, a hotelier, and a man who happened to have business interests in the manufacturing of bedding.

Bronfman owned fifty percent of Winnipeg's Globe Bedding, the biggest bedding and mattress company in Western Canada. Cynics said Bronfman used his mattresses as a cover to smuggle booze across the American border. Who knows? Nonetheless, Bronfman, was president and chairman of Globe Bedding.

His partner, and the chief executive officer at Globe Bedding, was Berel Keller, chairman of the Isaac Loeb Peretz Folk School, and, of course, an old socialist. Keller was rough and tough; he berated his employees and boxed their ears; he refused them a union; he refused them any real respect. His workers, with their blazing blue Polish and Ukrainian eyes, complained bitterly. Keller, however, opined that he was really a teacher; he was only treating his workers wretchedly so that they would hate him and, propelled by true hatred, dump capitalism and become true socialists.

When Keller died suddenly from a heart attack (which was provoked by a vigorous mattress-testing session within which he was jumping on them like they were trampolines), Bronf-man asked my father to make all the formal arrangements for the funeral presentation. As a result, my father wrote the *Hespet*, the official lamentation, and chose me to deliver it.

I memorized the *Hespet* easily and arrived at the Isaac Loeb Peretz Folk School auditorium an hour early. Already it was jam-packed, and loudspeakers had been assembled for those stuck outside in the schoolyard (most of his workers hated Keller, all respected him). I wasn't nervous or fearful. The funeral settings were pleasant and subdued, marked by a closed six-foot-long dark oak box and two microphones.

I was silently rehearsing my lines when a stocky man smoking a huge cigar approached me. "Hi, kid," he said. "I'm Sam Bronfman and by fuck, you're the Zholf boy."

"Yessir," I said.

"Are you ready?" asked Bronfman, chomping on his cigar.

"Yes, ready," I replied.

"You realize this is a fucking funeral for one of the Peretz School's fucking socialist greats. Keller had the fucking best mattress handles in Canada. I want you to be extra careful."

I said I would.

"You better be," said Bronfman. "Keller's in that fucking big box, and he'll be watching you, too."

Now I was no longer confident.

Sam Bronfman had scared the shit out of me. I could feel Keller giving me the Evil Eye from his coffin. Terrified, I looked around for my mother. I wanted to tell her that I had found the Evil Eye. But it was too late to run. I was in tears when I started to deliver my father's *Hespet*, his lamentation for Berel Keller.

Oddly enough, while Keller's exploited workers watched a small child weep for their bastard boss, they forgot their just grievances and wept along, too.

Sam Bronfman was ecstatic. "Didya ever see such a fucking bully, such a fucking tightwad like Keller get such a fucking send-off to eternity? Didya see the kid, the kid redeemed him? I say I'll book the fucking Zholf kid for my own fucking funeral now!"

Sam Bronfman, King of the Jews, tweaked me (where else?) on both angelic cheeks and he almost, but not quite, kissed me on the *schnozz*.

People in the neighbourhood were soon heard to say that I could raise the dead.

Digressions, incontestably, are the sunshine;—they are the life, the soul of reading!—take them out of this book, for instance,—you might as well take the book along with them;—one cold eternal winter would reign in every page of it; restore them to the writer;— he steps forth like a bridegroom,—bids All-hail; brings in variety, and forbids the appetite to fail.

— *STERNE*

NOT SO DAMN FAST

Early in the summer of 1945, my sister took a paying job. Because she had this job, she could no longer be a counsellor at the B'nai Brith camp and because she was no longer a counsellor at the camp, she could no longer be my sponsor and so I could no longer freeload for the summer. My father came up with the least expensive of alternatives: Kvutzah, a summer camp run by the Habonim, the youth wing of David Ben-Gurion's Palestine-based socialist labour party, Mapai.

My father had his reservations about Ben-Gurion and Camp Kvutzah. Not only was my summer at that camp going to cost him fifty dollars but the Habonim, like the *yishuv* in Palestine, was unilingually Hebrew. The Habonim, ruthlessly intent on founding a Jewish state, ridiculed Yiddish. They called it "jargon," a "remorseless babble." They were determined to eradicate it. Nor did my increasingly orthodox father appreciate the way Ben-Gurion joyously flaunted Judaism's sacred kosher laws: pig farms, also known as "White Meat" farms, were common in the *yishuv*. As such, my father was certain that Camp Kvutzah not only had hog pens in the yard but compliant sows in its communal barns.

My mother hugged me goodbye at Union Station and gave me four delicate and piquant smoked meat sandwiches on rye, wrapped in waxed paper. She warned me to watch out for my sandwiches, to be on the lookout for our notorious local train thieves. I looked warily around the station hall and lit upon only one suspect: Saul Todres. A hillbilly slob of the Hebrew persuasion, he was the eldest son of farmers from southern Manitoba; the family had struck it rich in ways regarded as most mysterious.

Saul's family lived in a sprawling mansion where live chickens ran loose and shat loose; dishes were piled up in alpine columns; food scraps lay banked against the baseboards. I looked hard at Saul, who was sinking his bicuspids into a soggy, floppy white bread tomato sandwich. "Saul could be the one," I said to myself, and clutched my sandwiches to my breast throughout the train ride to Sandy Hook, Manitoba.

Upon arrival, we fledgling campers were greeted by a bevy of long-legged females who were singing spirited Zionist ditties:

> O, ye sons of Moses,
> Lift up your crooked noses,
> Fight, fight, fight for Palestine.

Beryl Fox, who later became a legendary documentary filmmaker and a colleague on the CBC flagship public affairs program, *This Hour Has Seven Days*, was not only a camp counsellor but sensual beauty on the hoof. Her sidekick was Arda Spritzer from Great Neck, New Jersey. Arda let us know right away that she wore no panties. Immediately someone among the greeters told us that Arda boasted an enormous dark bush, that her bush had been the original set for the movie *King Kong*. Others quickly reported that this bush was an international sanctuary for ferrets. "No! No!" Zionist fanatics assured us – Arda's bush was, plain and simple, pure Palestinian culture.

As we milled about the train station, Beryl and Arda began the camp's orientation program. The British Labour Party, we were told, long friendly to the Jews, had stopped being so in 1945; additionally, the party's foreign secretary, Ernest Bevin, was a self-confessed anti-Semite. At this point, we were mobilized into groups, some of which were designated by Arda of the Dark Bush to posture as British. I was so designated. I wore a monocle provided by Beryl. I called myself Jew Jeeves. Arda then led us on a death march from the train station to Camp Kvutzah. For two hours, we walked through wet, lumpy reeds and sodden grass. Arda of the Dark Bush cheered us on: "*Chaverim*! Comrades! If we can walk through this Manitoba swamp without losing a single camper, we Habonimers can outflank the soft-bellied British Labour Party and the yellow-bellied British forces in Palestine."

We arrived at Camp Kvutzah in time for the evening meal, a decidedly secular affair – Clark's strictly unkosher pork and beans and Canada Packers' strictly unkosher hot dogs, washed down with milk and capped with Jell-O for dessert. After we wolfed down our forbidden meal, Arda of the Dark Bush, a very plain woman, spoke beautifully on behalf of Labour Zionism and the fight with the British for Palestine.

Said Arda of the Dark Bush: "As I look over this wonderful sea of Jewish faces, I can only say: Britain, watch out. The fighting Jews of the Winnipeg ghetto are training to get you, to kick you out of Palestine. And to do our duty, we have a secret weapon!"

A hush fell over the Camp Kvutzah dining hall.

"What is Zionism," she asked, "if not to share and share alike? Rich and poor Jews are to share alike. What's yours is mine and what's mine is yours. In the name of Labour Zionism, I give what I have to my fellow Jewish pioneers, my fellow Habonim, my fellow Palestine freedom fighters." Arda of the Dark Bush paused. "In a socialist camp like Camp Kvutzah, no one owns anything. No pure property exists; no personal property exists. What's yours is ours, what's ours is yours."

All gifts, said Arda, including all food gifts, were to be turned over to *Kupa* – the cooperative camp treasury. Once collected, the gifts would be distributed at random, thereby assuring that the legions of poor campers among us would not be shamed.

I watched in horror as Saul – mansion dweller – handed over four sloppy, soggy tomato sandwiches. I then watched as I – shack dweller – gave my four waxed-paper wrapped pastrami sandwiches to the storm troopers of *Kupa*.

Arda of the Dark Bush presented my sandwiches to Saul Todres, and gave me the four soggy tomato sandwiches.

I uttered a wild animal shriek of outrage, a scream that vowed vengeance. I swore injury to all socialists, their loyalists and followers. My revenge plot, however, was interrupted by the lovely Beryl Fox.

"There's a lot of boning going on at the hog barn tonight," she said with discerning candour. She wondered if I would like to watch her and her friends *in flagrante delecto*.

That night, the young women who took to the floor of the hog barn were terrific. While engaged in close coupling with a girl named Sadie, Calman, a pre-med student, twice called out Jewry's ancient cry: "*Am Yisroal Chai!* The People of Israel Live!"

Ziv, whose dream was to be a Zionist sniper for the Palmach, cried, "Catch him on the rise!"

I soon tired of watching what seemed to be copulatory escapades and headed back to the camp's dining hall where counsellors and staff were locked arm-in-arm dancing the Hora. I joined in. Soon, Beryl and Calman were beside me, grabbing my hands during this tribal dance (I cannot now hear *Hava Nagila* without going bonkers). I told her how angry I was about losing my smoked meat sandwiches, how I had been subjected to an exchange more appropriate to capitalism – wherein the poor feedeth the rich – than socialism. She was poutily sympathetic (her quivering lower lip drove me crazy), but she did not disavow *Kupa*. Instead, she told me that she was part of a study group in which various campers picked to be refugees trying to smuggle themselves into Palestine.

"We're short a Jewish refugee," said Beryl. "Do you know anybody, Leibele?"

"How about disgusting Saul? He'd make a great Jewish refugee!"

"Why not?" said Beryl. "The deal is done. We'll make the raid as British Coastal Patrol at about 4 a.m. We won't tell you which day."

One night at precisely 4 a.m., there came a knock on our cabin door. Beryl Fox, dressed in British khaki battle fatigues, identified herself: "British Shore Police! Are you hiding Jewish illegals in your cabin?!"

Total silence was broken by someone yelling, "Yeah! Saul! He's right here! He's a Jewish illegal, that's for sure!"

Saul was taken away and incarcerated in a top-secret room somewhere in the camp.

At breakfast, Beryl hugged and squeezed me. "Leibele," she said, "you make a lousy socialist and the worst Zionist. But that was the best British raid on Jewish illegals we've ever had in Camp Kvutzah."

From my taste bud wrenching lesson in ideological eco-
nomics to my little act of bittersweet betrayal, camp life
proved to be a profound learning experience for me: I looked
into and yet was not vanquished by the dark delta of the
female bush; I witnessed and yet discreetly withdrew from
the sight of avid coupling; I got the hang of Palestine politics;
I learned to share and share alike, and how to be righteously
wronged yet graceless about it; I learned to cope with international intrigue and betrayal; I learned about those deeply
ingrained habits of the official ideological mind, Zionism
and capitalism. I did all this without surrendering my loyalty
to myself, or my loyalty to my father, my family, Canada and
the British Empire. And so, when the sun set on Lake Winnipeg and the campers and counsellors gathered on its banks,
when everybody sang:

Goodbye
America,
Goodbye forever.
We are going to Palestine.

I thought, "Not so fast. I ain't going nowhere. Not so
damn fast. My whole family's right here."

—Angels and ministers of grace defend us! cried my father,—can any soul withstand this shock?—No wonder the intellectual web is so rent and tattered as we see it; and that so many of our best heads are no better than a puzzled skein of silk,—all perplexity,—all confusion within-side.

— STERNE

THE NAMING

By the spring of 1947, when I was thirteen, our North Winnipeg schools – our schoolyard fields of fury – had become so tough that they'd been given the names of jailhouses: Aberdeen School was Alcatraz; Strathcona was Folsom State Prison; and Machray was Leavenworth Penitentiary.

As a graduate of the Isaac Loeb Peretz Folk School where I had been a star student for seven years, I had learned to read and write English, Yiddish and Hebrew, and I was steeped in the Yiddish literature of Sholem Asch, Isaac Bashevis Singer, Joseph Opatoshu, Daniel Charney, and of course, Isaac Loeb Peretz. I'd even read, in Yiddish, the novels of Charles Dickens. The school had given me a terrific grounding in Canadian and English literature and history.

My classmates at the Isaac Loeb Peretz Folk School, however, had been Jewish. All of them. Since, in my new school, there was going to be a Uke (or twelve here), a Polack (or fourteen there), six Krauts, four-to-seven Griks, and several clusters of British partridges in our local pear tree, I was happy to be going to Leavenworth, to Machray School. There, as a born Canadian, I would be able to meet the muddled masses and learn about Canada and how the country works.

My first day:

In the school playground, I was asked my name. "Leibele," I said.

"Mabel," chanted Stanley Blaschowitz, a 240-pound Polish twelve-year-old, "Mabel shit on the kitchen table!"

"Label, Label! His mom is called Mabel. She fucks all the sheep in a *sheeny's* stable!" said another Polish wit.

I was only thirteen but, with my nose for disaster – and believe me, on this day my nose was tingling – I knew that my whole life could be warped if not ruined by my Jewish moniker, Leibele.

I asked a snub-nosed Jewish boy what his name was.

"Larry Kussin," he said.

When it came time to sign in for class, self-consciously and for the first time, I took my life in my hands and signed the register: "Larry Zolf."

Leibele of the *shtetl* was gone – not unlike the *h* that, courtesy of the nuns at his birth had been dismissed, the *h* that he might have carried on his back like a hump.

At thirteen, I had now truly begun the process of becoming my own man.

Huzzah!

In my last act as a child wizard, as an *eilu*, I had named myself.

—Here, reader, you must have a little patience. I have undertaken, you see, to write not only my life, but my opinions also; hoping and expecting that your knowledge of my character, and of what kind of a mortal I am, by the one, would give you a better relish for the other: as you proceed farther with me, the slight acquaintance, which is now beginning betwixt us, will grow into familiarity; and that, unless one of us is in fault, will terminate in friendship.—O diem praeclarum!—then nothing which has touched me will be thought trifling in its nature, or tedious in its telling. Therefore, my dear friend and companion—bear with me,—and let me go on, and tell my story my own way:—Or, if I should seem now and then to trifle upon the road —or should sometimes put on a fool's cap with a bell to it, for a moment or two as we pass along,—don't fly off,—but rather courteously give me credit for a little more wisdom than appears upon my outside;—and as we jog on, either laugh with me, or at me, or in short, do any thing,—only keep your temper.—

— *STERNE*

AT LEAVENWORTH

My classroom teacher was Mr. Wellwood, a veteran of the Royal Winnipeg Rifles, a tough World War II regiment. He seemed amiable enough as I chose a seat close to the class cloakroom. Ahead of me was Irving Gershbein, a scarecrow kid we Jewish boys called "*Beindel*," meaning "bones." The class athlete, Morley Mogul, nephew of the Canadian Football League immortal, Lou Mogul, sat himself beside Beindel.

"God Save the King" had just played over the intercom.

Beindel said to Mogul, "Morley, go fuck yourself."

Morley replied, "Fuck you, weasel."

Mr. Wellwood stomped up the aisle. "You little Jew bastards shitting your little Jew shit balls all over the place and you expect me to fuckin' pail and shovel your shit and clean it up."

Then he banged Beindel's head against Morley's head, knocking Beindel cold.

I threw up my breakfast.

Wellwood was furious.

He rubbed my wondrous fabled nose in my vomit, then he took me into the cloakroom and strapped me four times on each hand.

Next class. I had never heard of the Dewey Decimal System. Miss Charlton, the school librarian, gave our class a Dewey Decimal test. I scored zero out of one hundred. It was the first time I had failed anything. Fuming, Miss Charlton complained that Jewish parochial students were "poorly prepared."

Next class. Miss Currie, the art teacher, wandered around the room carrying a huge bristol board inscribed with the words "Board of Education." I knew how to mix metaphors but I couldn't mix colours; I was hopeless. I got a sharp smack across the brow from Miss Currie's Board of Education.

My hands and head throbbed with pain.

I took my pain home for lunch. My mother said nothing. She made me a chicken sandwich, smiled her *La Gioconda* smile, and sent me back.

I lined up with other kids outside the school's woodworking shop. Mr. Cormack, another soldiering sort, seemed wired for fury. He said he wanted to set the right tone for our class, and asked everyone to hold out their hands palms up. Then he beat our palms with a strap.

I was given a length of board and a wood plane, and told to plane the board level. I planed away. I planed and planed. Wood shavings mounted into curls of impending disaster as I reduced the sixteen-inch-wide board to kindling.

The board that I had reduced to nothing, said Mr. Cormack, had cost a dollar — and my father would have to pay up the money. But that wasn't the extent of my punishment. Mr. Cormack said I lacked military discipline. He told me to remove my pants and shorts, and to bend over. He then produced a cane and began to beat me while shouting: "One: Private; two: Private First Class; three: Lance Corporal; four: Corporal First Class; five: Sergeant; six: Sergeant Major; seven: Regimental Sergeant Major; eight: Company Sergeant Major; nine: Lieutenant; ten: Lieutenant First Class."

Half-crippled and in terrible pain, I was let out of class early and told not to forget to get the one dollar from my father.

My father, having been a school teacher, always took the word of other teachers above the word of his own children. When I told him my tale of woe, he slapped me hard four times on each cheek. More than anything else that day, *that* hurt. He then gave me one dollar to take to school, and said, "Go to bed."

My bruises shone in the darkness of my room.

I quietly wept. At the time, I wasn't sure why, but I've since realized that I was weeping at the sudden awareness of my first experience of real loss: loss forever of the guileless days I had had in my father's Jewish school, loss of school as a place where I could learn and enjoy learning. My new school was brutish and any future based on such schooling might turn brutish, too. I understood in a flash that the only way I would ever survive would be to get smarter, sharper, and more articulate than my teachers – those sometimes good, often mediocre, always innately furious men and women.

—Never mind, he would say, consoling, we shall
have another war break out again some of these days;
and when it does,—the belligerent powers—I defy
'em to take countries without taking towns,—or
towns without sieges.

– *STERNE*

KOSHER WARS

One Saturday morning just before the outbreak of World War II, Reuben Parness, an upstanding and pious kosher butcher, amidst a moment of meditation and severe penance, began to feel that something strange was happening to him. He thought he heard the sanctuary in the synagogue talking to him. Reuben shrugged off the voice as mere stress – after all, he worked eleven hours every day except the Sabbath; he paid the *Kehila* – the Council of Orthodox Rabbis – a small fortune to make sure that his meat was kosher; and he'd been undergoing a daily barrage of complaints from his wife, Mindel, that he, Reuben, was not man enough for her between the sheets.

Reuben cocked his ear to the sanctuary. There it was again, a voice from God above, saying, "Reuben, the *Kehila* is robbing you blind. They are a monopoly, a conspiracy in restraint of free trade. Do something, Reuben. Don't let those rabbis get away with it."

Reuben was impressed.

He told his kosher butcher friends. They, too, were impressed.

The next day, a meeting was held in the damp basement of the butchers' synagogue on Derby Street. The kosher butchers decided they needed a rabbi of their own to make their meat both kosher and cheaper. They also needed allies. Reuben, now heavy with the Word of the Lord upon him, wondered if Velvel Grober, the kosher salami king of Winnipeg, could be such an ally.

Grober looked smug as he welcomed the dissident kosher butchers into his office. On the walls were six portraits of Grober: oak frames, ornate gold-leaf frames. A seventh framed artefact was a six-foot scroll proclaiming that one Velvel Grober was sponsor of the official kosher salami book for North America: *The Sacred Sausage of God: Jews and Salamis Over the Centuries.*

Grober listened very, very carefully as Reuben and his pious friends pled their cause. Then Grober spoke unto them: "Comrades" – Grober had once been a communist and found using this designation always got and held people's attention – "I think I have a solution to your problems. But first, let's get a few things straight. In the future, you and your fellow butchers will stock only my salamis in your butcher stores. Granted, this will be a salami monopoly – but it will be your salami monopoly, too. I will bring in a rabbi. His rates will be one-third of the *Kehila.* Secondly, you now have no rabbi at the butchers' synagogue. My rabbi will be your rabbi and he will only cost you $10,000 a year. The *Kehila* will fight back. Therefore, each of you will make a $500 donation to our strike fund."

Grober was given the go-ahead to find a rebel rabbi.

Meanwhile, World War II had begun.

On the last getaway boat from Gdansk, one Rabbi Saten and his family fled Hitler and sailed for Canada. They were greeted at the Winnipeg CPR station by a stately delegation of kosher butchers decked out in *shtreimels* and long black gabardine coats, led by Reuben Parness and the salami king, Velvel Grober. Rabbi Saten promised the butchers "peace and prosperity."

Velvel Grober then herded the rabbi and his family into Grober's Cadillac and drove them to an opulent house on Boyd Avenue in the heart of North Winnipeg. The good rabbi's first words to his wife as he entered the door were: "SORA, A GLASS OF TEA AND COOKIES! NOW!"

Grober was as good as his word: Rabbi Saten charged only a third of the *Kehila* rates. The dissident butchers lowered their prices accordingly. Soon, all of North Winnipeg was frequenting the rebel butchers' shops and the *Kehila* stores stood cold and empty.

Rabbi Saten, regularly paid off on all sides, it did well: he had a nice house and he drove a Packard; the fur of his *shtreimel* was mink, the gabardine of his long waistcoat was Italian, and his shoes were mail-ordered from Church's in London.

The *Kehila* did not take all this lying down. One morning, thirty-six of its sons and disciples divided themselves into two picket lines positioned along the front and back of Grober's kosher sausage factory. Other sons and disciples took up similarly arranged picket duty at the dozen rebel butchers' stores. The *Kehila* picketers were well behaved and smartly dressed. Their curly forelocks were combed, their caftans were neat and pressed. On their heads, they, too, wore elegant fur (but not mink) *shtreimels*. Their picket signs were of good design and purest lucidity (on one side Yiddish, on the other English):

ONLY KEHILA-ENDORSED
MEAT IS KOSHER.
GROBER'S KOSHER SAUSAGE
IS NOT KEHILA-ENDORSED.
NEITHER IS THE MEAT BEING SOLD
AT THIS BUTCHER'S STORE.
NEITHER IS RABBI HERSCHELE SATEN.

A holy war ensued. The rebel kosher butchers fought the *Kehila* picketers, yanking at their forelocks, kicking them in the *tuchus*. And the *Kehila* banished the dissident butchers to limbo (not technically a Jewish place but if a group of outcasts want to call their lonely place limbo, who's to quibble?). The *Kehila* then moved to secondary boycott tactics: it took out newspaper ads, urging any and all gentiles who might have a taste, yea, even a longing for tasty kosher meat, to avoid the shops of the recusant butchers.

Women who shopped at the rebel butchers' stores, women like my mother, found themselves under some pressure. Our favourite butcher was a dissident and one day, as my mother and I came out of his store, our meat wrapped in waxed butcher paper and leaking blood, a pious pasty-faced Chassid said to my mother: "Mrs. Zholf, it does not pass, the wife of a socialist, buying unkosher meat from a scab butcher."

"Mr. Basovsky is a good and honest man. You are nothing but a trickster," said my mother, narrowing one eye. And on our way we went.

Finally, in Montreal, presiding King of the Jews, Samuel Bronfman, caught wind of the dispute.

"Fuck," he said. "Hitler is killing and fucking the Jews in Europe and we are killing and fucking each other over a few fucking scraps of kosher meat."

Bronfman called in the parties. He brought them to heel.

A compliant Grober agreed that his rabbi, Herschele Saten, would charge kosher-services rates competitive with the *Kehila*. Rabbi Saten would also become a full, paid-up member of the *Kehila*. The holy war was over.

My father had watched the conflict with a keen eye and said nothing. He was now well into his Orthodox gambit and as such, loved all rabbis. As the years passed, Rabbi Saten became his closest advisor and friend. In the fullness of their time, he and the good rabbi could be seen strolling arm-in-arm every Saturday afternoon.

In particular, my father came to relish the good rabbi's pro-business and ultra-free-enterprise views. Rabbi Saten introduced my father to Ricardo's Iron Law of Wages and Darwin's "survival of the fittest." As for matters in Palestine, the good rabbi favoured the battle-ready Irgun insurgents and the terror tactics of Ze'ev Jabotinsky. My father, himself a former Jewish self-defence fighter, approved of the rabbi's harsh views of the Grand Mufti and the Palestinian rabble.

All the better, then, that the good rabbi loved my father's writing. For weeks, Saten praised him from the pulpit. On Saturday mornings, tables were set up at the butchers' synagogue and they were stacked with Joshua Falek Zholf's books. When my father suggested that I might go into the rabbinate, Rabbi Saten offered to give me Talmud lessons, free of charge.

In my father's mind, I had become Isaac to his Abraham. Offering me up as a rabbi would allow him – in search of justification – to atone for his past socialist sins (there was no guarantee that an angel would intervene on my behalf at the last minute).

At Rabbi Saten's house, I was asked all kinds of loaded questions about socialism. Not yet having been to summer camp, I defended the faith.

"Good boy! Good boy!" the rabbi said. "The boy has the dialectics, *Chaver* Zolf. The boy will do well in Talmud."

On the way home, my father listed all the rabbinical advantages – a Packard car, a big house, the best of garments and shoes, obedient daughters, and a dutiful wife like Sora.

Being also my mother's son, I said nothing.

Talmud class at Rabbi Saten's was small, a mentorship designed only for the select few. One boy was the son of a communist who had died in the Spanish Civil War; the second was the son of a poor garment factory pants presser; the third was Rabbi Saten's hapless youngest son; and the fourth – that was me, a very unhappy fourth.

Every class was preceded by an hour of prayer, prayers that consisted of flipping pages backwards and forwards for no apparent reason. I could understand the Hebrew of the prayers but I often felt paralyzed, unable to find the right pages. At that point, the good rabbi would box my ears. One day, after such a boxing, he said to me: "A woman faints on the Sabbath. She is five thousand feet from the sanctuary. On the Sabbath, it is forbidden to walk more than four thousand feet. What do you do?"

"I'll tell you what I would do, Rabbi," I said. "I would pick up the woman and carry her to sanctuary."

Rabbi Saten erupted. He jumped across the room and slapped me across the face. "Your answer is socialist garbage," he said. "The answer is that the law of life is more sacred than the law of the Sabbath – that's why you can pick up the woman and carry her to sanctuary."

Whenever any one of us blundered like this, Rabbi Saten would invoke the name of his son, Saul, who was studying at a *yeshiva*, in Chicago. "Saul will soon be here," the rabbi announced. "Saul will show you, you socialist *drek*, what it means to be a true Talmud scholar."

Saul arrived. He was greeted by Rabbi Saten with open arms, and seated on a footstool of honour in front of his father. As Saul joined us in prayer service, I couldn't help but notice that while he flipped through the pages with aplomb – with real flair – he stumbled over more than a few Hebrew words.

Rabbi Saten did not notice; he was eager to begin the Talmud class. The rabbi started his Talmud colloquy with me, then moved on to the two working-class boys (though penniless, too, I was the son of an intellectual). All of us read our portions with competence, and were more or less sharp in our answers.

"Not bad, boys, not bad," said the rabbi. "Now let's hear a master do it."

Saul seemed nervous, apprehensive, as he started to read. In the first sentence alone, he mangled ten words.

A bitter, glowering Rabbi Saten understood instantly that Saul had in fact spent the last few years playing truant; he wasn't attending his *yeshiva* lessons – he was hanging around Chicago poolrooms and bordellos, chasing *shiksas*.

The betrayal was too much for the good rabbi. He needed catharsis – never mind that the concept emerged out of ancient Greece – and catharsis he found.

Rabbi Saten (yet another teacher possessed by innate fury) lunged at Saul, kicked him to the floor, and delivered two vicious blows to his son's nose, breaking it in several places. As the blood poured, a regular geyser, the rabbi began kicking his son in the ribs.

The class dispersed.

I ran home at top speed. My hatred for the Orthodoxy, rabbis, and pious bullies peaked as I burst through the front door, crying and out of breath. Meyer, who had been listening to the radio, and my father, who had been writing one of his stories for the local Yiddish newspaper, took me into the kitchen. I told them what had happened. I told them I hated being forced to be a rabbi, to be Orthodox.

My father tried to console me: "Rabbis are the leaders of the Jewish people, my son. They have much to worry about. Sometimes they get out of hand."

"I hate rabbis! I hate them, I hate them!" I shouted.

This blasphemy infuriated my father. He grabbed a Grober kosher salami that was hanging on the wall and swung it at me, opening a huge gash in my brow.

Meyer intervened. "Leibele is not going to any more rabbis, Pa! Let Leibele have a normal teenage life for a change!"

My father said nothing.

My brother took me to the hospital for six stitches.

—Here is the glass for pedagogues, preceptors, tutors, governors, gerund-grinders, and bear-leaders to view themselves in, in their true dimensions.—

Oh! there is a husk and shell which grows up with learning, which unskilfulness knows not how to fling away!

—Much may be learned by rote, but Wisdom not.

— STERNE

BIRTH OF A SALESMAN

After the success of his memoir in 1945, my father began to explore the possibilities of an entrepreneurial triumph that would not only deliver the Zholfs from the slums of Winnipeg but ultimately deliver him from the clutches of the Isaac Loeb Peretz Folk School, its Mothers' Union and the Jewish socialist clique that ran the place. Those years – the C.D. Howe – Louis St. Laurent years, 1948-1957 – developed into a happy time for the Zholfs. My father, energized by his new Orthodoxy, cast out those last vestiges of socialism still inhabiting his soul. His new relationship with God dovetailed neatly with the end of World War II and the boom prosperity that came with C.D. Howe's form of corporate liberalism. Joshua Falek quite naturally concluded that since Canada's prosperity had closely followed his conversion from socialism to Orthodoxy, these two events were inextricably linked and, therefore, had caused one another. Jewish Orthodoxy, my father believed, now belonged to the Jewish Elect.

A Jewish businessman had told my father: "Dress like a businessman – and soon you will be one."

My father had taken such sagery to heart.

Soon, he boasted four suits, all double-breasted. His black patent-leather shoes were covered by the finest of Bond Street's charcoal grey spats. A homburg rested jauntily on his head. Terms like "inventory," "depletion allowance," "capital cost allowance," and "marketing and public relations," came trippingly off his tongue. He started tipping his homburg to all the lovely Jewish ladies who he passed along Selkirk and Main. Often, he would offer them a market tip fresh from Namak's Barber Shop.

Freda felt that my father, in his snappy new C.D. Howe-inspired business garb, had gone balmy. She refused to be seen with him on the streets. And, as if to further bewilder her, it wasn't long before she could no longer get extensions to her butcher bill, her grocery bill, her milk delivery bill. "Before you ask me for credit, Madam Zholf, let your pluto-crat husband sell one of his many suits," proprietors would say. "Then you'll have enough money to pay me for a year!"

In the mirror, however, Joshua Falek took only an approving note of his grey serge double-breasted suit and grey spats, the red boutonniere in his right lapel. And he asked himself, "What do I have to sell that is truly unique, that no one else can come up with, something that would interest everyone, something I could easily do and then sell?"

The answer came as in a blinding light: "You, Joshua Falek Zholf – teacher, ex-socialist, former German prisoner of war, former revolutionary, slum *boulevardier*, Yiddish *sprechmeister* and wit, up-to-date gossip and Zionist supreme – your life story would make a great autobiography, a great book. Such a book would sell like griddle cakes!"

In less than a year, he had written and edited his epic life story. In even less time, he had persuaded several top-class Jewish tycoons across the city to pony up for the printing of his autobiography. The first run produced five thousand copies; books sold at five dollars apiece. The title, *On Foreign*

Soil: Tales of a Wandering Jew, had particular resonance for my father. All his life, he told his readers, he had lived on foreign soil. Tsarist Russia did not belong to him. The quasi-fascist Republic of Poland had been forced on him. And as for Canada, my father was grateful to the country for saving his life and the lives of his family members, but it, too, was foreign soil: a cold land where, more often than not, Jews got the cold shoulder.

Written in excellent Yiddish, *On Foreign Soil* was carefully aimed at both the rootless cosmopolitan Jewish communities scattered over the prairie frontier, and the teeming, huddled masses hunkered down in the country's largest ghettoes. To one and all my father said: "*ON FOREIGN SOIL* IS THE GREATEST JEWISH STORY EVER TOLD! I've told it because no one else has had the guts to do so. It should be made into a movie. John Garfield would be perfect to play me as a young man; Paul Muni would be perfect to play the mature me, the thoughtful and kind me, the Jewish man of action."

His tales – life in his Polish *shtetl*, the horrors of famine and pogroms, a murderous war followed by a worse civil war, and a savage, knuckle-headed revolution followed by the poverty and hardship of slum life in Canada – made for a great Yiddish page-turner. Most of the print run sold.

Itching for new book markets, he went westward-ho toward the mountains, convinced that the Jewish colonists scattered across the frontier in esoteric crossroad towns – Plum Coulee, Neepawa, Indian Head, Dominion City, Weyburn, Wadena, Edenbridge – would be natural born readers of *On Foreign Soil*. He packed his books into six satchels and turned his face to the open road. He became a drummer – always selling, selling, selling. Ironically, however, he was going down this road just as many Jews were leaving the small towns and farming hamlets of Western Canada: sons and daughters of the colonists were heading for Winnipeg or Toronto, or skipping over the mountains to Vancouver to study pharmacy, medicine, nursing, accounting.

To those left in the outpost towns, the remaining silent, stoic Jews on the margins of prairie life, my father made his way. They could still read Yiddish and they still "got the joke" – they could laugh at his insights and witticisms, his tales of the perils of war, immigration and racism. *On Foreign Soil* became a bestseller in all the remote parts of the prairies. By the hundreds upon hundreds, Jewish prairie pioneers bought the book and whiled away what free time they had by lamplight, reading the story of *père schnozz* aloud to their kith and kin.

Having, in a short time, criss-crossed the prairies, my father decided to detour east to the large Jewish communities of Toronto, Montreal and New York. There, his sales pitch touched a raw nerve among the ex-*shtetl* masses; in droves they laid down their tools and bought his book. *On Foreign Soil* was so popular that it was the only book on the Yiddish bestseller list.

For the publication of his second book, *The Last of a Generation*, my father enlisted me in many of his travels. One day, during a tour stop in Calgary, we found ourselves seated at the head table in a large crowded auditorium. There were huge piles of books on the table. My father beamed approvingly as he watched his Calgary friends sell his books to the guests who entered the hall. He was not perturbed when many of the guests, who could barely read English, never mind Yiddish, bought the books and then handed them over to the waiters to do with what they wished.

A sale was a sale.

When the master of ceremonies, who delivered his address in Yiddish, spoke of my father's genius for three-quarters of an hour, my father glowed with warmth and gratitude. When the master of ceremonies then delivered a thirty-minute sales pitch on behalf of the book, my father could barely conceal his approving sentiments. When the Belzbergs, Supersteens, Singers, and other tycoons in the auditorium, restless and hungry, began throwing their bread rolls, butter pats, cutlery and napkins at the master of ceremonies, my father barely moved a muscle. When the master of ceremonies went on to compare my father most favourably to Isaac Loeb Peretz and Sholem Aleichem, my father beamed even as the tycoons stamped their feet and shouted: "Who cares! Who cares! Let's eat!!" And when the tycoons then stampeded to the buffet table, my father only smiled benevolently, believing that such unprovoked hostility only made his book more attractive, even more saleable.

The long and short of this: my father put a down payment on a one-and-a-half-storey bungalow on Lansdowne Avenue, which was in a much better neighbourhood. This meant we were about to say goodbye to our home on Aikins Street: no longer would we have to play hide-and-seek with bedbugs and cockroaches; no longer would I hear the soft, pitter-patter of rats under the bed that I shared with my brother; no longer would Judith sleep on a small cot in our bedroom; no longer would my tiny backyard playground operate under a cloud cover of chicken feathers caused by the nefarious plucking practices of the professional chicken plucker next door. In our new house, we would have an electric stove and fridge instead of a wood stove and icebox, Judith would have her own bedroom, and though my brother and I would still have to share a bedroom, we would finally have our own beds – bunk beds.

As a best-selling man of the book, my father was no longer at the mercy of the Isaac Loeb Peretz Folk School socialists who were always trying to tell him what to think, what to believe, and what and how to teach. No, success had turned Joshua Falek loose; he had become a fervent lover of the politics of the negotiated deal, an advocate of the sale, the come-on, the canvas, the close. He had become a true believer, a free enterpriser in love with the invisible handjob of the marketplace.

But my mother, always wary of the Evil Eye, was having none of the dewy-eyed, wild optimism of her husband and children. For her, change was always for the worse. Her lavish family mansion in the old country had been replaced by a North Winnipeg dump; even still, she had managed to live in this dump with the man she loved, and she had lived there for years, surrounded by children, friends and good neighbours.

My mother was convinced that everyone in our imminent new land of lawnmowers and water sprinklers, rockery stones painted white and sofas encased in plastic, was a stranger.

As Mama sat crouched on the front stoop at Aikins Street looking as if she were under a catatonic spell, we hoisted chairs and tables, hauled mattresses, boxed books, carried clothes hangers weighted with coats and dresses, and rattled pots and pans; we loaded up everything around her, took off for the new address, and unloaded the evidence of our lives. Then we went back to the old house, plucked my mother from her stoop, perched her in the truck, and brought her to her new home – a series of scenes, tableaux – though Ma Joad was never catatonic – from a Yiddish *The Grapes of Wrath*.

As a family, we had suddenly entered into the years of post-war prosperity. Rose was still married to her humble jeweller; Judith, owner of the largest collection of mohair sweaters this side of Angora, was now dating the most eligible of Jewish frat brothers from the university at Fort Garry; and, like a light unto the Zholfs, true resurrection and redemption was soon to be ours because Meyer was on the cusp of becoming – not the biggest *shiksa*-chaser east of the Rockies – but the first Jewish chartered accountant to plunk his abacus down in the recently discovered oil fields of Leduc, Alberta.

Joshua Falek's joy passed all understanding. My brother the auditor, was no longer the strolling stud of Selkirk Avenue, a blonde delight on each arm; instead, he and my father, two proud and accomplished free enterprisers, strutted the streets of Winnipeg, talking of capital investments, accelerated cost allowances, inventory depletion and fast write-offs.

My mother, of course, remained not just dutiful but admiring of the man she loved. She did not, however, partake in all of the opinions he now offered from under cover of his homburg hat.

It was a consuming vexation to my father, that my mother never asked the meaning of a thing she did not understand.

—That she is not a woman of politics or science, my father would say—is her misfortune—but she might ask a question.—

My mother never did.—In short, when she went out of the world at last she went without knowing whether it turned round, or stood still.—My father had officiously told her a thousand times which way it was,—but she always forgot.

For these reasons, a discourse seldom went on much further betwixt them, than a proposition,—a reply, and a rejoinder; at the end of which, it generally took breath for a few minutes (as the affair of the breeches), and then went on again.

— *STERNE*

THE DUMMY *DUMA*

Given that I was a failure (my father despised any kind of failure) at woodworking, and anything having to do with the placement of decimals, I was shipped out of Machray School and sent to St. John's Technical High School where I was welcomed with open arms by other misfits into the "dummy' class, a class that happened to appeal to my subterranean wit and anarcho-syndicalist tendencies. Being earnest and socialist, I found it easy to identify with my fellow travelling dummies, true proletarians who were crying out for Marxist dictatorship – and with my nose extending itself towards politics, I soon became their man.

I was boisterously at ease with the school bounders, rounders, spastics and jerks, anyone who'd been born for the rope. I quickly put together a political machine discovering my natural best – to be the presence behind power – the informer of those wanting to be informed – in fact, I became so accomplished at working the halls, the phones and the toilet stalls, that I almost got my fellow dummy, Conrad Tittler, the football team's German-Canadian fullback, elected as student president. My brilliant ad hoc campaign on his behalf, however, gave rise to an inevitable dialectical response: the establishment – that is, the teachers and the rich-bitch students (male and female) – was determined to keep the presidency out of the blunt-fingered hands of my dummies. The principal called the whole school together in a special assembly and warned that the presidency of the student body was a very complex and difficult job, calling "for a strong mind, not a strong back; for a scholar, not a full-back; steady hands at the till, not heavy hands in the till; for someone going somewhere instead of someone born to be nowhere."

We, the dummies, who were expected to lose, indeed lost – but only after two recounts.

As a burgeoning maker and shaker, I had found my own candidate, created my own political machine and fought the establishment to a standstill. And I suffered an added thrill: for the first time, I had worked against the conventional wisdom of the conventional Jewish line, against the received opinion of the rabbis and my fellow Jews, and this gave me, as Tittler's campaign manager and speech writer, the feeling that I was a true socialist. I wasn't some politico standing prudently apart in thought, dress and deportment, a rootless cosmopolitan at work only for the Jews and himself. Like Trotsky, I was doing my best for the working class,

It was also comforting to find out that politically, I could scare people; I could manipulate them in the name of a good and higher cause. All power to the dummy *Duma*!

Truthfully, of course, I was not so dumb for a dummy – I was only "passing" as such.

Others knew this, including Miss Christie, who was both my homeroom and English teacher. She had extra long arms, and in her rather horny-toed stocking feet, she stood six feet four inches tall. She was the best English teacher at St. John's Technical High School. Over and over again, she told me that I was a fake, that I was playing the dummy to the hilt, that I was the only one to blame for my problems. And I would say: "Miss Christie, students in my 'dummy' class are my comrades, my vanguard of the proletariat. I will never leave them, nor will I abandon them to the clutches of an over-agitated, gangly spinster engaged in agitprop."

Nasty lines of this sort were below the belt. Everyone knew Miss Christie had lost the one throbbing love of her life to the air wars over France shortly after D-Day.

She would only smile wanly.

One day, she sat me down and said, "You have the gift of leadership, but it's at the bottom of a chalice otherwise full of poison. You are your own worst enemy."

"Not when you're around," I shot back.

She gave me that wan, knowing smile, and said, "What a shame, when you could be your own best friend."

"Mind you," I said, so that she would not, in fact, think that I was stupid, "I do know who my real enemies are, Miss Christie. Mr. George Reeve, the school principal, is no friend of mine. Vice-Principal Ridd is my sworn enemy. And my father, no matter his protestations of love, has – with my failures in class – become my executioner: ever since my "dummy" des-ignatim, I have been cut off, amputated in my own home, made to eat my meals alone upstairs because my father will not look upon me at his table. And you, Miss Christie, say that all I have to do is exercise my will – 'will' it – and I will be free of indenture and immolation. That's bull, my sweet gangly, and you know it."

But Miss Christie had a trick up the sleeve of her long arm.

In the spring of my first year at St. John's, all grade eleven students, whether in accelerated or non-accelerated pro-grams, had to write the same standard English exam. Over a hundred students wrote that exam. I received a mark of 87%, the highest mark in the school.

Miss Christie, in a fit of colic, said to the class: "I hated giving Larry Zolf this mark. Larry is destroying himself with nihilistic bitterness and anger. He is immoral, a social deviant, and good marks cannot help him unless he changes his attitude."

I quickly replied, "Miss Christie, you can take that mark of 87% and shove it where the sun don't shine."

Girls gasped. Boys clapped.

Miss Christie slapped the back of my head and with sarcasm, said, "Keep up the good work, Larry!"

The dummies were proud of me. And I was in seventh heaven. Not only was I, the *schnozz*, a politician – the dummies' appointed political representative – but given my exam mark, I was the triumphant *schnozz* among all the accelerated grade eleven goody two-shoe suck-hole *schnorers*, those *in vitro* Jewish scholars, those soon-to-be dentists, accountants and doctors.

I took my exam home to my mother. She was happy for me and together, we waited in the living room for my father to finish eating his double-helping supper. After a few easeful burps, he came into the living room and settled in to read *Der Tag*.

"Pa," I said, excitedly. "All the accelerated and non-accelerated grade eleven students had to write the same English exam. I got 87%, the highest mark in the entire school. I beat out over a hundred kids! See for yourself."

Closing one eye as if to better concentrate, he perused the marked examination paper. Line by line. Not a muscle in his face moved. Not a hair in his moustache twitched. Then, as a twenty-year veteran of the classroom, he said, "I see that your teacher made no personal remarks of any kind on your paper. That speaks volumes. We teachers have all seen one-day, one-week, one-month, wonders! You are not the first!"

Then he stood up, hands trembling with anger. "Today, my son, you are still a dummy, still a bum! Next week, the same! Next year, more of the same! O GOD, LORD, MASTER OF THE UNIVERSE: WHEN WILL THE SHAME ON THIS HOUSE END?!" With that sitting-*shiva* look in his eyes, it seemed he wanted only to rend his garments and say prayers for the dead, to name me dead. "O Lord of Lords," he cried. "Rid my life and my house forever of this failure!"

I bolted from the house, tears streaming down my face. I ran to Nordic's Pool Hall, chanting: "ALL POWER TO THE DUMMY *DUMA*."

As many pictures as have been given of my father, how like him soever in different airs and attitudes,— not one, or all of them, can ever help the reader to any kind of pre-conceptions of how my father would think, speak, or act, upon any untried occasion or occurrence of life,—There was that infinitude of odd- ities in him, and of chances along with it, by which handle he would take a thing,—it baffled, Sir, all cal- culations.—The truth was, his road lay so very far on one side, from that wherein most men travelled,— there every object before him presented a face and section of itself to his eye, altogether different from the plan and elevation of it seen by the rest of mankind.— In other words, 'twas different object, and in course was differently considered.

— STERNE

THE HOLOCAUST
CHILDREN

After spending five years in concentration camps, a group of Holocaust children arrived at our high school. Because the Holocaust children could not speak English, the education authorities at St. John's Technical decided that the best place to put them was in our "dummy" class.

The Holocaust children could only speak Yiddish. The only other person in our class who could speak Yiddish was me.

One day, I overheard two Holocaust boys, bored to death, playing a very odd game.

One pointed to the numbers tattooed on his left inner arm and said to his desk mate, "I've got three sevens. What do you have?"

His partner looked at the numbers tattooed on his own inner arm and said, "I've got four eights."

"You win!" said the boy with the sevens, and they both laughed.

When I laughed, they turned to me and asked, "*Redt* Yiddish?"

I said yes and asked the name of the game they had just played.

"It's Auschwitz poker!" they said, and we howled with laughter.

Soon, I had my own private squad of Holocaust children to back me up in my mischief and larceny.

Then, miracle of miracles, I began to grow rapidly. I gained eleven inches in height. Pubic hairs arrived. I was showering and pissing with the big boys; paradise was mine. I attributed these miraculous changes to the arrival of the Holocaust children. I ached for the chance to repay them for their presence, as well as their affection and increasing loyalty.

Our physical education teacher, Russ Pastuk, himself only five feet tall, had an obsession with tumbling – especially the tumbling of Jewish bodies – and often began class by directing us to the tumbling mats set up on the gymnasium floor.

Baruch, a heavy, big-boned survivor of the death camps, refused to tumble. He explained to me, "I have lived and fought among the partisans. I have parachuted from an airplane behind enemy lines. I have starved. I have lived with lice. I am not a coward. I won't do a stupid front roll. Even in Auschwitz, they didn't make me do a front roll!"

I passed the message on to Pastuk.

The class stood assembled in the gym, waiting.

Pastuk said, "No exceptions."

I looked at Conrad Tittler, the friend I'd almost gotten elected student body president. He looked at me. I farted. He responded by making a similar noise with his mouth. Then one by one, each student in the class, simulating very loud fart sounds, cupped their hands under their armpits and squeezed in curious harmony.

> Well, said Gymnast, I have failed,—I will undo this leap; then with a marvellous strength and agility, turning towards the right-hand, he fetched another frisking gambol as before; which done, he set his right-hand thumb upon air, poising and upholding his whole weight upon the muscle and nerve of the said thumb,

and so turned and whirled himself about three times:
at the fourth, reversing his body, and overturning it
upside down, and fore-side back, without touching any
thing, he brought himself betwixt the horse's two ears,
and then giving himself a jerking swing, he seated himself upon the crupper—

— *STERNE*

The Holocaust children and the Great Yiddish Mouthpiece
(as I came to be known, by them) made a good team. We
learned from each other. We helped each other. But above all,
we had a sense of pure fun and gallows laughter. One of our
favourite ploys was to go to Eaton's, the major department
store in Winnipeg, and challenge its official credo: "The cus-
tomer's always right."

One day, on the crowded main floor, in the midst of the
Ukrainians, Poles, and Germans who shopped at Eaton's but
weren't allowed to work there, Baruch suddenly collapsed
on the floor, eyes glazed, tongue protruding, spittle running
out of his mouth and down his shirt.

I pointed to the tattoo on his inner arm and, in perfect
English, yelled at the top of my lungs: "Auschwitz survivor!
Severe case of malnutrition!"

The Holocaust children and I, the Great Yiddish Mouthpiece, watched as staff engaged in a mad scramble to get
Baruch off the floor and into the cafeteria. Then we fled and
waited outside for Baruch.

He emerged an hour later.

"What did you have, Baruch?" I asked.

"Chicken pot pie, scalloped potatoes, pot roast, hot cross
buns and six butter tarts," Baruch said.

"Goniff! Thief!" I cried, to the laughter of the Holocaust-niks.

I was also able to bring the Holocaust children home. Their excellent Yiddish warmed my father's cockles, and their survival stories renewed his faith in God and the Jewish people. Furthermore, my father took pride – however grudgingly – in the fact that I was their mouthpiece, their go-between in school and about town, and this took some of the edge off his rage at my bad marks, my constant delinquency, my demonstrable dumminess.

Then, the Holocaust entered my life in another manner.

One of my best friends was "Shimmy" Altman, so nicknamed for his fancy footwork on the dance floor. Into Shimmy's house moved a lodger, Harry Hyman. He, too, had the telltale tattoo on his inner arm.

Such a lodger the North End had never seen before. He had the muscles of an Adonis, but his nose had been broken three or four times by the butts of Nazi rifles. Before the war, he had been the welterweight champion of Germany. His personal specialty – a pleasure he had left unspoken the day he was sent to the concentration camp – was knocking blue-eyed Germans unconscious in front of angry Jew-hating crowds. "That was a great feeling," Harry said, his English broken but passable. "It is hard to describe!" His boxing skills, he told us, helped keep him alive in the camps. He didn't say how. In fact, none of us had ever seen him box.

Tough as he was, however, Harry preferred love to hate, and he had the air of a man who knew a lot about sex. As if he were an elder brother, he patiently answered all of the sex questions by which we'd been baffled. Harry, who worked as a cutter in a downtown garment factory, became our Dr. Ruth. The women he dated were also fun, and they loved us, the little Jewish terrors who were always hanging around and following Harry.

But not everybody in Winnipeg loved little Jewish terrors. One day Baruch, myself, and a friend of ours, Herschel, decided to take in a double feature at the neighbourhood College Theatre. We walked arm-in-arm down Main Street, as if we were the Three Musketeers, the Three Caballeros.

Suddenly, I was picked up and, with great force, hurled into the closed door of the theatre. Badly bruised, I looked up at my attacker. He was huge – at least six-foot-four – and angry. "You fucking Jews don't own the sidewalks!" he yelled. "Go back to Palestine where you came from!"

Then he moved on.

Baruch and Herschel began to yell at the bully in Yiddish: "Bastard, choke on your own vomit! May your foreskin turn cancerous!"

Oddly enough, the bully seemed to understand Yiddish. He turned around and headed towards us.

Baruch, Herschel and I beat a retreat.

It was Friday night and the Jewish hangout, appropriately named, This Is It, was at the end of the street. Hearing the commotion, several boys and men spilled out onto the sidewalk – including Harry. They formed a line across the sidewalk; the bully was not allowed to cross. The bully tried. He grabbed hold of Harry's shirt sleeve, the one covering the tattoo.

Harry, in his best broken English, said, "Get your goddamn hands off my good shirt!"

The bully stood his ground.

Harry sent a vicious right cross to the bully's jaw, then a left hook and another right cross. Teeth clattered and the bully's knees buckled.

Two cops, who had been watching the scene from their squad car across the street, decided things had gone too far. They approached, removed the bully, and drove away.

The sidewalk cleared.

I was so moved I wept. At last, the Great Yiddish Mouthpiece had a champion he could relate to – someone even better than John Garfield (whose left hook was only exercised during the boxing movies in which he starred). Harry was the real deal. When he threw a left hook, it resonated. And his left arm carried a full house out of the camps: two twos and three threes.

—No doubt, Sir,— there is a whole chapter wanting here—and a chasm of ten pages made in the book by it—but the book is more perfect and complete by wanting the chapter,—

– STERNE

95% IN LOGIC

It was Friday night, Sabbath dinner. I was lying on my bed, waiting for my mother to deliver my dinner plate, as my father still refused to share the table with me and all of my failures, sins, oversights, foibles. I was, therefore, flabbergasted, when I heard him call for me to come down to the dinner table.

"What do you want to do with your life now that high school is done and you start university?" he asked.

My heart nearly burst. The words poured out of me: "I would like to study literature and politics. I would like to immerse myself in Canadian history and Canadian politics, in philosophy and in the classics."

"Why?" he asked temperately.

"Because," I said, "I would like to be a proud Canadian and a proud Jew. I will study hard. I will do anything, Papa, to be a somebody."

"You have until the Christmas exams. Fail by even one mark and I will yank you out of university and put you smack in the middle of a garment factory, where you shall toil for the rest of your so-called life!"

I excused myself from the kitchen table. "I have some studying to do, Pa."

Joshua Falek Zholf looked dubious, but he said nothing. He said nothing for a month.

That term, my 95% in logic gave me a straight-A average. I was number one at United College.

In fact, I was number one among the entire student body at the University of Manitoba.

No longer was I an outcast in my own home. I was once again the *wunderkind*, beloved by both my mother and father.

I wish I could look at him—
There can be no sin in looking at him.
—I will look at him.

– *STERNE*

THE PRODIGAL

After the official publication of my grades, life with father took an extraordinary turn. Phone calls of congratulations poured into the house. The prodigal son, once an outcast who had to walk ten steps behind even the swine, was now a scholar, his name on the lips of every somebody in North End Winnipeg. Overnight, my father became my social secretary, accepting or declining invitations on my behalf. He cried out that he loved me, and he loved saying so. He also loved his secretarial job, and was good at it. He had no difficulty hitching his swayback horse of old socialist ideals to my unexpected public success. Indeed, he now took credit for my success with the same depth of emotion that he had once spent decrying my delinquency.

As my father saw it, my failures had been a wilful aberration on my part. For his part, I was his creation and now he was prepared to pronounce that his creation was good. Moreover, my triumph represented vindication – hard on the heels of all the humiliation he had suffered at the stubby little hands of the Isaac Loeb Peretz Folk School's godless socialists. They had ridiculed and belittled his talents; they had suggested he was no longer a *chaver*, a comrade; and they had trampled his Orthodox ideas and beliefs. Now, however, out of the manger of his mind, he had given rise to his own redeemer, an avenging angel, a *schnozz* with wings, an awe-inspiring *schnozz* made in his own image, a *schnozz* of high repute who would smite the city's socialist fat cats and cast them out of the workers' temple to the four corners of the earth.

His anger, the contempt and loathing that had been my lot, was replaced by cheer and a reverent, almost religious, trust in me, not to mention his own overt indulgence in self-love.

Somehow, however, I couldn't forgive or forget. For my *bar mitzvah*, a time of celebration, when I was still the prodigy, my father had given me a copy of his autobiography. Inside the book, he had written: "My beloved, so very dear to my heart, my little son, Leibele: I beg you to read with enthusiasm and love this book of mine. You will perhaps learn something from it – not only about your father and all the very heavy, bitter dilemmas and soul-wranglings he has experienced in his life, but also about the generations of Jews who carried their Jewishness with pride, respect, and a willingness to sacrifice their lives if necessary.

"Walk in the paths of these proud Jews, my son.

Then, toward the end of my turbulent, failure-ridden high-school years, there was that night in Banff Springs, when my father stripped me of all dignity with the horrible, hurtful things he said about me, as a person, a Jew, or a Canadian, in front of my family and the strangers that were assembled. I had no redeeming qualities, he cried out. My eighteen years of life – and this, he shouted to the rafters of the Banff Springs Hotel – were devoid of any contribution, any skill, any insight, any truth. He referred to my unwanted birth and he cursed himself for not delivering me to the abortionist. He called me a liar and a cheat, a poolroom lout and a gambling loafer. But above all, he emphasized my dumminess, my lack of brains, my general stupidity, my laziness – and he stressed my wilfulness, my deliberate desire to divest him of all joy as a father, an author, a teacher. "You've robbed me of my life!" he shouted. "You are my personal pogrom-chik, an enemy of your own family, an enemy of your own people!"

Stunned, I had said nothing, not one word in defence or reply.

As a consequence of this condemnation, I'd had to live at home in alienation and isolation, hidden away, from my father, who felt that my very existence heaped scorn and rebuke upon his head.

As a result, I had drawn even closer to my mother. It was she who had never asked me what I had done to enhance the Zholf name. It was she who had made sure I was fed once my father left the dinner table each evening. It was she who had snuck me into the house all those late nights, while my father snored soundly on his pillow. It was she who had shown me all the tiny considerations that constitute love.

PISSING ON MY PARADE

One Saturday afternoon at Nordic's Pool Hall, known gambler, closet communist, and prince of pool sharks, Coke Lander, shouted that the papers were full of my name. And what a read it was! I had won the University of Manitoba's Marcus Hyman Memorial Scholarship for being the top student in second year. I had also received honourable mentions for six other scholarships (in those days, you could take home only one scholarship per year; an honourable mention meant that you were the real winner of the scholarship in question unable to accept it). Coke read out my name and my awards. The pool hall rocked with applause. I was so shocked and moved by this affection that I burst into tears just as Coke said, "Larry's glory is the glory of all those among us who have pulled a cue from a rack, laid it on the table to check its level, then broken the balls and stroked a game."

I was ecstatically happy, yet the imp of perversity had hold of me. I had no desire to be with my family. Instead, I moved from bottle to bottle; I stayed out for more than forty-eight hours. I did not phone home, once. I felt that my family – namely my father – wasn't worthy of my triumphs.

By the time I entered the front door of my house, I had a three-day beard and I reeked. My clothes were stained, my *schnozz* was in blossom, and spittle was stuck to my lips. My father, clutching a bunch of congratulatory telegrams, rushed to greet me. He did not say a word about my absence, my intoxicated state. Instead, he talked loudly, boastfully, about the rich Jews of River Heights, and the MPs and MLAs, the rabbis, the big shot socialists from the Isaac Loeb Peretz Folk School, who had called to congratulate him for having me, me, as a son. Even the Premier had phoned. Beaming with ethereal approval and self-satisfied beatitude, and wholly unaware of my disarray, my father handed me the telegrams.

I threw the letters to the floor and stomped on them, calling on anger, self-pity and despair: "You wouldn't talk to me for four years! Now you're proud of me? Well, take your telegrams and shove them up your ass!"

I leapt at him, my hands at his throat, and toppled him to the ground.

But nothing could put a crimp in the *noches*, the joyful sense of good luck that my triumph had brought him. He got up and waved off my attack, as if my efforts to choke him had been mere nerves on my part. Then, stroking his nose with satisfaction, he spoke of the Isaac Loeb Peretz Folk School socialists – how my achievement had forced them to offer my father congratulations. "This," he said, "is sweet vengeance. You, my son, have given me my revenge."

I was astonished. I'd been bullied to death by the man. Now I was being loved to death.

Death is death!

The smartest man I had ever known understood nothing.

Prejudice of education, he would say, is the devil,—
and the multitudes of them which we suck in with our
mother's milk—are the devil and all.—We are haunted
with them in all our lucubrations and researches; and
was a man fool enough to submit tamely to what they
obtruded upon him,—would his book be? Nothing,
—he would add, throwing his pen away with a
vengeance,—but a farrago of the clack of nurses, and
of the nonsense of the old women (of both sexes)
throughout the kingdom.

This is the best account I am determined to give of
the slow progress my father made in his Tristra-paedia;
at which (as I said) he was three years, and something
more, indefatigably at work, and, at last, had scarce
completed, by his own reckoning, one half of his
undertaking: the misfortune was, that I was all that
time totally neglected and abandoned to my mother:
and what was almost as bad, by the very delay, the first
part of the work, upon which my father had spent the
most of his pains, was rendered entirely useless,—every
day a page or two became of no consequence.—

— *STERNE*

THE PING-PONG AFFAIR

She was standing on her toes. She was peeking through a transom window at dirty movies. The movies were being screened by the Manitoba Censor Board in the basement of the Manitoba Legislative Building, where I was working at a summer job. It was 1955 and I was one year away from completing my Bachelor of Arts. The calves of her legs were taut. Her flapper haircut set off a very handsome face, and her quirky curiosity set off my own. I joined her on tiptoe. The movie was *Lover Boy Meets the Sex Kitten Bandit*, starring no one. My calves hurt. I could stand on my toes for only a minute.

Flat-footed, I could see that the young lady had a fine figure.

"I'm Larry Zolf," I said. "I'm the shipper's assistant in the Department of Education. I go to United College. My majors are history and poli-sci. You?"

"I'm Patricia Legge. I'm an assistant to the Minister of Mines and Natural Resources. I'm also at United; I go to the Fort Garry campus. My majors are mathematics and physics."

Wow. I had always hated mathematics; it was the one subject that was totally resistant to my capacity for bafflegab. I had failed it twice in high school. In fact, mathematics had helped put me in the "dummy" class – I was too stupid to take physics.

Patricia Legge. My daydream was upon me: I would become the Clarence Darrow of the 1960s, and she would be my

forensic expert, my science advisor. Together, we would con-
quer.

But first things first.

"Would you like a cup of coffee?" I asked with a little
woo on my mind.

"Sure."

Patricia Legge was the women's table tennis champion
at the University of Manitoba. I had been taught to play
ping-pong back in high school, by Holocaust children. After
the Americans had liberated the concentration camps, the
first items they'd brought survivors were bushels of food;
second were ping-pong tables so that the survivors could
play while they awaited repatriation. I had never met a
teenaged camp survivor who wasn't an absolute ping-pong
shark. These survivors had taught me to play hard and fast
– back apace from the table, rapid fire, constantly spiking
the ball.

The next time I saw Patricia Legge, she was at her porno
peephole. The flick was *Hand Job to Paradise*; it starred an ex-
sumo wrestler.

"I hear you play a little ping-pong," I said. "How about if
I play you a game or two?"

Over the ping-pong table at the Students' Union, I fired
one spike after another at the head, shoulders and ample
chest of the lovely Patricia Legge. All my spikes were quietly
and quickly returned. At the end of the day, I had lost each
and every game.

The race for her heart was on full tilt. I took her to museums, art galleries, impromptu campus debates (in which I
starred), intramural basketball games (in which I held my
own), pool halls and gambling emporia, and bowling
alleys. We drank beer in the ladies and escorts section of the

Bell Hotel, and visited the odd after-hours club. We went to movies, lots of them, and we did not stand on tiptoes. *Au contraire.*

I had not laid a finger on Patricia. I didn't want to jeopardize our friendship. With my huge hooter and skin-and-bones body, I was no prize package. But we kissed and miracle of miracles, our teeth did not collide. Patricia Beatrice Legge put her tongue in my mouth (no one had ever done that before) and leaves fell, trees bent, sparrows fled. I was head over heels in love. Beauty had aroused the Beast. But because the pill had not yet been invented, and condoms and diaphragms were not common among the mostly uninitiated, oral sex was our delight of choice. We'd sixty-nine in the back seats of cars, in front of the legislative buildings late at night, in the last row of the Capitol and Garrick movie theatres, in the laundry room of her apartment building. We groped on elevators and escalators.

We also studied together, and went to parties and dinners together. We were inseparable.

Pat's mother, however, was not keen on me. Though Mama Legge, an American woman from Wisconsin, was amiable enough during our first meeting, she was wary, and by the end of the visit, disapproval was in the air.

"I'm Larry Zolf. Is Patricia home?"

"Yes, of course! Come on in. Have a cup of tea. How are you? How's the university?"

"I'm fine. So is the university."

"Have you known Pat for very long, Mr. Zolf?"

"Three weeks, four days, eighteen hours and twenty minutes – and I've never had so much fun in my life."

Images of "fun" popped into Mama Legge's mind. The images looked very much like stills from a porno movie.

"Isn't today Yom Kippur?" she asked, trying to clear her head. "My associate, Mr. Flink, took the day off to fast. Can you have tea and cookies?"

"I'm a socialist, Mrs. Legge, and to be a socialist, you have to eat every day, even on Yom Kippur, so that you are strong enough to bite the capitalist enemy – like James Richardson and Sons – in the throat. Pat tells me that your husband slaved for the Richardson family for thirty years before he passed away. And, if I'm not mistaken, there was no pension. This wealthy cartel that holds Winnipeg by the throat provided no help to you, the widow!"

My odd looks, my socialist views and my quasi-vampire attitude repelled her.

Later, Mama Legge felt obliged to inform Pat that Jews were descendants of the Devil, that Jews cast spells on beautiful gentile girls in order to do with those girls what they wanted. Pat and Mama Legge quarrelled bitterly. Hair was pulled, blouses ripped, ankles kicked, faces slapped.

"Patsy," I said, when told of the episode, "if I could cast spells don't you think I would have gotten rid of my *schnozz*?"

With tenderness and affection, Pat fondled my nose, my spare sex organ.

So: that left only my wonderfully tolerant family to contend with.

Said my father, partly correcting himself—she is but tenant for life—

 —That makes a great difference—said my mother—

 —In a fool's head, replied my father—

 Unless she should happen to have a child—said my mother—

— Sterne

THE BELLS TOLL

It was hot and steamy through the summer of 1956. I'd been dating Pat for one year, but my father still did not know that I had a gentile girlfriend. He had to be told.

The argument went on, nose to nose, for hours.

Joshua Falek said that I owed it to the Jewish people, my love of Israel, and my hatred of anti-Semitism to drop this liaison at once.

"I love Israel and I love the Jewish people," I replied, "but Patricia's love for me has stopped my psoriasis dead in its tracks and my gout is now almost gone."

Exhausted, we headed for our beds.

My father had been known to sleep through hurricanes, tornadoes, trench warfare and the odd pogrom.

I, however, was a light sleeper like my mother, and even in my dreams I was looking over my shoulder.

I saw my father's face. He was trying to wake me up. I was asleep. It was a nightmare. I was used to nightmares. I rolled over. It was no nightmare. My father was yelling: "Wake up, Leibele! Wake up!" It was 5 a.m. I was told to get dressed, that we were going for a walk.

In solemn, wary silence, we came to rest in St. John's Park, scene of many a heated public debate on Jewish matters in which my father had always shone.

What I told him – leaving out all reference to sex, of course – was this: my love for Patricia was an affirmation of socialism and of Patricia's working-class roots. As a young socialist, he himself had wooed and won the strong and silent Freda Rachel Pasternak; now I, as a young socialist, had wooed and won the strong and silent Patricia Beatrice Legge.

"Socialism," said my father, as he circled me, "is a great snare and a delusion. Socialism says everybody is the same. Try telling that to the Nazis. Blood is thicker than water. The Jewish people have survived the Holocaust. The Jewish people will die if their sons and daughters marry gentiles."

"Moses married a gentile. And Boaz married the gentile Ruth, she of 'whither thou goest, I will go,'" I said jauntily.

"The Talmud cautions us that neither marriage came to a good end," said my father.

"Pat has offered to convert."

"Mixed marriages don't work," said my father. "You'll wake up in the middle of the night craving a salami sandwich; she'll wake up in the middle of the night craving – pork!"

(Ah, pork! Pork, my mother had often told me, gave the gentiles constipation, ulcers, glaucoma, heart attacks, to say nothing of trichinosis.)

My father picked up the pace. "You'll be walking with Patricia down Selkirk or Main or Portage and you'll both hear the pealing of church bells," he said. "The sound of the bells will remind you of the pogroms, the beatings inflicted on the Jewish people by *goyische* Christians. Your Pat will hear the church bells and in her subconscious, she will come to need the partaking of communion. Pat will leave your side and answer the call of the bells. The bells are ringing for Pat but they are tolling for you," my father warned.

"I guess I'll just have to give up salami and walking near churches."

At that, Joshua Falek decided Pat ought to meet the family – the whole family.

I agreed.

The locale was Rose's modest bungalow in West Kildonan, the lower-middle-class suburb where she and Harry lived with their children. Meyer, now a happily married father and high-profile tax advisor to tycoons like the Belzbergs and the Singers, flew in from Edmonton. And Judith, along with her husband Jack, flew in from Sioux City, Iowa.

The Zholf family sat on the sofa and chairs that had been assembled in a single row. I – the Great Yiddish Mouthpiece – and the lovely Patricia Beatrice Legge – a Christian woman prepared to embrace Judaism for the good of all man-and womankind – sat facing them.

Meyer, whose successes rendered him the respected family favourite, led off: "If you marry Pat, aren't you worried that your children will marry Negroes?"

Pat burst into tears.

My mother shook her head sadly, as if such should not be happening in her home.

"If the Nazis came here," Judith snapped, "whose side would *you* be on?"

Patsy burst into tears again.

My mother now shook her head in sorrow.

I rose to the occasion in my own way: "First, Pat would kill Mama. Then Papa. Then Rose and her children. Then Meyer and his children. For the climax, so to speak, Pat would kill you, Judy, and then throw your babies up in the air and catch them one by one on her bayonet."

This outburst led to a half-hearted scuffle between Meyer and myself, which ended when our father began to speak.

"Why do you want my son, Leibele?" he asked. "He's lazy; he sleeps all morning whenever he gets the chance. His nose is so large that he could hold a party in it, and he's a dreadful dresser. He can't swim or dance. He doesn't brush his teeth. When he eats, his narrow chest is a forest of crumbs. He's sarcastic and has a foul temper; he's fickle and could easily leave you; he talks too much and never listens. And his socialism is phoney – he wouldn't give a beggar a dime. Can't you see that a beautiful, clever girl like yourself needs a better partner than my hapless son, Leibele?"

Patricia burst into tears again.

My father was not used to making beautiful women cry. He could see that the confrontation had stumbled to a halt. As the Zholf family sat chewing their lower lips – the curse of intermarriage staring them in the face – my father realized that there was nothing he could do. Reluctantly, he said that he'd somehow learn to live with the situation. Everyone nodded warily. Tea and cookies were served, politics were discussed. Patricia dried her tears and ate my mother's sponge cake. The Zholf family was once again something of a unit – and my Patricia, for better or for worse, was now a part of it.

Thrice happy book! thou wilt have two pages, at least, within thy covers, which Malice will not blacken, and which Ignorance cannot misrepresent.

— *STERNE*

THE DANCER DANCING

Following his secret conversion to Orthodoxy, the moral odyssey upon which my father embarked extended well beyond his rabbinical plans for me. The logic and truth of my father's position, as he saw it, drove him straight to the hearts and souls of the little Jewish boys who, every evening, were sent by their socialist parents to visit my father for socialist succour at the Isaac Loeb Peretz Folk School.

For these Jewish boys, my father prepared a feast of Orthodoxy that they had never before encountered.

First, Falek would check the halls to make sure none of the hated socialist bosses were still around.

When Falek found no one, he would open his satchel and distribute prayer books, prayer shawls and skullcaps, as well as pocketbook versions of the Talmuds – a popular history of rabbinical wizardry from the fall of the Temple to the rise of the Wilner Gaon. Stories of how Jewish socialists helped round up illegal Jews in Israel and dissident Jews in Russia for the purpose of camp imprisonment soon followed. Explicit name-calling of powerful and beloved local socialists also took place – in an amiable and jocular fashion, of course. The British Labour Party and the CCF were declared forces, and socialism was declared the opiate of the Jewish people. Only loyalty to God would get the Chosen People anywhere, Falek told his captive audience.

My father had suicidally crossed the Rubicon. He was secretly subverting a Jewish socialist school and getting paid by socialists to do it. Sooner or later, he would be caught.

Sooner came earlier rather than later. His secret Orthodox laboratory for Jewish socialist boys was hardly on a par with the strict confidentiality with which the development of the atom bomb was treated. Indeed, my father's activities were quickly becoming more intensive, and often required co-conspirators.

For example, he decided the best way to rescue the boys from the pit of socialism was to give them *bar mitzvah* training. For this, he had to smuggle into the school some Orthodox cantors and musicologists, not to mention cumbersome Torah scrolls and other accoutrements of the faith.

To show the boys the beauties of Orthodox Judaism, he arranged outings so that they could participate in the celebration of *Succoth*, the Feast of Tabernacles: he took them to the synagogue, where they watched the waving of the four species: citron, twigs of willow and myrtle, and the frond of a palm; and he took them to the houses of those Orthodox neighbours who had erected temporary *sukkah* structures in their backyards. To show the richness of Orthodox Judaism, he taught them the wonders of Jewish voodoo and mysticism.

The pupils tended to like the Orthodox rituals that my father was peddling. Many were from well-off socialist families, and they were eager to try out what they had learned on their unsuspecting parents.

Itzikel Levine, the socialist atheist realtor's son, spoke to his parents about the wonders of *Succoth*, and described the *Sukkah* tabernacle that Rabbi Berl Zadek had built in his backyard. "We should have one, too, Daddy," said Itzikel.

"We could keep an Auschwitz orphan there…" Mr. Levine was stunned.

Not as stunned as the Dorfmans! Beindele, their thirteen-year-old, waltzed into the living room one day with a large bag from which squawking noises were emanating. Beindele hauled a live chicken from the bag, wrung its neck, and then waved the carcass around the living room with gusto.

"My God, what are you doing?" his mother asked in sheer terror.

"I'm beating off the evil spirits. Somebody has to!"

"And where did you get that piece of nonsense?" Mr. Dorfman asked.

"From Mr. Zholf's Dialectics of Socialism class at the Peretz School," Beindele answered dutifully.

Indeed, the neighbourhood's children were quickly turning delinquent. Velvele Schtifer gave his mother the Evil Eye; she'd to take to bed for a week. Motke Goldberg stayed out all night and then said to his parents the following morning: "I'm thirteen; according to Jewish law, I'm a man. I don't have to tell you anything about what I'm doing."

The community was stunned.

My father was particularly proud of Menachem Mendelsohn, the furrier's youngest son; he delighted in Menachem's in-class performance of the *maftir* Torah portion. "It's wonderful," my father said. "Sing it everywhere, Menachem, and the world will be your oyster."

Mr. Mendelsohn was a staunch Jewish Bundist – that is, a socialist and an atheist. He wangled a solo for his Menachem to sing at the Rosa Luxemburg Memorial Anniversary Banquet and Dance, which was being held at the Isaac Loeb Peretz Folk School. Menachem was assigned the communist anthem, "The Internationale."

When it was Menachem's turn to sing, he donned a skull-cap and prayer shawl, and wound a few phylacteries around his arms and legs. Then Menachem mounted centre stage and sang from memory his total *maftir* Torah portion.

The audience of radicals was stunned.

"How could you do it?" Menachem's father asked.

"Teacher Zolf made me do it, Pa," said Menachem.

It's fair to say that my father wasn't surprised when the authorities at the school finally put two and two together and caught up with him. He was ready for his socialist golgotha.

Berta Gladik, a broad-shouldered woman with a muscular chest, and enormous hands and feet, chaired the inquisition. As the wife of Velvel Gladik, the city's toughest socialist loan shark, Berta was the perfect socialist woman for the tricky job of interrogating my God-ridden father.

The following scene, involving arguments that were not necessarily coherent, ensued:

Berta: "*Chaver* Zolf, do you believe in the non-existence of God?"

Chaver Zolf: "Of course I do, *Chaver* Berta. I am a good socialist and I believe that the brightest, smartest, most talented, and most beautiful like yourself, *Chaver* Berta, should have the wisdom of socialism to steer you. But the lazy, the useless, the indolent, the jobless, the helpless, the wretched, the homeless, and the poor, they need God to believe in. They need God to help them. Believe me, God is the only one who will take these losers on!"

Berta: "Is God a man or a woman, *Chaver* Zolf?"

Chaver Zolf: "Oh, a woman, *Chaver* Berta. Certainly a socialist woman.

Socialism cannot work unless God is a woman. Everyone knows the best rent collectors, the best collectors of high interest on outstanding loans, are the socialist members of the Mothers' Union. Everyone knows that the socialist members of the Jewish Mothers' Union were always able to obtain for their husbands the best workers at the lowest wages. Everyone knows that the Isaac Loeb Peretz Folk School is kept alive by the socialist members of the Jewish Mothers' Union."

My father was brilliant. His final argument was a lulu. He told the Mothers' Union that the reason he was taking his students through Orthodox methodology was to make them better socialists. Jewish socialism, my father said, came from Jewish Chassidism. To know the latter was better to understand the former, he insisted. The Mothers' Union was not amused.

Finally, my father offended the Jewish socialist establishment by writing his autobiography – "on school time," said the Mothers' Union. On school time, they said, he had written the book and raised money to pay for its publication. On school time, they said, he'd had book launches. On school time, they said, he sold the book door-to-door in Winnipeg (they didn't seem to be aware of his trips to the outback).

They fired him.

It is said in Aristotle's Mast Piece, "That when a man doth think of any thing which is past—he looketh down upon the ground;—but that when he thinketh of something that is to come, he looketh up towards the heavens."

— Sterne

THE TROUBLE WITH HARRY

In 1958, two years after I'd completed my Bachelor of Arts, the liberalism that had made United College a famous institution across the land came to an abrupt end: dark forces at the college had found a way to kick socialists off the campus block.

A veteran socialist history professor, Harry Crowe, had written a personal letter to a colleague at Queen's University, which he placed in the United College post box. The letter, however, never left campus; someone took it and secretly turned it over to the principal of the college, Wilfrid C. Lockhart. Prior to his position at the college, Lockhart had been the pastor of Kingsway-Lambton United Church, which was located in a wealthy Toronto suburb.

Principal Lockhart was not amused by the animated socialist discussions that took place between socialist professors and their North End socialist Jewish students at Tony's, the school cafeteria. Lockhart was a staunch Anglo-Saxon free enterpriser, and he was determined to put all this Marxist-Leninist nonsense and simple-minded tolerance in its proper place – outside the doors of United College.

The Crowe letter was exactly what Lockhart had been looking for. In it, Crowe had attacked, ridiculed and blasphemed the greatest Calvinist of them all – God, in all His Predestined Glory.

Though the letter was private, Lockhart took the high ground. He called Harry Crowe on the carpet and demanded that Crowe apologize to Lockhart personally, the college at large, and God Himself – for this Bolshevist atheist blasphemy.

Crowe, a tough, fearless man who had been awarded a Military Cross for valour behind enemy lines in the Second World War, told Lockhart to stuff it.

Frustrated, Lockhart decided to put the fear of the Lord into United College faculty members by firing Harry Crowe.

The story made the front pages of all the major newspapers and was the lead news item of TV and radio broadcasts across the country. The infamous "Harry Crowe Affair" became the biggest *cause célèbre* in the land and, ultimately, made its way into history books: Lockhart the Heavy versus Crowe the Victim.

◎◇◎

I remember the day I first laid eyes on Harry Crowe. He was a stocky, moustached man, with a point of view on everything from tiddlywinks to the Tolpuddle Martyrs. McCarthyism, however, was Harry's obsession. He hated Senator Joe McCarthy so much that his American history course began with a three-week denunciation of the Wisconsin senator. Then, out of breath, he let his course slowly work its way backwards to the Pilgrim Fathers and their Salem witch hunts, an image (he agreed with Arthur Miller) of McCarthyism rooted in time.

Harry had quickly warmed to me because I brought him a copy of the *Winnipeg Tribune* news clipping that mentioned my communist cousin, Jerry Zalph, the chief proofreader at the *New York Times*, upon whom McCarthy had pounced.

Harry read the clipping and asked me a few questions about Jerry. Then, he devoted half the class to the wonders of my brave commie cousin, this man of integrity who had pled the Fifth Amendment while fighting off the malevolent McCarthy, his thug Hoover, the FBI and other such sewer rats.

Another day, Harry described how he – as a Canadian soldier – had shot down two Nazis bearing the white flags of surrender during the re-taking of France. The class gasped, appalled. My admiration for Harry, however, soared: he did not have a sentimental, apologetic bone in his body. When he invited me to the history club that he hosted at his home so that I could hear doctoral student, Ramsay Cook (later, a distinguished professor himself), give a paper on Canada First, I knew I had entered into socialist high society, and for the first time, I had made it on my own merits.

◎◎

Simply put, Harry was the best teacher I ever had. He taught me how to have an historic sense of events in time, an historic sense that has animated everything I've ever done in my life. He also tried (and failed) to teach me that history should be a hanging judge, that the world was and is divided between heroes and villains – that the job of the alert historian is to extirpate the villains.

Harry was no scholar, but he made me love history.

It was not hard to see that as a lover, he was blinkered. He didn't like Sir John A. Macdonald, so Sir John was nothing but a drunk. And he felt that Joe McCarthy was an unalloyed monster – versus a malevolent yet hapless drunk, a man hopelessly out of his depth who, with good public intentions, righteously, stupidly and opportunistically set out to destroy lives.

According to Harry, only socialists were good and true; only socialists had the answers.

In graduate school at the University of Toronto, I soon outgrew Harry's view of history. But I have never outgrown his love for history, his love for scenarios, fact play and historical recreation. He thrilled to certain moments in history as a man thrills to certain women. I am no hanging-judge historian, yet I am prone to follow in Harry's footsteps. For without enthusiasm, laughter, a sense of shock and a sense of dismay, history is dry as dust and totally uninspiring. Harry gave me the love of scholarship, the heartfelt fun in it, the buffeting-about of reputations and interpretations – all of which turned out to be Harry's greatest gift to me – love of politics and the politics of love.

There are some trains of certain ideas which leave prints of themselves about our eyes and eye-brows; and there is a consciousness of it, somewhere about the heart—we see, spell, and put them together without a dictionary.

— *STERNE*

BLOOD LEIBELE

It was Harry Crowe who agreed to give Patricia (whose family was nowhere to be found) away at our upcoming wedding – so long as he could use the occasion to deliver a major speech on the inequities of Joe McCarthy, the shallowness of Mackenzie King and the Liberal Party of Canada, the duplicity of Principal Lockhart, and the general viciousness of the German people.

When I finally told my father of my wedding plans, I invoked Harry Crowe's name, his war record, his academic stature, and his crystalline socialism as proof that what I was about to do was acceptable in the highest academic and socialist circles.

My father, as usual, leapt to two conflicted conclusions.

On one hand, no one had more faith in academics than my father, and since he now felt that a professional academic career was in the offing for me, he was obliged to believe that Professor Crowe could only be a help.

Somehow my father – still unable to accommodate what he knew was going to happen – managed to come to the conclusion that the gentile girl I was going to marry had to be a blood relative – perhaps even a daughter – of Professor Crowe. Why else would he be the one willing to give the bride away? My father concluded that the good professor had chosen my bride for me and arranged the marriage, that I was a helpless victim of a socialist-Christian kidnapping plot.

My father told all of this to my sister, Judith. She, walking in the shadow of my father's perversity, called Harry Crowe in the middle of the night to denounce his proselytizing of innocent little Jewish boys like her kid brother, a guileless young man, she said, who was obviously being led by his ample nose to the trough of assimilation, cultural genocide, and mixed marriage.

Later, I told Harry how sorry I was.

He shrugged it off. "I haven't had so many laughs since I wiped out those white-flag-waving Nazis just outside of Antwerp near the end of the war!"

Every thing in this world, said my father, is big with jest,—and has wit in it, and instruction too,—if we can but find it out. Yes—

Imagine this to yourself;—

Besides the many nautical uses of long noses enumerated by Erasmus, the dialogist affirmeth that a long nose is not without its domestic conveniences also; for that in a case of distress—and for want of a pair of bellows, it will do excellently well, ad exitandum focum (to stir up the fire).—but then I had better begin a new chapter.

— *STERNE*

THE FLAMING RED RABBI

It was the spring of 1958.

Patsy and I had been living in Toronto for a year. I had just finished my first year at Osgoode Hall Law School; Patsy was the household breadwinner.

"Do you, Ruth (Patsy) Beatrice Legge, take this man, Larry Zolf, to be your lawfully wedded husband, to love, honour and cherish, all your living life until death do you part?" asked Toronto's Rabbi Abraham L. Feinberg, rabbi emeritus of Holy Blossom Temple, the largest Reform synagogue in the country.

Rabbi Feinberg had helped fight the notorious racism and segregation with which black people were acutely oppressed in Dresden, Ontario; he fought to ban the bomb everywhere; he fought for peace everywhere; he fought also for abortion rights, women's rights, and freedom of sexual expression. And he was rumoured to be writing a Jewish sex manual, *Torah Between the Sheets*. (He would ultimately go on to write three books: *Storm the Gates of Jericho* (1961); *Hanoi Diary* (1967); and *Sex and the Pulpit* (1981), which became the recommended rabbinical book on sexual practices among the elderly and sexual lore in Judaism.)

The Red Rabbi was pure *huzzah*, pure show biz. In the early 1930s, he had been the radio singing star, Tony Frome. When he returned to his rabbinical career, fame continued to follow. In 1967, he journeyed to Hanoi with two other holy men so that they could see for themselves the ravaged state in which the American bombing had left North Vietnam. There, he famously befriended Ho Chi Minh. Feinberg's insistent protestations of the war garnered much opposition, including death threats, and the nickname "The Flaming Red Rabbi." And in 1969, he visited John Lennon and Yoko Ono at their Bed-In For Peace, where he performed various spiritual services, and recorded "Give Peace a Chance," along with Lennon, Ono, Timothy Leary, Petula Clark, and others.

Not surprisingly, he loved women; the brighter the better. (The long-legged beauteous journalist, June Callwood, once told me that after a disarmament rally, the Red Rabbi had chased her around the Holy Blossom sanctuary.) Being a lover, he was willing to officiate such marriages as ours in synagogues – in fact, he was the only rabbi in Canada who would do so – and so he was the rabbi of choice among many couples.

When Patsy and I had gone to see him, he asked whether we intended to have a civil ceremony if he declined to marry us.

"For sure, Rabbi," I said.

"In that case," said Rabbi Feinberg, "it is better that I perform the wedding in a house of God."

I told him, "Patricia is very brainy. You're going to love her. She's crazy about Jews and Israel. What's even better, she's for peace, nuclear disarmament, racial integration and unions. She's also against pollution and capital punishment. She's your kind of woman, Rabbi."

He took a quick, intense look at Patsy's magnificent face and figure, and readily agreed that she was his kind of woman.

Patsy spent a week pouring through stacks of books and then went to visit the rabbi. After an hour, she was home with the news: "I'm a Jew. God, it's hard to believe. Rabbi Feinberg said I would be an asset to the Jewish community. He said I was a worthy namesake for the Bible's Ruth. So that's now my Jewish name: Ruth. And then he looked me over closely – and said I was really cute!"

The wedding, almost spectral for its want of living witnesses, was performed at the Holy Blossom Temple. The Red Rabbi, who had sight in only one eye, used a magnifying glass to read the service. I held the glass for him. "And do you, Larry Zolf, take this woman, Ruth Beatrice Legge, to love, honour and cherish – sorry, I missed a line – to be your lawfully wedded wife, to love, honour and cherish all your living life, until death do you part?"

"I do." I felt assured that, in that very moment, *dybbuks* were dancing along the outskirts of Zastavia and *golems* were gambolling in fields that were growing greener by the second all the way down to the Pasternak pond.

I let my eye wander over the cavernous, empty Holy Blossom Temple, and felt some sadness creep in. Harry was there. Neither my family nor Patsy's were present.

I had kept my promise: my father had asked that I wait a year after moving to Toronto before marrying Patsy. And in fact, we had lived apart for that year, having taken single rooms at two separate dwellings on Wells Avenue in the Annex, an immigrant and working-class enclave where fellow tenants were known to stash their babies in open bureau drawers.

Patsy had given up university to work as a clerk so that she could support us while I was studying at Osgoode Hall. Her wages had not been enough with two rents to pay.

Though my father had promised a small subsidy, it hadn't come. We'd had no money to go anywhere. Our only form of entertainment was our rented television set. We'd curl up in front of it and hurl insults at the curling matches, the Jackie Rae Show, Hockey Night in Canada, Wayne and Schuster, and the nation's songstress, as she was called, "pet" Juliette.

Just before the wedding, I had decided to move Papa from conventional to nuclear warfare. I'd wired him the following provocative telegram: "The wedding reception will be this Friday in the vestry of the Martyred Saints Roman Catholic Church, Etobicoke. Obviously, I cannot afford to live a Jewish life now; perhaps a Christian one will be more rewarding for Patsy and I. You and Mother are of course welcome to attend."

There was no reception.

A week later, we received our wedding gift in the mail: the rental subsidy, and with it, a stern letter condemning such wedding brinksmanship.

When a man gives himself up to the government of a ruling passion,—or, in other words, when his Hobby-Horse grows headstrong,—farewell cool reason and fair discretion!

— *STERNE*

ONTO THE GOOD SHIP
LOLLIPOP

In the spring of 1959 I made my first radio broadcast.

A friend of mine, Michael John Nimchuk – an occasional playwright and poet, and a somewhat notorious campus hanger-on at the University of Toronto (where I was now, having left Osgoode to pursue my Masters degree in Canadian history) and actually drove his very own Volkswagen – suggested that Patsy and I join him on a road trip to Louisiana and the Deep South of the United States. Nimchuk also said he had a way of financing the trip: "We'll go see Harry Boyle at the CBC. I've got some great ideas that I'm sure he'll buy. If he does, he'll cover our expenses, and supply the tape recorder and tapes."

Nimchuk and I entered a dingy old red brick building on Jarvis Street (since renewed the building is now the primary residence of Canada's National Ballet School), and walked down a narrow basement hall that reeked of hard-boiled eggs and stale coffee.

Harry Boyle's office was unusual for two reasons.

First, there was his secretary, Barbara Burns. She was a large, raucous woman, a hard drinker, and she was tough as nails and often direct to the point of wounding. "Are you back again, Nimchuk?" she bellowed. "What is it you want to record this time? Ukrainian bird calls or a Polish wedding where you're talking to the bride whose holding a bowling ball?"

Nimchuk was half-Ukrainian and half-Polish.

The second unusual thing about Harry Boyle's office was the waiting bench; it was located inside his office rather than in the reception area that housed Barbara's desk. Nimchuk and I sat on the waiting bench and watched Boyle demolish some poor hapless freelancer whose ideas did not pass muster.

As our shot with Boyle neared, Nimchuk turned to me. "Let me do the talking. Harry don't like academic types like you, Larry."

"Doesn't," I said, correcting his grammar.

Nimchuk approached Boyle's desk. "How about an interview with a Mississippi steamboat captain?" Nimchuk asked.

"Nope, not interested," said Boyle.

"How about an interview with a real southern belle?"

"Nope."

"How about a chat with a Klansman as he sets fire to a wooden cross?!"

"Nope." Boyle turned his attention to me. "What do you do?"

"I'm a graduate student studying Canadian history at the University of Toronto, if it's any of your business," I shot back.

"Here," said Harry. He threw a book at me, landing it on my lap. "Review it," he said.

"For what?" I asked.

"For my radio program, *Assignment*. I'll produce you personally. Come back in four days with your review script. Goodbye."

The book was the recently released *Brown of the Globe, Vol. One: The Voice of Upper Canada, 1818-1859*, by J.M.S. Careless, the distinguished professor of Canadian history at the University of Toronto. I asked if I could also interview J.M.S. Careless on the program.

"You're on!" said Boyle.

I slaved over my script for three days. It was over-wrought, full of circumlocutions and convolutions, more-overs to the left and howevers to the right, every last one of them footnoted.

I presented my single-spaced seven-page script to Harry Boyle, and watched him tackle it in a manner that was very strange to me. He read the first paragraph, and then cut it in half. The next paragraph, the same, and so on and so forth until what was left was a succinct four-minute script.

"You get paid for doing this?!" I said.

Boyle chuckled.

In the studio, I read my script flawlessly. Then, Professor Careless and I had a very good chat. My segment on *Assignment* was fifteen minutes long and, joy of joys, it was heard in Winnipeg.

Almost immediately after the broadcast, I phoned my father. He had been under the weather for some time and was not doing well: skin pale and loose, nose and beard life-less, he'd had a recurrence of precancerous bowel polyps and was facing another major operation at the Mayo Clinic in Rochester, Minnesota. On the phone, he sounded out of breath (reminding me that, as a child seated in his lap, my head on his chest, I loved listening to him breathe). He said I was authoritative on the radio, wise in my wit rather than glib, tonally better than Lorne Greene, the CBC's "Voice of Doom," as he'd been nicknamed during World War II, and H.V. Kaltenborn, the popular American radio commentator. "Broadcasting could be your life's work, my son."

Always (especially at moments when I was charged up anew with love for him) the contrarian when it came to my father, I said: "The CBC is a Wasp world, Pop. White-bread

Brits. The good ship *Lollipop*. A nice Jewish boy like me is safer at university."

My father went into a coughing spell.

My mother, sounding drained herself, said goodbye for him.

My mother was going very gingerly in the dark along the passage which led to the parlour—holding in her breath, and bending her head a little downwards, with a twist of her neck—she listened with all her powers:—

—'Twas to his wife,—as so said my father.

Who made Man, with powers which dart him from earth to heaven in a moment—that great, that most excellent, and most noble creature of the world—the miracle of nature, as Zoroaster in his book called him—the Skekinah of the divine presence, as Chrysostom—the image of God, as Moses—to go sneaking on at this pitiful—pimping—pettifogging rate?"

— *STERNE*

LOLLIPOP, LOLLIPOP

I had been brought up in poverty among the fellow dirt-poor in Winnipeg's North End. Things had been tough, and I knew what was said about the poor: they were the bad drunks on my street who beat their wives and children without remorse or restraint; the poor who stole our meagre goods, the poor preying on the poor, the poor who were stupid and bigoted; the poor who told my father that he, who shared his bed with me and my brother, was secretly rich, getting money from the Rothschilds every month.

Shared received opinion! Yes – sometimes evidence of bigotry – but also some containing truths, hard learned.

In our hard-scrabble schoolyards, the poor might well beat somebody like myself senseless – with impunity. They might well steal my marbles when I played agates on the boulevard and inform on any one of us to the police when we did something wrong. The poor, more often than not, were Hobbesian rather than Utopian. The poor, as I'd come to know and be among them, bore watching for safety's sake.

Such ideas, whatever their worth, had not prepared me for a life of middle-class moil and toil in the media in the early 1960s. The emerging New Left extolled the virtues of the poor, the meek, and the downtrodden – laudations that had not been in circulation since the Great Depression's canonization of dispossessed Okies, railroad hobos and ten-cents-a-dance girls, the days when Ma Joad was Madonna.

In search of a provocative interview – an emotional moment, a whiff of sex or sodomy, a controlled breakdown – the investigative journalism of the early sixties by definition exalted the people and scorned the rich and powerful. To tap into this temper of the times, CBC Television's *This Hour Has Seven Days* instituted a segment called Hot Seat: the rich and powerful were to be challenged, if not ridiculed, before the nation; the people, on the other hand, were to be revealed, in all earnestness, as unfortunate in their circumstances, and beleaguered but not entirely broken, possessing, as they did, the plain-spoken wisdom of those who had nothing left to lose.

I was assigned to a *This Hour Has Seven Days* documentary that had the working title, "Loneliness." The director-producer was a World War II German survivor, a self-confessed conscientious objector to Nazism who had somehow lived through Nazi incarceration and ultimately made his way to Canada. Horst was his name.

My job was to find Horst a suitably despondent, suitably lonely and suitably suicidal person to interview on camera. Of course, these days, such assignments are routine; both public and private television boast dozens of loneliness-cum-suicide stories daily. But in the early sixties, the marketplace of despair had not yet been oversubscribed.

Within a week, I burst into Horst's office brimming with good news. "I found a woman. She's Jewish, forty-five years of age. She has tattoo numbers on her left arm, a hunchback and a club foot. And boy, is she lonely!" I gushed like a teenager who had been French-kissed for the first time.

Horst, a true practitioner in the marketplace of despair, offered a thin, all-knowing smile, a smile that, in the years ahead, I would come to see often on the faces of media gurus. Said Horst: "I realize she's Jewish, forty-five years of age, has tattoo marks on her left arm, is a hunchback with a club foot, and is no doubt lonely. BUT FOR OUR PURPOSES SHE'S *NOT QUITE LONELY ENOUGH!*"

I realized, then, that I was truly in the presence of a maven of loneliness, a Darwinian of the School of Survival of the Loneliest. I skulked out of Horst's office and headed to Bloor and Yonge for a much-needed drink or two or ten.

I needed to revise my search strategy.

I began to hit the streets methodically, especially the bars of downtown Toronto, in pursuit of the Lonelies. Weeks passed.

One day, I found myself in a pest-hole bar on the Danforth called Eton House. I was nursing my third double scotch when a pleasant-faced, Anglo-Saxon woman of an uncertain age with a pronounced limp sat down beside me at the bar.

After a drink or two, she asked me what I did for amusement. I confessed to hunting for lonely people for some Hun producer at the CBC. I told her the Horst "not quite lonely enough" story, and she laughed.

Lillian then told me how lonely she was, how people stared at her limp and laughed at her behind her back. She said that it often made her feel as though life was not worth living.

I liked Lillian a great deal at once, and listened to her story with interest. At the same time, however, I felt that I was doing something wrong – that I had inappropriately pried into her private life. I shared these feelings with Lillian.

"That's your job, Larry," she said. "How about me? Am I lonely enough for your TV show?"

Horst brought an army of technicians to the tiny room that Lillian called home in Toronto's east end. I wore a neck mic; I was the off-camera interviewer. All I had to do was toughen myself, forget my North Winnipeg roots and meek-of-the-earth socialism, and the nagging feeling that I was poking into the private life of a woman who, said my gut, should be left alone. It helped that my journalistic instincts told me that was perfect for the "Loneliness" show.

I swallowed my scruples and quietly and gently began to guide Lillian through her story. At times, her tale was so touching, so gutsy, that it literally took my breath away and I would say nothing for some time, unwittingly providing pregnant pauses for the use of producer Horst, the Darwinist of Loneliness.

As Lillian's story neared climax, the room was so quiet you could hear a pin drop. The cameraman, the sound record-ist – the entire army of technicians – were utterly rapt. I was just about to ask the Question That Had To Be Asked, God-dammit, when Horst broke the spell. "LAHR!" he shouted. *"IT'S TIME FOR THE SUICIDE QUESTION!"*

I turned white with anger. Lillian noticed and said sim-ply: "Yes, Larry, it *is* time for the suicide question."

◎◎

During that period, I was dragooned for dyspeptic duty in the Hot Seat, and at the time, the hotspot in the country was Quebec. Producer Patrick Watson assigned myself and emerging political presence, Pierre Elliott Trudeau, to grill Quebec cabinet minister, René Lévesque, who was then rumoured to be a separatist. Trudeau wore a woollen turtle-neck sweater. His pockmarked face seemed to denote some childhood disease. He was extremely shy when he and I met with Watson to plan the interview.

I didn't know then that Lévesque and Trudeau were old friends and sparring partners. All I knew was that Trudeau was uncomfortable with the role he had been asked to perform in the Hot Seat. He was to play the "heavy," the one the program counted on for drama, effect and ratings.

My role was secondary. I was to play the nice guy and moderator, when necessary, to ensure that the interview turned smoothly.

Lévesque was a former CBC Radio-Canada star performer and had been among the leaders of the bitter Radio-Canada producers' strike that occurred in the late 1950s. The Radio-Canada studio crew worshipped Lévesque and loathed both Trudeau and I. The atmosphere was tense, to say the least.

The interview began badly, with Trudeau asking soft questions about Quebec's forest industry and economy – and, ten minutes into taping I was handed a note by the floor director. It was from Watson in the control room. The message was simple: "Drop Trudeau. Take over the interview. Do the dirty work."

So I did. Playing the heavy, I asked Lévesque if he was a separatist. I said he looked like a separatist, walked and talked like a separatist and, therefore, must be a separatist. I said English Canada would not stand idly by as Lévesque ripped the country apart.

I noticed a look of surprise on Trudeau's face. He jumped in, asking if separatism could be accomplished without violence. Lévesque fielded both our questions easily and effortlessly. The give-and-take had edge, wit and authenticity. Lévesque had been stung, but only a little; he had come out of the fray looking fine. Watson was pleased.

President J. Alphonse Quimet and the CBC brass, however, were not happy. They asked that we do a second interview with Lévesque; they wanted something more tamped down, less responsive to Lévesque's character. Lévesque showed up late and in a bad mood. After Trudeau asked the first question, he said: "I'm too busy to listen to fools," and stomped out of the studio.

◎◇◎

The Lévesque Hot Seat interview, with me as heavy and Trudeau as constrained professor, had gone to air. So, too, had Horst's documentary, "Lillian's Loneliness."

Mary Lowrey Ross, the erudite critic for *Saturday Night*, wrote a scathing condemnation of the Lévesque Hot Seat and the role that I'd played. Said Ross: "If these CBC terrors want to learn something about the art of interviewing, they should look to the gentle, sensitive, anonymous interviewer who handled *This Hour's* documentary 'Lillian's Loneliness.'"

Exhilarated by a success that had come so easily – and not yet jaded enough to be suspicious of such an air of ease and well-being among my well-wishing producers – I nonetheless heard a whisper on the wind – was it a warning, an intimation? – whatever it was, I didn't heed it, I didn't pay attention. I had, however, heard it: "Larry it *is* time for the suicide question."

You cry out, he would say, we are ruined, undone.
Why? he would ask, making use of the sorites or syl-
logism of Zeno and Chrysippus, without knowing it
belonged to them.—Why? why are we ruined? however Because we are corrupted.—Whence is it, dear
Sir, that we are corrupted?—Because we are needy;—
our poverty, and not our wills, consent,—And where-
fore, he would add, are we needy? —From neglect, he
would answer.—

– *STERNE*

TEN SIR JOHNS

By the fall of 1959 I was seated almost every day deep in carrels of the University of Toronto, in pursuit of my first love, Canadian history. I was two subjects short of the coursework required for my graduate degree – Historiography, and the History of 20th Century Canadian Politics. These two courses, plus my completed Masters thesis on Ontario Liberal Premier Mitchell Hepburn (who held office from 1934-1942) and a French reading test, would give me my Masters degree in Canadian history.

Patsy and I decided I would get some sort of academic job – teaching assistant, library assistant – and complete my course requirements at the same time. With the extra money, we would be able to move to more civilized living quarters.

I approached my history professors at the University of Toronto and told them of my plans. They responded quickly, telling me that the Archives of Ontario had a vacancy at the lowest level, Archivist I; it paid $4,200 a year. Dr. Spragge, the head archivist, a man with a mouth like a hen's ovipositor, allowed me to take one course on Wednesdays from 12-2 p.m., and the other course on Fridays from 4-6 p.m.

My first day on the job was an eye-opener. Conservative Premier Leslie Frost – the Silver Fox, as he was called – had arranged that the archives of the *Orillia Packet & Times*, the newspaper of his birthplace, a newspaper that had been in business for over one hundred years, be donated to the Archives of Ontario. In return a microfilm containing every single page of past *Packet & Times* would be given to the newspaper. Frost – to all appearances down-home country, a vigorously courteous man – was actually tough as nails. At the microfilm screening, Frost pressed the flesh of the persons present with a welcoming shyness, making those gathered feel at home. Then, the mood changed completely: on the screen, Premier Frost saw page fifty from an 1864 edition of the *Packet & Times*, followed by page twelve from a 1917 edition, two pages that had been fed upside down, and finally two pages that had been fed sideways and scanned via image inversion – all impossible to read. Frost turned to Spragge and said with ice-cold finality: "This won't do, Dr. Spragge. We'll have to start again and this time, under proper supervision. You have a new archivist on staff, a Mr. Zolf, have you not? I hear he's a brilliant history student. Why not let him supervise the microfilming?"

Dr. Spragge, mustering a certain fussiness, insisted his regular staff could handle the Orillia problem.

The Premier said, "How about it, Mr. Zolf? Are you keen?"

"Very keen, Premier, very keen indeed," I replied.

The next morning, I reported to work at the Archives, ready to take on my new responsibilities. The mircofilmer's name was Mossop – and only Mossop – and his room was in the basement. There, I found Mossop holding a huge geological map of northern Ontario's mining country. He wasn't moving. It was nine in the morning and he was very drunk, trying to sleep it off while standing up. He stirred but took no notice of me. Instead he lay down and covered himself with the map. At twelve noon, I roused him.

Mossop opened his bloodshot eyes, located me, blinked, and shouted, "You're a Jew!"

"And you're a drunk!" I shouted back.

I made a deal with Mossop.

He would have his mornings free and could drink if he wanted to, but at twelve noon he was mine, and he was to be sober. We went to work. Before each and every shot, I checked to make sure that the pages were chronologically and sequentially okay, and right-side up, before I let Mossop push the treadle on the microfilm machine.

In no time at all, over a hundred years of the *Orillia Packet & Times* had been microfilmed. Another special screening was held for the Silver Fox.

"You've done wonderful work, Mr. Zolf," he said. "Come and see me at my office sometime. I'd like to talk to you about a few things."

Dr. Spragge, left dangling in his own musty disarray, was doing a slow burn. He did not like my emerging romance with the Premier. I knew that he would try to hurt me if he could.

In his outer office, Premier Frost pointed to ten clay maquettes. They ranged from three to twelve feet in height. They took up enormous space. They were white and ghostly, cheerless presences. A sculptor had used the maquettes to arrive at his final rendering of Canada's first prime minister, Sir John A. Macdonald. Something of a brother, a man with a pronounced *schnozz* for power and booze, Sir John now stood in bronze at the apex of Queen's Park Crescent.

"How much are these worth, Mr. Zolf?" the Premier asked me.

"It's hard to say, sir. At least $500 each, I'd say."

"They are cluttering up my office, Mr. Zolf. Will you find homes for these ten Sir Johns?"

"I'll try, sir, but let me say one thing right off the bat: if you're planning to destroy any of these models, think again!! If the press were to catch wind, the publicity would be overwhelmingly negative. A *Toronto Telegram* headline might read: TORY PREMIER TAKES AXE AND GIVES THE GREATEST TORY OF THEM ALL FORTY WHACKS."

"I hear you, Mr. Zolf. I hear you loud and clear," said the Silver Fox.

Faculty clubs and associations all over Ontario, including various Canadian Legions and the Albany Club, became foster parents to eight of the ten Sir Johns.

I went back to the Premier hoping for a reprieve.

"I'm sorry, Mr. Zolf, but those last two Sir Johns are the biggest of the lot. They have got to go."

"Give me a panel truck and one helper."

"Done," said the Silver Fox.

"I'll take care of it after dark," I said.

Along with Wasyl, my helper, I drove into the deepest, darkest woodiest area of Toronto's High Park. In the 2 a.m. silence, the tall, white Sir Johns, almost luminescent in the moonlight, were attacked with sledgehammers. We crushed their backbones and cracked their skulls, then gathered the debris and scattered it all over High Park so that no one would ever be able to identify or trace the remains.

In the morning, I found a personally signed letter of thanks from the Premier waiting for me on my desk.

Word of my talents as an archivist spread. Sam Resnick, the secretary-treasurer of the Ontario Woodsworth Memorial Foundation asked to see me. He was a storyteller and during our first meeting he told me many tales of the socialist activism for which Spadina Avenue, the main thoroughfare of Toronto radicalism, was known. Then he gave me a $100 cheque, hiring me as the Foundation's archivist. Another $100, he said, would come my way at the end of the summer project.

But the end of the project came faster than I had anticipated. One day, I discovered that Sam's office at the Foundation had been padlocked. Sam had run off with the Foundation's money. Though he was a successful lawyer, he had made some very bad investments, accrued huge debts, and paid those debts with Ontario Woodsworth Memorial Foundation money.

There was talk that Sam had contemplated suicide.

In fact, Sam had lit out for Israel. Once there, like the gangster Meyer Lansky, Sam had invoked Israel's famous Law of Return, hoping that his newfound citizenship would protect him from the Canadian courts.

I cannot think of Sam Resnick and socialism on Spadina Avenue without remembering Maxie Federman, the Jewish Zionist Canadian labour negotiator, leader of the Chicago-based, communist-controlled International Fur and Leather Workers' Union (which, around this time in the arcane world of unions, dissolved into the Amalgamated Meat Cutters and Butcher Workmen of North America). I had no sooner left the Foundation and gone to work for the Toronto and York Region Labour Council, than the country hit hard times under the governance of John Diefenbaker. Maxie, who liked to see himself as a peacemaker, got to his feet in the Labour Temple and made one of his characteristic dovish speeches:

"Brudders and sisters, you all know me, Maxie Federman, leader of de foie and ledder voikers of Canada. Dis veek, de foie ohners and de foie voikers came to a kollectif aghreement. Ve did so peacefully and kvietly, so kvietly not a mouse on Spadina Avenue moved even a teeny muscle in his teeny baudy.

"So I suggest we form a komittee from all de fakshins of de Taranto Labour Council. Den ve shud go to Yuhnion Stashun and take a train to Ottava. In Ottava ve shud den take taxicabs to Pahrliament Hill.

"Ven ve get to Pahrliament Hill, ve shud ask dey jondarm at de front door of de Centre Block vere is Deefenbaker's office. Den ven ve get de anser, ve shud go at vonce to see Deefenbaker."

Maxie's bald head was wet with sweat, his huge eyes were bulging out of their sockets, and his fingers were wagging in all directions, as he anticipated meeting the Great Plainsman, John George Diefenbaker.

"Den, brudders and sisters, ven ve at last see Deefenbaker in de flesh, face to face, we shud calmly and kvickly look him in de eye and say: 'DEEFENBAKER, YU SONNAVABITCH! VAT DE FUCK ARE YU DOING TO US VOIKERS!'"

Through such contacts with my brothers and sisters in Labour Council, I also met the legendary Sam Carr (Schmil Kogan), the man who allegedly organized the Canadian passport that Ramón Mercader had used to enter Mexico and assassinate Leon Trotsky. This was the same Sam Carr who, when stopped and questioned by the Mounties just as he was about to board a flight to Moscow, had said: "Ghenteelmen, I am karing in dee briefcase dee sekrits of a bohmb that vil blow up dee hole vide voild."

The Mounties had laughed heartily and let Carr go – to give the Soviet Union the secrets of a bomb that could indeed blow up "dee hole vide voild."

Of course, with the later defection to Canada of the Russian intelligence clerk, Igor Gouzenko, and the 1946 spy trials that followed, Sam Carr and several other suspects including Jewish communist Member of Parliament from Montreal's

Cartier riding – Fred Rose – were convicted of treason and sentenced to prison.

In 1962, when I had begun working on another TV documentary – "Whither the Party," a one-hour CBC look at the Communist Party of Canada – Sam Carr was no longer sewing mailbags in Kingston Penitentiary. Still a communist, Sam had become the business manager for Kern's Jewellery, then located at College and Yonge.

I approached Sam for an interview.

"Nah! Vhat, arre yu crazy!? I need publicity like dee Sohviet Uhnion needs annuder five-yeer plan," Sam said.

Then Sam Carr, master spy and traitor, a man who had been incarcerated by his country, for seven long years, who I expected to be bitter and angry at politicians and the police, asked the strangest question: "Do you know Neel Leeroy?"

"Yes, Sam, I do. Mr. LeRoy used to be the president of my union the CCAA."

"Aturs and Aktors my ass!" said Sam. "LEEROY IS A DEADBEAT. AFTAH ALL DESE YEARS HE OWZ ME TWO HUNDRED AND TVELF DOHLARS AND TOITEEN CENTS. TELL HIM DAT VHEN YOU SEE HIM! YOU TELL HIM, HE'S A DEADBEAT!"

He was shaking his fist.

Tell me, ye learned,—

Are we for ever to be twisting, and untwisting the same rope? for ever in the same track—for ever at the same pace?

Shall we be destined to the days of eternity, on holy-days, as well as working-days, to be shewing the relics of learning, as monks do the relics of their saints—without working one—one single miracle with them?

— *STERNE*

IN THE GOOD OLD DAYS

In 1961 at the University of Toronto, I was a successful writer for the student newspaper, *The Varsity*, and a socialist cabinet minister in the school's student-run model parliament. Additionally, I spent a lot of time at the U of T student watering hole – the King Cole Room in the Park Plaza Hotel, where I performed stand-up comedy rants, heaping wit, scorn, and outright abuse upon Trinity College, Victoria College and that blighted bastion of the *nouveau riche*, Forest Hill.

During this time a female student at Victoria College decided to take the "mickey" out of me via the University of Toronto's campus magazine. She drew a comic strip for the magazine, wherein two women don't know what to do on a Saturday night, the loneliest night of the week.

Says one woman to the other: "Sometimes we went to the King Cole Room & drank 10¢ draft, to watch Larry Zolf talk."

"scintillate"
"quip"
"sparkle"

"zzz"

"gosh... I bet he could go on like that for 20 years..."

The author of the Larry Zolf cartoon was none other than poet, wit, and scholar, Margaret Atwood.

MY FATHER
AT THE MAYO CLINIC

At the world-famous Mayo Clinic, my father propelled him-self around the halls of the hospital in his wheelchair, talking to patients in his broken English, reassuring them, trying to build up their courage and confidence as only a corner debater and teacher might.

Once, on one of his wheelchair tours, sitting on the in-flated rubber donut that kept his rear end comfortable, my father greeted a man he thought was a lost friend.

"You look familiar," he said. "Have I seen you before? Maybe in Winnipeg? Perhaps Toronto? New York possibly?"

"You might have seen me in a movie. My name is Fred MacMurray. I'm a Hollywood actor."

His wife, Lillian Lamont, was in the Mayo Clinic dying of cancer of the liver.

"Fred MacMurray? The name doesn't ring a bell," my father said. "Well if you're a Hollywood actor you must have acted with beautiful women. Give me their names and I'll see if I remember."

Fred MacMurray, though impatient, acquiesced.

"Let me see… I acted with Katherine Hepburn in *Alice Adams* and with Sylvia Sidney in *The Trail of the Lonesome Pine*."

"Sylvia Sidney – she's a Jewish girl, isn't she?" my father asked, cocking a suspicious eye. "You're not married to a Jewish woman, are you?"

"I believe Sylvia Sidney is Jewish but I'm not married to a Jewish woman. That, of course, does not mean," he added defensively, "that I wouldn't marry a Jewish woman under the right circumstances."

My father, fierce enemy of mixed marriages, was relieved.

"Any other actresses you can tell me about?"

"Well, I did *Double Indemnity* with Barbara Stanwyck."

"Barbara Stanwyck, you say! She's good!"

Then my father showed Fred MacMurray a copy of *On Foreign Soil.*

"In New York, people call *On Foreign Soil* the Yiddish *Gone With the Wind*. It would make a great Jewish movie, a minor epic," my father said. "Paul Muni could play the present me, John Garfield could play the younger me – both speak excellent Yiddish! Could you please talk to them, Mr. MacMurray, on my behalf?"

An exasperated Fred MacMurray said he would try to do so.

Finally, my father said that he was sorry, but that there would be no part for MacMurray in the Yiddish *Gone with the Wind*.

"That's okay by me," said Fred MacMurray.

A happy Falek Zholf then wheeled away from Fred Mac-Murray and, perched on his rubber donut, propelled himself, nose into the wind, down the hall.

Philosophy has a fine saying for every thing.—For Death it has an entire set; 'twas difficult to string them together—I took them as they came.

"'Tis an inevitable chance—the first statute in Magna Charta—it is an everlasting act of parliament—All must die.

"—To die, is the great debt and tribute due unto nature:—

Is it not better to be freed from cares and agues, from love and melancholy, and the other hot and cold fits of life,—

There is no terror—only the blowing of noses and the wiping away of tears with the bottoms of curtains in a dying man's room.—

— *STERNE*

JOSHUA FALEK ZHOLF, GONE

Joshua Falek, whose precancerous bowel polyps had twice sent him under the operating-table knife, died not of cancer but of an infection acquired within the walls of the world-famous Mayo Clinic during his second visit.

Papa was dead!

Hard words to hold on the tongue: *my father is dead,* hard words to give music to: *my father is dead* (only Samuel Beckett has been able to make laughter out of the blunt language of birth, of death).

Joshua Falek: Kerensky's captain, ardent lover, and sharpshooter in the trenches; fearless immigrant and obsessive storyteller; a socialist turned capitalist; a would-be abortionist turned doting father; First Knight of the Order of the Nose.

Gone!

His ex-Isaac Loeb Peretz Folk School bosses – those bouffant-bewigged socialist ladies of the Mothers' Union, and their powerful, steely-eyed socialist husbands – decided to treat Falek in death the opposite of how they had treated him in life: with respect, and as one of the great Jewish legends of the time. Four scholarships were pledged in his name. At the funeral, his old students read aloud from his books. The *Hespet*, the official lamentation, was given by Velvel Gladik, mogul, and chairman of the board at the Isaac Loeb Peretz

Folk School. This man whose wife, Berta, had years ago led the very inquisition that ultimately saw my father fired, described my father as: "a man of the people." My brother and I listened with our eyes shut. Our mouths shut. We were pallbearers. The other pallbearers were various socialist bosses and peers who father had come to hate.

In silence, in love, my brother and I lowered our father into the grave.

—Tread lightly on his ashes, ye men of genius,—for he was your kinsman:

Weed his grave clean, ye men of goodness, for he was your brother—alas! alas! alas! in spite of reverences—the occasion is lost—for thou art gone;—the genius fled up to the stars from whence it came;—and that warm heart of thine, with all its generous and open vessels, compressed into a clod of the valley!

—But what—what is this, to that future and dreaded page—where—all my father's systems shall be baffled by his sorrows; and, in spite of his philosophy, I shall behold him twice taking his spectacles from off his nose, to wipe away the dew which nature had shed upon them—

— *STERNE*

HALLEHLUJAH,
I BECOME A BUM

Ever since my father grudgingly agreed to send me to university, I'd been stricken by fear of failure – of, in effect, being banished to my bedroom again – and as a result, had been seized by a fury to succeed. I had come to believe deep in my bones that by succeeding, I would at last atone for my sin(s) against my father.

This need for atonement and approval only intensified after I moved to Toronto to pursue graduate studies. Morning, noon and night after sleepless night, I studied like a maniac – my nose always in a reference book or history tome.

Disapproval is a terrible weapon.

And because I had not married a woman of the tribe, because I had separated myself from the ghetto, I further tried to compensate by turning the very good woman with whom I shared a marriage bed into – in the eyes of others, especially my family – a perfect woman, a veritable saint. My wife, I'd repeatedly insist to my father, might indeed be a *shiksa* but she was the finest *shiksa* in the land, and he should be pleased.

Silent disapproval cuts to the quick.

There's a lot of pain in the quick.

The day that I hauled his coffin on my shoulder, however, I was overwhelmed with an eerie sense of relief: Joshua Falek Zholf would no longer be able to work his dark magic on me. Having crossed him, gone against his grain numerous times, and having experienced the often physically and emotionally violent consequences of these infractions – having most recently spent three years living in Toronto in near abject poverty, trying desperately to not only accommodate but realize his ambitions – I suddenly realized that the tiresome manoeuvring through dark waters was finally over.

At the same time, however, I felt a sense of blessing for having known this incredible figure, this almost mythic presence, this man, who had shaped me, molded me, loved me, driven me crazy, disapproved of me even as he sought my approval of him, this man who had banished me yet embraced me. I now had to face the hard fact that my father would no longer be there *for* me. Perverse though he'd often been, he had always been *for* me. Yes, a force *for* me.

My father's death, of course, changed my life. Drained and devastated as I was, I simultaneously felt university life paled – I could barely spend an hour, let alone a day, writing my thesis. In fact, I wasn't interested in writing anything, be it an article for *The Varsity* or a piece for the CBC. I felt like a prize fighter who, though still punching, has no idea how many rounds he's already gone, how many rounds he has left, or even what the prize is.

Determined to retire from the ring – retire from any and all responsibility, especially the responsibility to atone for myself – I headed out of my house and eventually out of my marriage, choosing instead to settle into that place of cultural discombobulation, that place of hippies and dropouts and bums: Yorkville.

LOSERS IN THE NIGHT

Yorkville: a squalid crossroads of coffeehouses, blues bars, and chess cafés. While junkies and booze hounds slept on and between the lawn chairs that decorated the grounds of the neighbourhood old folks' home, dope pushers, gigolos, undercover cops, moochers, scam artists, folky guitar strummers, kneecappers, rootless immigrant women of real flash, and part-time prostitutes strolled the streets.

As I eased into life on the street, I inadvertently found myself a protégé: one Zalman Yanovsky, son of a strict disciplinarian and bloody-minded communist. Zalman, aged sixteen, had fled to Yorkville. He had no place to stay so I brought him home. He came, he went; he came, he went. Patsy liked him, but sometimes, if someone else was staying the night in our narrow cot of a guest bed, he'd sleep in the dryer at the neighbourhood laundromat. He'd get into the dryer for an hour's snooze, paying a quarter each time.

Zalman told me that he would like to play the guitar but he didn't own one. So, I shook down a wealthy Canadian Press reporter, a Jewish American who ultimately became part of my growing entourage. That entourage included Zal, Earl Pomerantz – who later became an ace Hollywood writer for shows like *Mary Tyler Moore, Taxi,* and *Cheers* – and his brother Hart Pomerantz – who famously partnered with producer Lorne Michaels in the 1970s to create the smash-hit comedic *Saturday Night Live* variety show – and Jackie Burroughs, the actress who married Zal as soon as he was of legal age, and went on to become a famed Canadian actress.

Zal, of course, became the lead guitarist for those great bands, The Lovin' Spoonful, The Halifax Three, and the Mugwumps (along with Denny Doherty and Cass Elliot, who would go on to form The Mamas and the Papas). In fact, Zal became such a renowned musician that in 1970, he was invited to participate in Cynthia Albriton's infamous Plaster Caster project – an arts endeavour that saw her casting the penises of famous rock stars in plaster.

Together, Zal, Earl, Jackie and I would stay up till dawn drinking with Tom Druge, Pat the Pimp, and Alfred: Boy Nazi.

Zal became the kid brother I never had, the kid brother I truly loved, not just because of his high, throaty laughter, but because he was the author of my favourite Yorkville ditty: (a riff on the 1918 show tune, "I'm Forever Blowing Bubbles"):

I'm forever blowing bubbles,
Bubbles is
Forever blowing me.

Alfred: Boy Nazi was a poet, pool shark, and – so he said – violinist. He assured me that it was the Jews, the controllers of the Toronto Symphony Orchestra, who were preventing him from playing his violin. He would shuffle around Yorkville for nine deranged hours a day, hectoring, explaining, declaiming and whining – Jews, Jews, Jews – until 2 a.m. sharp, when his wisp of a mother would arrive, clasp him to her bosom, whisper in his ear, and take him home, her Alfred, the Neo-Nazi mama's boy.

Alfred's unlikely sidekick (we were all, of course, unlikely), Tom Drudge, spent his days slumped in an old

Canadian army uniform. It had never been cleaned, nor had Tom – it seemed – ever seen soap. His father, a Sergeant Norman Drudge of the Canadian Army, had beaten Tom silly every evening for over twenty years. Now, Tom, who not only stank but often foamed at the mouth, passed his time plunked on a curb or a stoop, reading Holocaust books – the work of Bruno Bettleheim, *The Diary of Anne Frank*, Elie Wiesel's *Night* – saying these stories made him laugh.

Of course, nothing made Tom laugh more than Pat the Pimp, who – at twenty-four years of age – wasn't much of a pimp. He lived off the occasional B&E and the uncertain avails of a scrawny, plain-looking part-time prostitute. Pat was a natural dancer. He'd pull out his false teeth, plunk a corn-cob pipe in his mouth, and – while croaking out the tune to "I'm Popeye the Sailor Man" – pirouette and leap from one Yorkville stoop to another, all with madcap grace. Unfortunately, having been raised a ward of the state, in a string of foster homes, he had a hair-trigger temper, and if anyone he spun past made a snide comment, he would wheel out of his dance and come back swinging, brutal with rage.

Pat the Pimp loved my *shtick*, my gab, my egalitarianism, and my socialism, but mostly he loved my open and aggressive defence of the downtrodden. He would follow my swelling entourage, everywhere, to the neighbourhood coffeehouses and the pubs on Yonge Street near Yorkville – the Pilot Tavern and the Bohemian Embassy – where I, as jester to the juiced and the junkies, often held court.

Novelist and journalist Barry Callaghan, who was also drifting around Yorkville in his own distanced, contemplative kind of way, recalled in his 1998 memoir, *Barrelhouse Kings*, seeing me, the *schnozz*, at play at my work.

I often ran into Larry Zolf in the cafés. He was an extraordinary young man.

In many ways, Zolf was the best of what I saw my city becoming: a place of acerbic loners entrenched in the lore of the country and the local politics, men who were self-absorbed but only so that they could be more public spirited, men who were profoundly parochial but only so they could be entirely at ease in the world.

As my grandmother Minn would have said, "Zolf was forthright to a fault. He wore his heart on his sleeve."

He believed he could be forthright and get away with it.

"My father," Zolf had said, "saw the American Dream this way – to be Jewish and human was to be American. As I see the American Dream operating in Black America and Yellow Vietnam, I am forced to conclude that somehow, to be really human, is to be neither Jewish nor American. Today the Jewish community in America is indeed a participant and more than an equal in the power elite of White America. The Jews are close to the top in education, affluence, status. But to Black America, the Jew is as much Whitey as anyone else. The American Jew lives in a white neighbourhood, worships in a white, cavernous temple, eats white kosher Chinese food at white Chinese restaurants, has white directors for his white *bar mitzvah* movies. He likes it that way and is sure everyone will understand.

"I must admit that my stomach feels queasy when I hear Nicholas Katzenbach gloating over the Viet

Cong kill toll, when I hear Jews gloating over Six-Day War Arab losses. It saddens me to see how the American Dream and the melting pot has coarsened and vulgarized my racial *confrères*. I prefer the *schlemiel* wisdom of Gimpel the Fool to the Sammy Glick-*shtick* of Norman Podhoretz."

There were Jews in Toronto who said Zolf was an anti-Semite. They were the same Jews who said Mordecai Richler and Philip Roth were anti-Semites.

One evening, I sat in the Penny Farthing as eight or nine young, beautiful Germans arrived for their usual aperitifs, the men all looking like my friend Dieter, from the tax assessment office. Then Zolf came through the narrow door to poolside. He waved hello. Behind him, his entourage. Wherever and whenever Zolf performed, he had his travelling entourage: one gimp who was a lawyer, one club foot (the painter, Gershon Iskowitz, who had survived Auschwitz), one dwarf (a comedienne), and two very fat women who never wore bras, letting their great breasts loll. The troupe trucked in and sat around a table at the end of the pool opposite the young Germans.

After coffees and chocolachinos, Zolf suddenly rose, and in a high nasal drawl, he intoned, at the top of his voice, "Auschwitz, Auschwitz, I know nothing of Auschwitz. I vork at Dachau."

It was as if the young Germans had been pole-axed.

No one moved.

Not a word was said.

Zolf sat down.

His entourage snickered quietly.

A moment passed, and the Germans, trying not to glance over their shoulders, stumbled back into conversation.

Zolf rose.

They saw him rise.

They waited.

He intoned, "Vee Nazis and Jews must stick together."

There were gasps. The dwarf began to laugh hysterically. Half the Germans leapt to their feet and fled.

I thought, he's going to clean the joint out…

There was a long silence. Hardly anyone spoke at either end of the pool. Iskowitz stood up. He had a sad face, a mournful smile. Dragging his foot, he got to the edge of the pool. He looked like he was going to jump in, but he stood staring at the iridescent turquoise water. What was he thinking, staring into the stillness of water this man who had been a child in the camps? I realized I had never seen anyone swim in that water. I had never seen a ripple on that water. It was just there. The Germans were there. Zolf was there. He rose. He intoned, "Be ze first one on your block to turn in Anne Frank…"

The Germans fled. Zolf's entourage laughed and giggled. In a little while, they left, too, but not before the owner chastised Zolf: "After all, they were too young to do what their fathers did."

I felt sad for the young Germans. I felt triumphant glee for Zolf and his entourage…

One evening, I saw a man who looked like Jean-Paul Belmondo sit down at a table on the patio of the Penny Farthing. With him were two Jewish ladies of a certain age and deportment, somewhere between forty-seven and fifty-five. The man, lean of leg, was suited up entirely in black leather except for a ruffled white shirt. He ordered for the ladies: Tom Collins cream-capped chocalachino espressos. He told them slightly risqué jokes, waited for the ladies to stop shuddering with coy laughter, and then told them sexier jokes from behind the back of his own coy hand.

He was Yorkville's dancing gigolo, a Frenchman at ease with the bolero, the tango, and all the waltzes his footloose Jewish divorcees and housewives wanted to dance. His name was Henri Borecki. His best friend was Werner Graeber, a Berliner who had fled that divided city to live openly in his own Yorkville coffeehouse with a woman named Toba, the wife of a Jewish dentist. Werner and Henri could be very sweet, both of them, but Henri's constant, bitter denunciation of the Jews always left me feeling a little queasy (and what – I wondered – did his ladies think, flat on their backs, as he whispered his Jew-baiting love messages in their ears?).

The amazing thing about Henri, aside from his *klatch* of Jewish ladies, was that he knew a great deal about Jews: their international affairs and history, the names of all the rich Toronto Jewish families, and which rich Jewish wives were about to cheat on their husbands. Words were whispered in his ear and he would sit back and wait for such wives to come to him, some for simple social event escort services, some for moments of unbridled laughter, and others for raw sex.

One day, he took me to meet a Dutch couple who, he said, had lived through World War II as members of Amsterdam's underground resistance. Both husband and wife looked Aryan like Henri, but they were, in fact, Dutch Jews. Not only underground resistance fighters, they had also been members of the Irgun, the right-wing Jewish underground army in Palestine. They said they had run guns around the British blockade of Palestine in the forties, and that they were responsible for several terrorist killings – attacks on travellers, diplomats, and peasant villagers. They were tough. Hardened. Like the Irgun, they favoured some sort of fascist state for Israel.

The biggest surprise, however, was that Henri Belmondo, the anti-Semitic dancing gigolo, was also Jewish, and had been a member of the Irgun.

During the Second World War, the Gestapo had tortured Henri's father, breaking all the bones in his body. Henri, meanwhile, had been hidden by Belgian priests in a school. The other children hated him; they called him a Judas goat, a goat who would attract the Nazis, and they beat him up almost every day. But they never betrayed him; they never turned him in.

That afternoon in the Dutch couple's house, Henri still said terrible, critical things about the Jews, but he was also full of Jewish pride, calling the Jews the master race and naming himself a proud member.

Somehow, confessing his Jewishness to me eased some deeply debilitating darkness in Henri and his confession drew me closer to him – I could feel only compassion for his confusion, his fear of the abyss he carried in his own heart. Not long after our intense talks, he decided that he would put his dancing shoes away and enrol as a mature student at

York University. He asked for my help; I knew the Dean of Arts at York University.

As he waited for acceptance, Henri read books, went to poetry and fiction readings, and talked to the graduate students on campus. It was a new Henri, optimism and hope on his lips. He started reading books aloud to me. He said he was going to read all of Moses Maimonodes.

The answer to his application came back: he did not fit York University's mature student requirements. Henry got up and left the patio of the Penny Farthing. He said he wanted to be by himself.

I never did see Henri again.

Overwhelmed, I suppose, by rejection, deeply ambivalent about his Jewishness, and sick of living on the margins, Henri climbed the Bloor Street Viaduct.

"Toronto's first LSD suicide," the *Toronto Telegram* proclaimed.

Among his Yorkville friends, there was heavy sadness. Henri took a part of me with him on his fateful leap into oblivion. To this day, every time I hear tango music, I expect to see Henri, ladies in tow, step out onto the dance floor, while envious bully-boys surround and slang him. Henri Borecki, lean of leg, so very much the torn-apart Jew of his time, totally confused in his loyalties, yet for some reason loyal to me. A loyalty I'm not sure I deserved.

◎◎

As I did more stand-up comedy in the Yorkville coffeehouses, I developed, to my surprise, a following among budding actors and writers who shared a dark, sharp sense of humour – a humour that reflected our attitude not only towards the present moment but the Holocaust. For example, a friend, Ray Jessel, who is now a cabaret performer, came up with this incredible line for *Spring Thaw* – Toronto's celebrated annual satirical revue (directed and produced by Mavor Moore, son of Dora) – which was delivered by an actor playing a Nazi war criminal who has just been confronted with *The Diary of Anne Frank*: "Are yu going to believe me – an Obergruppenfüehrer of the S.S. – or do yu take ze vord of some fourteen-year-old Jewish girl vannabee writer instead?"

This was tough stuff. So, too, was the following routine of mine: I acted as if I were a Fox Movietone newsreel come-alive in which Americans were forcing Germans who lived near Buchenwald concentration camp to view the pile of dead Jewish bodies. Upon seeing the skeletal remains, one German says to another: "See, Hanz, I tohld yu. Ze Jews really do shtick togezzer!"

Wearing a pullover sweater, a tam, and dark glasses, I would sit on a stool at the Purple Onion or the Bohemian Embassy, and perform routines that reflected my pet loves (interfaith and interracial marriage) and pet hates (the Nazis, the Holocaust, and those fanatic anti-communists, the McCarthyites and the RCMP, who were always hunting for Reds under beds).

My Yorkville audience was often divided between curious suburban day-trippers, rich Jewish tourists from Forest Hill, and WASP tourists from Rosedale, all of whom came to Yorkville to gawk or laugh at the freaks and losers, the drop-outs, druggies, dope fiends, twitchers, and spastics of the streets.

The Forest Hill klatch sat in stony silence through my poem, "Christmas in Auschwitz":

It vas ze night before Christmas
And all through ze camp,
Ze inmates were shivering,
Ze wezer was damp.
One thousand would die
The following day
In ze usual jazzy
Gazzy
Nazee
Way.
It was Eichmann's
Christmas gift
To Himmler, his boss.
When it comes to playing
Saint Nikoloss,
You just can't beat
Our Auschwitz commandant,
Jolly old
Rudolf Hoss.

During several Purple Onion performances, my rendering of this poem led to the throwing of chairs by angry Jews who somehow felt I must be a Nazi lover. To placate these irate people, I would stage my *Hitler's Wedding* sketch:

Announcer: Achtung! Achtung! Achtung! Deutsche Reichs-Rvndfunk-Gesellschaft, German Empire Broastcasting Corporation. Erewacht, wake up, fellow Nazis. It is April 20, 1945, 2 a.m. Ve take you now to der Führer's bunker where der Führer's marriage to his beloved consort, Eva Braun, is about to take place. Reich Minister of Propaganda, Dr. Josef Goebbels will perform the ceremony. Reich Party Minister, Martin Bormann, is the best man – and the ring bearer.

Goebbels: Do you, my beloved Führer, take this woman, Eva Braun, to be your lawfully wedded Führeress – to love, honour and cherish – until death do yu part?

At this juncture, Hitler's German Shepherd, Blondi, barks out a cacophony of approval.

Hitler: Jawohl, Reich Minister Goebbels, I do.

Goebbels: Do you, Eva Braun, take our beloved Führer to be your lawfully wedded Führer and husband – to love, honour and cherish – until death do yu part?

Eva Braun: Jawohl. I do.

Goebbels: Obergruppenführer and Reich Party Minister, Martin Bormann, the rings please!

Goebbels turns to Hitler.

Now, my Führer, slip the ring on the pinky finger of your beloved Eva Braun.
(Goebbels turns to Eva Braun)
Eva, slip your ring on the Führer's pinky finger. Good! I now pronounce you husband and wife, Führer and Führeress! My Führer, you can now kiss the bride.

Hitler proceeds to kiss the bride. Blondi barks out another cacophony of approval.

> Obergruppenführer Martin Bormann, the poisoned chalices please!

Goebbels turns to Hitler, Eva Braun and Blondi.

> Drink up! Mein Führer and Führeress, and you, too, Blondi, are now kaput.

> My fellow Nazis, dis is vone hellufa vay to begin a marriage!

To stress my liberal roots and my love of life at its most American, I did a radio sketch in the voices of two of my "characters" that ended like this:

Bill Budd: Tell me, Helmut, do you have any favourite Hollywood stars?

Helmut
 Kalbfleisch: Oh, tons of them, Mr. Budd.

Bill Budd: Will you tell our listeners who they are?

Helmut
 Kalbfleisch: Glad to, Mr. Budd. My favourite Hollywood stars are…

Narrator: Kalbfleisch, quite bizarrely, extends his right arm in a stiff salute.

Maximilian Schell
Maria Schell
Marlene Dietrich
Horst Buchholtz
Eric Von Stroheim
Curt Jurgens
Oskar Werner
Hardy Kruger
Werner Klemperer
Conrad Veidt
Helmut Dantine
Otto Preminger
Wolfgang Preiss
Wolfgang Buttner
Peter Van Eyck
Gert Fräbe
Peter Lorre
Armin Mueller-Stahl
Karl Maria Brandauer

Only Nathan Cohen, the acerbic drama critic for the *Toronto Star*, seemed to get the inner joke – the names I had rattled off were liberal German anti-Nazis and/or German-Jewish refugee actors who had fled to the open arms of Hollywood.

The fair Beguine continued rubbing with her whole hand under my knee—till I feared her zeal would weary her—"I would do a thousand times more," said she, "for the love of Christ"—In saying which, she passed her hand across the flannel, to the part above my knee, which I had equally complained of, and rubbed it also.

I perceived, then, I was beginning to be in love—

As she continued rub-rub-rubbing—I felt it spread from under her hand, an' please your honour, to every part of my frame—

The more she rubbed, and the longer strokes she took—the more the fire kindled in my veins—till at length, by two or three strokes longer than the rest— my passion rose to the highest pitch—I seized her hand—

And then clapped'st it to my lips,—and madest a speech.

— *STERNE*

275

NATALIA'S ROOM

Having stopped being an academic, I'd become a *luftmensch* – a man of air, a hippie, a bum, cadging a bed and a meal where I could. Every night, during the stand-up comedy routines that I performed between blues singers at the Purple Onion and poets at the Bohemian Embassy, I would get drunk, very drunk, and then have supper in the wee hours of the morning at No Foo Ling's, a Chinese restaurant in Gerrard Village.

One night, the proprietor of the Bohemian Embassy, Don Cullen, had in tow a short young woman with nice legs and a marvellous posterior. "I'm Natalia," she said.

Later, during the meal at No Foo Ling's, I did ten minutes of badinage displaying my awesome wit and cutting tongue.

Natalia responded by saying that I was a bohemian deadbeat, an immature adolescent, and offered me the tagline "Senility Comes to Andy Hardy." That got a big laugh. Then Natalia said she was a Ukrainian girl from Edmonton.

"Ukrainians are all too familiar to me," I said. "I grew up among thousands of them in the North End of Winnipeg. Our oppressive landlord, Mr. Wasko, was Ukrainian, and his beautiful daughter married a handsome Jewish medical student, a former pupil of my father's. Our cleaning lady was a Ukrainian who loved to argue politics with my mother. This was easy enough to do because my mother never said anything back, not even when the cleaning lady shouted at the top of her lungs: 'Vate til Hitler cohm heir; he's going to make you Jews pay!' We didn't care about her anti-Semitism because our favourite neighbourhood ditties were about Ukrainians. For example:

> Loohk lak mhonkee,
> Voik lak dohnkey,
> Must be honkey.

"We didn't care," I said, actually making no sense at all, "because the Ukrainians were mostly singers and dancers. In fact, the men carried their mandolins and balalaikas on their backs even when they went out to plow the fields. If a plow broke, they would dig up the soil with their musical instruments." I went on, explaining that my mother had always been terrified of Ukrainians. "Before she would leave the house, I had to survey the outdoors. I would stand on the veranda and look left, look right, look straight down the centre of the street. Then, I would shout to my mother who was all dressed up in her best Sabbath suit: 'Ma, you're safe! There is no one hiding up in the trees! The Ukrainians are all in some church basement having an accordion concert!'"

This interminable monologue broke up Natalia. We began to talk. She was a student at the Ontario College of Art. She said she lived in a single basement room facing Jarvis Street. As it turned out, this was the basement to a three-storey edifice chock-full of female hookers and gay male weightlifters. I took to coming around to her room, playing the role of gentleman caller. Every time I showed up, the hookers in the lobby applauded and cheered. Natalia and I were the only straight couple to be seen in the place.

One night, Natalia made love to me. From that point on, her room became my love nest. The lovemaking was easy and pleasurable; time stood still. I, however, was on the edge of stagnant. Doing nothing myself, no writing at all, I became jealous of Natalia, jealous of the totally committed and concentrated way that she painted. Once, while she was in the bathroom, I carved up one of her canvases. When she returned and discovered what I'd done, she laughed and effortlessly painted a new canvas.

Out and about in the bars around Yorkville, we became a team; if patrons liked our comic patter we shook them down for free drinks. I got to meet artists Robert Hedrick, Gordon Rayner, Graham Coughtry and Joyce Wieland. It was exciting, and my relationship with Natalia deepened. In Natalia's room, our laughter was loud, boisterous. We were in love and did not notice how loud we were in our loving.

One night, we came home to find a cluster of angry gay men waiting for us. Their leader, a muscular young man, shoved me, slapped me, punched me. He looked like he wanted to spit on me. I promised to suppress my laughter – and did over the days to come.

My bohemian life, however, was beginning to get me down. I hadn't worked or read a book in months; I hadn't written a single word for a long, long time. The future seemed to be receding into the past. My worries, anxiety, and sense of belittlement began robbing me of my sleep and destroying my appetite. I was miserable: the nose knew he was going nowhere. I felt trapped. Additionally, we were desperately short of money. Natalia had a small allowance, but I had nothing. Things were so tough that we began trying to charge double for the funny jokes and stories we told at the bars. Nobody wanted to pay double. Natalia toyed with the idea of becoming an exotic dancer, a little bump and grind at Starvin' Marvin's Burlesque Palace. I was becoming more depressed by the day. I still loved Natalia but could not stand my life, could not stand me. I dreamed of holes, a hollow. I started hearing silence. It echoed, a cruel ominous music. My father? He fixed me with a fierce rabbinical look.

I told this to my beloved.

She fixed me with a fierce Cossack look. And then saw through me completely when I said that I would be gone for a few days.

She said nothing.

Contrite, I returned to my home and my marriage, flush with awkwardness and confusion. I asked consideration and so granted, I settled with my wife. I felt a sudden lightness of relief, a freedom in my heart – I could breathe again. The cruel echo of silence ceased. I could hear my thoughts with clarity, a certain calmness.

I decided to visit Natalia to square things, close with her, and perhaps pay final respect to what had once been, what had been lost between us: a gaiety of love.

There was no Natalia.

There was a tall, handsome black man, her new man, preparing supper.

A thousand of my father's most subtle syllogisms could not have said more for celibacy.

— STERNE

—Inconsistent soul that man is!—languishing under wounds, which he has the power to heal!—his whole life a contradiction to his knowledge!—his reason serving but to sharpen his sensibilities—to multiply his pains, and render him more melancholy and uneasy under them!—Poor unhappy creature, that he should do so!—Are not the necessary causes of misery in this life enow, but he must add voluntary ones to his stock of sorrow;—struggle against evils which cannot be avoided, and submit to others, which a tenth part of the trouble they create him would remove from his heart for ever?

— STERNE

A POLISH JOKE:
THE VARSITY JEWS

My sojourn in Yorkville as a stand-up comedian had led, in some Jewish quarters, to the charge that I was a *vendu,* a Jewish traitor, a Jewish self-hater, a man who played false to his own nose.

When I was still a graduate student at the University of Toronto and a regular contributor to the student newspaper, *The Varsity,* Mark Nichols, who became a distinguished *Maclean's* journalist, decided to put out a monthly student literary magazine, titled *Otherside.*

Mark was a shy, slouchy, heavy-drinking man who did not have a mean bone in his body – rather, he had a keen sense of the appropriateness of things. He asked me to contribute an essay to *Otherside.*

At the time, I was fascinated by the writings of Jewish liberal novelists and the short stories of Philip Roth, Joseph Heller and Bernard Malamud. Malamud, in particular, was my hero. His links to the work of Yiddish writers – Isaac Bashevis Singer, Israel Joshua Singer, Abraham Reisen, Isaac Loeb Peretz, Sholom Aleichem – endeared Malamud to me.

I was also intrigued by commercially successful writers like Herman Wouk, who espoused a contemporary current of Jewish revisionism that rejected the old Yiddish moral and ethical traditions. I was struck by the fact that the antagonists in Wouk's stories – the novel-writing and cowardly

Lieutenant Tom Keefer in *The Caine Mutiny* and the show-bizzy and cowardly Noel Ehrman (man of air) in *Marjorie Morningstar*, for example, were often lowercase "l" liberals. Wouk was saying that liberal writers like Roth and Heller who satirized suburban Jewish life were, at heart, Jewish self-haters, Jewish anti-Semites. Suburban Jews, Wouk argued, were the real Jews, the upright Jews, Jews with weapons in their hands.

For *Otherside*, I penned an essay: "Woukism: A Study in Suburban Jewish Babbittry." My essay was replete with pointed metaphors: "The suburban Jews," I wrote, "their noses bobbed, their minds circumcised." I referred to suburban Judaism as "Disneyish, more dwarfish than Snow White," and the suburban Jewish response to intermarriage as "a reverse racism of the worst kind."

While my byline in *The Varsity* had appeared quite frequently, I was not very well known to the Jewish students on campus, nor to their representative student organization, Hillel. I was at least four or five years older than these undergraduates, and I tended to fraternize with my fellow graduate students, nearly all of whom were gentile.

Angry letters appeared in *The Varsity* comparing one L. Zolf to incorrigible anti-Semites like Evelyn Waugh, who just happened to be one of my favourite writers.

I was flattered.

Then Nichols came to see me. He looked sad and dejected. My essay, he said, had not been well received by Student Council, which had authority over *The Varsity* and Nichols' literary magazine. "But that's not all," said Nichols. "Because of your essay, Hillel has laid a charge of anti-Semitism against *Otherside*. The hearing is tonight at seven o'clock. I want you to be my star witness."

Half of the student council membership was Jewish and belonged to Hillel. I had re-read my piece and still loved every rat-a-tat-tat metaphor in it. I was glad to be Nichols' number-one defence witness.

My life as a Polish joke was about to begin.

When I walked into the hearing, the sight of me – a thin, cadaverous Jew with a huge Jewish proboscis who ambled along like a ghetto rag picker – thoroughly stunned my would-be inquisitors.

They were stunned for only a second or two. When Nichols said, "Ladies and gentlemen, this is Larry Zolf, the main witness for my defence," everyone burst out laughing. It seems that Hillel had assumed, correctly, that Zolf was a Polish name, but incorrectly assumed that I was a Pole.

Publicly, the Hillel Jews were not going to take on another Jew.

Before I had a chance to say a word in my own defence, Student Council dismissed the Hillel charges and let Mark Nichols and I go free.

But my trial by Jewry – the charge of self-hating Jew uttered behind the hand, behind the closed door, had begun. It was to last my lifetime.

PENIS ENVY AND LOATHING AT THE U.S. SENATE URINAL

Though we were bereft of funds, Patsy and I decided we should indulge in a cheap honeymoon, the honeymoon we had never had. I called Jerry Zalph, my communist cousin in New York.

Jerry and his wife welcomed us, accommodating Patsy and I in the spare room in their Queen's apartment. I thanked Jerry so profusely that his wife spoke to me in my mother's tongue: "*Genug iz genug.*" Immediately, I felt at home. I told Jerry that we would stay in New York for the week, and then spend one day in Washington.

Cousin Jerry was great fun. Like me, he enjoyed arguing and meant nothing personal by it. One day, Jerry and I argued that age-old question: What makes a Jew?

"Judaism is a religion," said Jerry. "I'm not religious; I'm not Jewish. I'm a communist and an American and I'm proud of both."

"Tell that to Stalin," I said. "He's managed to find non-practising yet ethnically Jewish poets and writers to murder over the years!"

"Zionist propaganda," Jerry countered.

"If being Jewish is a religion," I said, "how come nobody looks Protestant or Catholic? Given my *schnozz*, I look ethnically Jewish and every anti-Semite knows I'm a Jew. Jews don't define who is Jewish. Anti-Semites and Nazis do. Want to know who the Jews are? Just ask your local Nazi. He'll know for sure!"

That evening, the Communist Party was having an affair for several of their leaders who were going to jail for sedition. Herman Lermer, the party's organizing genius, and Herbert Aptheker, the party's leading intellectual, would be making speeches. Both were risking prison stripes.

Jerry, his brother, Izzy, and Pat and I decided to attend the event.

As we approached St. Nicholas Arena, the scene of so many legendary prize fights that I had listened to on the radio, we were confronted by a raucous crowd of American Nazis wearing swastika insignias. The Nazis were chanting: "Ikey, Kikey, go to bed! Ikey, Kikey, wake up Red!"

Two squad cars of New York's finest Jewish and Italian cops were parked at the curb, keeping an eye on the Nazis' and the Reds' gathering cluster of attendees.

Jewish cops.

Italian cops.

A stand-off.

One afternoon late in the week, Jerry's son visited the apartment and brought with him his best friend, author, historian and Moscow sympathizer Paul Robeson Jr. Jerry's son was wearing a well-pressed U.S. Army uniform. Jerry was very proud of his son. "Communists are good American citizens and patriots," Jerry said. At a time when Jewish American Liberals were dodging the Vietnam war draft, Jerry's patriot son was proving that the Reds were no cowards.

I found it hard to argue with Jerry's sense of pride – he was a right-wing socialist who had respect for the military, for the bravery of soldiers. Jerry's son told us that he had been harassed in his army camp because of his father's constant appearances in the papers following the McCarthy attack. Private First Class Zalph, however, had fought back. He had broken some noses, he said.

On the day we were to depart by bus from New York, Patsy told me she had no money. I checked my pockets and found them empty, too. "We'll be okay, Pat," I said. We'll skip Washington. We'll cash in the difference on the tickets and have enough money for a good ride home."

At the bus depot, however, the bad news was final. The bus tickets could only be refunded in Toronto. Discouraged and frightened, we boarded the 10 p.m. bus to Washington. All the seats were taken so we had to stand, clutching the overhead straps, for six hours. Patsy developed a severe cramp in her leg. Sleepless, we arrived in the nation's capital on a Monday morning. Patsy just wanted to lie down and wait for the 11 p.m. bus to Toronto. My fatigue and anxiety, however, had disappeared and curiosity had taken over. I was in America's Rome. I was brimming with life. And I had a plan for survival.

Back in the spring, Senator John F. Kennedy had addressed the students of the University of Toronto. His oration had been terrific and I had almost forgiven him for his father's blatant and notorious anti-Semitism.

Surely the good senator would slip some money to a pair of starving, guileless Toronto disciples.

All we had to do was get to Kennedy. Bizarrely, Patsy agreed. No matter her cramped leg, she followed me to the Public Gallery of the Senate. The gallery was almost empty and we sat down in blessed relief. At two o'clock sharp, the bells rang, and in the chamber below us the U.S. Senate came to order. Richard M. Nixon, a shoe-in for the Republican nomination that year, was the presiding officer.

Kennedy made a fine speech, solidifying my hopes for the Great Kennedy Panhandle. One of the Senate cops told me that Kennedy would be leaving the Senate in about an hour; the Senator would then walk to his office which was about a block away.

I went to the Senate washroom to freshen up. As I was relieving myself at the urinal, the door opened wide. Four secret servicemen scoured the place, in search of drug pushers, army deserters and subversives. By the skin of my teeth, I was none of these – so it was safe for Vice President Nixon to enter the washroom. He was very tall, clean-shaven and, surprisingly, looked almost friendly. In my demonology in those days, Nixon was always holding hands with the likes of Stalin and Hitler. Now, here I was sharing a washroom with the Devil himself. Fear and loathing entered my frail body, tempered by a touch of pragmatism. Maybe I could tap old Richard for the odd shekel so that Patsy and I could have eggs for breakfast.

He went to the sink, and washed and dried his hands.

I did the same.

He then stuck out his hand and said, "I'm Richard Nixon and I'm going to be running for president. I'd very much like your vote."

I shook Nixon's hand. "Gee, sir," I said, "I'd really like to vote for you but I'm a Canadian; I can't vote here."

"That's all right, son. But you must have relatives in the United States? Why don't you get them to vote for me?"

"I'll try that, sir," I said, and tried to imagine Jerry and Izzy Zalph, their wives and children, voting for America's leading Red-baiter. I was so flustered, I forgot to ask Nixon for his loose change.

Patsy hobbled alongside me as we walked towards the Senate office building. Kennedy and his friend, Senator Mike

Mansfield of Montana, were walking just ahead of us. I caught up to them and to Kennedy, poured out my tale of woe.

"Senator Kennedy," I said, "we're starving students from the University of Toronto and we haven't eaten in a day. We're big fans of yours, Senator, and we have lots of relatives in the United States, we're going to make sure that they vote for you. I know that some people will never forgive your father's anti-Semitism. But Senator, I know that you're one of Israel's best friends. You're so right for the presidency. We only need a little money, Senator – it's just so that we can have breakfast. We're really hungry!"

"Never before has a Senator been so eloquently panhandled," said Kennedy.

He then pulled out his pants pockets and found them empty. He searched the inner and outer pockets of his seersucker suit and still came up with nothing. Senator Mansfield, however, produced $1.75, which Pat and I gratefully accepted.

The only food to be found nearby was a vending machine in the Senate office building. We bought what chocolate bars and soda pop and chips (salted) and more pop we could afford and wolfed the sickening sweetness down.

Then we sat on the knoll across from the Senate building until it was time to catch our bus.

At 11 p.m., we boarded our Toronto-bound bus. Thankfully, it was almost empty. Hours later, we finally crossed the Peace Bridge into Canada. We were exhausted and starved, but we both knew we would endure.

"Patsy," I said, "the 1960s have begun. And damn it, we're ready."

Sir—for in good truth, when a man is telling a story in the strange way I do mine, he is obliged continuously to be going backwards and forwards to keep all tight together in the reader's fancy—which, for my own part, there is so much unfixed and equivocal matter starting up, with so many breaks and gaps in it,—that now you see, I am a little lost myself!—

— *STERNE*

A PARTING OF THE RED SEA

The phone rang. It was Jim Guthro, the executive producer of the CBC television series, *Horizon*, which was hosted by the legendary J. Frank Willis. He asked me to come to his office.

Guthro and program organizer, John Kennedy, were in the midst of planning "Whither the Party," the one-hour CBC look at the Communist Party of Canada (for which I attempted to interview Sam Carr). Guthro wanted me to do all the research, all the interviews, and perform a three-minute stand-up monologue that took a satirical run at the Communist Party.

They wanted to know if $2,000 would be satisfactory.

Beside myself with joy, I parted a sea of Reds. As broadcast, I interviewed Maurice Spector, the Trotskyite, chairman of the Communist Party; William Kashtan, local Communist Party leader; and J.B. Salsberg, communist MPP. Throughout the program, J. Frank Willis respectfully referred to me as Mr. Zolf, warning the audience that Mr. Zolf would be back after the break, where they would find me on stage at an upstairs after-hours club, the local refuge for poets, the Bohemian Embassy. I did come back and I did three minutes of one-liners, closing my act with a solemn reading from Itzik Feffer's poetic tribute (I think it was titled simply "A Jew") to Stalin:

I am a Jew
And I have drunk
From Stalin's
Magic cup
Of joy and gladness.

I walk
With the peoples of the East.

The Russians are my brothers.
I am a Jew.
My pride lies in Jacob Sverdlov's name
And Koginovitch
Stalin's friends.

And to hell
With all our enemies
That are preparing
Graves for us.

I will plant
My own vineyard
And be the master
Of my own destiny.

For the day
Shall come
When I shall dance
A mad kazatska
On Hitler's grave.

I am a Jew.

I told the audience that Itzik Feffer had been executed by Stalin, but that the lingering worrisome question was: "Did Stalin liquidate Itzik because Itzik was a Jew – or did Stalin liquidate Itzik because he was a bad poet?"

That line, so out of tune with the pablum tenor of popular television commentary, got a roar of dark laughter.

My friend, talent agent Ed Cowan (who represented, among others, Canadian singer-songwriter Ian Tyson), brought Albert Grossman, Bob Dylan's manager, to my house to celebrate the show. Grossman, through much heavy breathing, spoke of a possible Mort Sahl future for me, and suggested a *bris* for the wart on my nose. In the *Toronto Star*, the august Nathan Cohen, national arts critic, announced that I was the Lenny Bruce of the North (he had never seen Bruce perform). And CBC's Beryl Fox and Doug Leiterman said, "Sign on the dotted line, Larry" – and I hired on as the first bona fide employee of their upcoming national public affairs program, *This Hour Has Seven Days*.

—Certainly it was ordained as a scourge upon the pride of human wisdom, That the wisest of us all should thus outwit himself, and eternally forego our purposes in the intemperate act of pursuing them.

In short, my father was so long in all his acts of resistance,—or in other words,—he advanced so very slow with his work, and I began to live and get forwards at such a rate, that if an event had not happened,—which, when we get to it, if it can be told with decency, shall not be concealed a moment from the reader—I verily believe, I had put by my father, and left him drawing a sun-dial, for no better purpose than to be buried under ground.

– STERNE

SCOOP

In the House of Commons, on Friday, March 4, 1966, the Honourable Lucien Cardin, Minister of Justice, was being abused, badgered and berated by Opposition Leader, John Diefenbaker, regarding Cardin's alleged mismanagement of an espionage case that had threatened national security. Fed up, Cardin stood and, fist shaking, declared: "[Diefenbaker] is the very last person who can afford to give advice on the handling of security cases in Canada!" He then demanded that "the Right Honourable gentleman" explain to the House "his participation in the Monseignor case when he was prime minister."

Of course, Cardin had meant Munsinger, as in the Gerda Munsinger Affair – the late-1950s sex-espionage scandal that Diefenbaker had, up until now, managed to keep out of the public eye. In fact, very few MPs in the House had heard of Munsinger. Older, grizzled members of the parliamentary press gallery knew, and so did Douglas Leiterman, boyish intrepid executive producer of *This Hour Has Seven Days*. He had been a Parliament Hill reporter for national newspaper service Southam Press in the late fifties, and he knew what "Monseignor" meant.

Leiterman told me that Gerda Munsinger, an alleged East German prostitute and Soviet secret agent, had lived in Canada from 1955-1961, at which time, she'd engaged in numerous affairs with various cabinet ministers in the Diefen-baker government – in particular, war hero and former Associate Defence Minister Pierre Sévigny. "Given Cardin's 'Monseignor' blurt this morning," said Leiterman, "we can jump on the Munsinger story right away. Sévigny lives at 33 Rosemount Avenue in Montreal's Westmount neighbourhood. He's a hard drinker and he has some unsavoury friends. Be careful!"

This was ambush time – ambush being the tactic of the political reporter who is a satirist at heart, one who, when confronted with the moral pretensions of those in power, knows that in the nature of things, there is nothing to be done about such powerful men, and so is morally outraged, not to the point of action, but to the point of laughter.

Montreal sources told me that Sévigny had already turned away reporters from the *Montreal Gazette*, *La Presse*, *Time* and *Maclean's*. Wondering about my legal position, I called Robert Shirriff, a close friend and senior partner at Fasken, Calvin, MacKenzie Williston & Swackhamer. Shirriff said, "Knock on Sévigny's door once, and you're like any other licensee. Knock on his door twice, and you could be considered a trespasser." That the camera would be rolling was legitimate, said Shirriff: "It's part of your trade, like a pencil and notebook for a print journalist."

I booked Jim Gratton, dean of Montreal's TV paparazzi, as cameraman. He had covered dozens of nationalist demonstrations and mob funerals in Montreal, and he was up for the Sévigny challenge. We'd use magnetic stripe film, Gratton told me. That way, no matter what happened, the sound would always be in sync.

My Montreal sources also told me that Sévigny was a very quarrelsome man. They, like Leiterman, stressed that he had many friends and associates in Montreal's lower depths.

My adrenalin was up, *schnozz* aquiver with the thrill of ambush.

Gratton parked our station wagon at the bottom of the Sévigny lawn. A long walkway led to the house. This open parking of the car out in the open was deliberate; it was in the best tradition of the ambush, making the ambush suddenly seem to be more of a singular gun fight at high noon than a sneak attack.

I was wearing a Burberry wool sport jacket and overcoat. I held the microphone in my right hand. I also carried a Frezzolini, a sixty pound device that, when activated, sheds a cold, harsh light on its subject, making any man look like a hardened criminal. I was to ask Sévigny in my finest *This Hour Has Seven Days* accusatory tone, if he knew and had slept with one Gerda Munsinger, knowing her to be a security risk at the time. If Sévigny denied the allegation, I was to confront him with the hard evidence that Leiterman had provided me. If Sévigny said that yes, he had slept with Gerda and was damn proud of it, I was to encourage a friendly interview with him by suggesting that, after all, even if Munsinger was a Soviet spy, she was a damn sexy one, and not even a former Associate Minister of Defence could be blamed for having his head turned and his libido roused by such beauty.

I knocked at the front door of the Sévigny mansion and activated the Fezzolini. It cast its very harsh light on Mrs. Sévigny, who answered the door. "Is Mr. Sévigny in?" I asked. "I'm Larry Zolf of *This Hour Has Seven Days*, and I would very much like to speak to your husband."

"He's not here," said Mrs. Sévigny.

I peered through the glass panes that framed the front door, and saw Sévigny seated in an easy chair in the living room, gulping down what I imagined to be a scotch and soda. I knew I was on thin ice. I told Gratton to join me in a withdrawal from the field. Inside the station wagon, he informed me that we hadn't been able to get an establishing shot, a shot identifying where we had been.

We returned a second time to the Sévigny mansion. It had begun to snow heavily. While I recorded background noise with the mic, Gratton proceeded to take a beautiful establishing shot. He panned across the cherubim statues that decorated the front lawn. Gratton's shot came at last to rest on the front door.

A man stood in the doorway, one hand holding a cane and the other in the air beckoning. Gratton yelled out: "Hey, Larry, he's at the front door. I think he wants to talk to you!"

My heart beat wildly. I was about to experience the wet dream of TV reporters everywhere: the dream ambush that made a scoop! I was about to outfox the world's press by getting Canada's top fucker to tell me, live to film, about his wham-bam with Canada's vampiest Soviet spy. I ran to the Sévigny front door, eager to engage my rendezvous with destiny.

Blinded by snow, I could barely make out what was happening as I rushed forward, microphone and Fezzolini in hand. Suddenly, I saw Sévigny raise his heavy cane and arc it for the middle of my head.

I ducked to save my life. The blow came hurtling down on my heavily padded shoulders and did me no damage. Sévigny continued to flail away with his cane.

I was furious; I blew my stack. "You fuckin' cocksucker!" I shouted at the top of my lungs. I kicked Sévigny hard on his left leg. To my utter surprise, my kick sent his leg – a wooden prosthetic – flying through the air; it landed on the far right of his front lawn. Cursed at and threatened by an enraged one-legged man, my crew and I beat a hasty retreat to the station wagon.

In the car, we took deep breaths and tried to calm down. Gratton handed me the can of film. Suddenly, we were startled by an explosive banging. There, beating his cane on the hood of our station wagon, was Westmount Citizen Cane, Pierre Sévigny.

I rolled down my window and yelled: "Look, asshole, you've got five seconds to get away from our car. Otherwise, my beloved Privy Councillor, we'll run right over you!"

We drove off. Certain that Sévigny would call the Westmount police, I went directly to Dorval Airport and took the first available flight home. In Toronto, I called Film Arts, the editing house for *This Hour Has Seven Days*, and told them I had some hot footage. When asked for a name for this footage, I said: "Call it 'Potato Famine: The Luck of the Irish.'"

That night, the same day of the Sévigny ambush, an assistant editor of Film Arts picked up a can labelled "Potato Famine: The Luck of the Irish," and screened the reel. The assistant could not believe what he was seeing – and hearing. The film had recorded, in sync, all my foul language, the insults I'd heaped upon Sévigny – war hero, Privy Councillor and ex-Associate Defence Minister.

As the assistant howled with laughter, other film editors gathered around. They, too, howled. Don Haig, who used to run Winnipeg's Yiddish movie hall, the State Theatre, was now the head of Film Arts. He decided that some of the language – in particular "fuck" and "cocksucker" – would really get me into hot water, so he replaced the swear words with the sounds of flamingos honking, monkeys chattering, and cows mooing.

Haig did something else. He edited the sequences so that the film opened with Gratton's establishing pass, cut to the front door and the interview with Mrs. Sévigny, cut back to the pass, and then ended on the caning. I appeared to have approached the Sévigny house only once, not twice.

When I visited Jacques Alleyne, chief legal counsel for the CBC, at his luxurious office in Ottawa, this detail was very important. "How many visits did you make to the Sévigny house?" Alleyne asked.

Abstract paintings by Paul-Émile Borduas and Jean-Paul Riopelle stared down at me, and my answer was just as abstract: "I'm not sure. One, maybe two, but no more than two."

"The film shows only one visit, Larry. Film never lies," said Alleyne. "You don't have any personal bias or malice towards Mr. Sévigny do you, Larry?"

"Considering Mr. Sévigny tried to kill me, no sir, I've no malice at all."

Alleyne liked my answers. He said nothing about the honking, chattering and mooing of flamingos, monkeys and cows.

A battle royal then ensued between *This Hour Has Seven Days* and CBC president, J. Alphonse Ouimet. Ultimately, Ouimet refused to allow the Sévigny episode on air. The press, however, got wind of it quickly enough, and I found myself on the front page of Vancouver newspaper *The Province*. To my immediate left was a photo of J. Alphonse Ouimet. To my immediate right was a photo of Pierre Sévigny. The headline read: "ZAM ZOWIE ZAP ZOLF ZEVIGNY!"

The cutline accompanying the pictures was: "I'm calling this my Citizen Cane period."

I revelled in my sudden notoriety as ambusher extraordinaire, with expectations about my future...

I did not know that the Sévigny caper would turn out to be the suicidal beginning of the end for *This Hour Has Seven Days*.

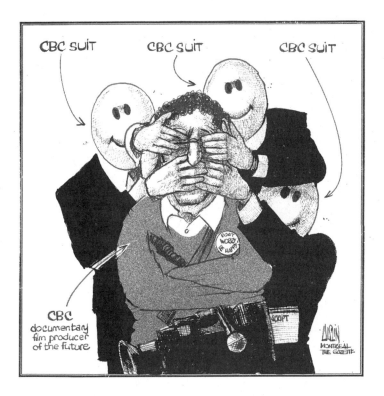

VIVA LA JOIA!
FIDON LA TRISTESSA!

A transient spark of amity shot across space—Why could I not live, and end my days thus? Just Disposer of our joys and sorrows, cried I, why could not a man sit down in the lap of content here—and dance, and sing, and say his prayers, and go on straight forwards, without digression or parenthesis—

I began thus—

— *STERNE*

A McCARTHYITE

Most people I knew were, for political and philosophical reasons, revolted by Senator Joe McCarthy. As was I. But I also had a personal animus. McCarthy had been a menace to the Zholf family's New York-based cousins, the Zalphs, having cast his gimlet eye on Jerry and Izzy, both active members of the Communist Party.

In 1934, Izzy Zalph had taken time out from composing dialogue for radio soap operas to write the American Communist Party's official history of the World War I veterans' Bonus March on Washington in 1932. At the ensuing Battle of Anacostica Flats, Major George Patton and Major Dwight D. Eisenhower (who in two decades, would become President of the United States), forcibly dispersed the Bonus Army – the nation's own war vets – with tear gas. Izzy's book was called *Veterans on the March* and it had a foreword by the great writer, John Dos Passos, then a radical. After publication, Izzy found that he was blacklisted, suddenly a former writer of radio soap operas, and so he became a rug merchant, selling valuable Persian weaves out of his Manhattan apartment.

Jerry Zalph was an entirely different case. Jerry was the chief proofreader for the *New York Times*. Jerry's wife, also a communist, was the chief proofreader at the *New York Herald Tribune*. McCarthy asked for their dismissal. Arthur Hays

Sulzberger of the *Times* and the Reid family of the *Herald Tribune* told McCarthy to get lost; the Zalphs were the best proofreaders in town.

McCarthy retaliated by tapping Jerry's phone and putting him under surveillance. Jerry was unfazed. He worked up a relationship with the man tapping his phone. During a brief visit I'd made while I was pursuing my undergraduate degree, I watched him pick up the phone and say: "Gary, I have a relative from Canada in town. We're taking in a show and having some dinner. Why don't you take a break now? We'll be back by midnight, I promise!"

To me, Jerry was the epitome of radical cool. He had much to teach frenetic me. He lived calmly under surveillance, he took being blacklisted in stride. He even had sympathetic words for Senator McCarthy: "He's really a drunken Irishman. You can't take him seriously!" But I had not yet experienced the sort of deep scarring and betrayal that enables one to take so large and benign a view. I took McCarthy very seriously, and the Kennedy family, too. The Kennedys had been gung-ho for McCarthy, for his fervent anti-Communism, and had taken part in his sweaty world of sleazy political bombast. Like McCarthy, Joseph Kennedy Sr. was a rich patriarchal fascist, a Catholic, an anti-Semite and a first-class Red-baiter; he was a staunch McCarthy backer. And his son, Bobby Kennedy, served as special counsel to McCarthy.

During my time at the University of Toronto, I became a zealous opponent of all things Kennedy. My hero was Adlai Stevenson, my heroine Eleanor Roosevelt. Nonetheless, like many liberals, I loathed Richard Nixon more than I loathed the Père Kennedy. I was at an age when I looked for signs. I saw the shadow on Nixon's jaw as the shadow of reactionary evil. So, with ideals twisting in the wind, I was glad when

Joseph Kennedy Sr. struck a deal with the Mafia to secure the West Virginia and Chicago votes that ultimately guaranteed his son's presidency. With JFK in office, a sense of hope, of freshness, began to circulate. His brand of charm got to me, and I'd near-excused him for his malignant, conniving father and corrupt brother. Mind you, I hadn't lost all good sense and perspective. When JFK, with seeming backbone and skill, stared down Soviet Premier Nikita Khrushchev, and handled the 1962 Cuban Missile Crisis, I had stroked my *schnozz* – always a sign of either perplexity or pleasure – and wondered how he could complain about Cuban missiles ninety miles from American shores when America had missiles in Turkey, ninety miles from Russia's shores.

By this time, however, I had knots of my own to unravel. The CBC was undergoing a crisis – innovation will do that to a corporation. Namely, the upheaval was between *This Hour Has Seven Days* and senior management. President J. Alphonse Ouimet, confronted with an actual innovative success that entailed notoriety – a notoriety that had not only stirred up public sentiment but had also stirred the backbones of the catatonic backbenchers in the House of Commons – came up with a blunt, yet surgical solution – he fired the program's four most talented people: Patrick Watson, Laurier La Pierre, Roy Faibish, and myself.

All my well-wishers suddenly wished me goodbye: they were alright, Jack, but I was gone. I had to scramble and scrounge to live. Then, Dalton Camp, the *eminence argent* of the Progressive Conservative Party, hired me to churn out propaganda for Premiers Duff Roblin and Robert Stanfield. A reprieve! Then, a phone call came: I was offered a whopping recompense to serve on the campaign of one Milton Shapp who was running for governor of Pennsylvania.

Pennsylvania. How, I wondered for a fleeting moment, had my journey come to this?

No matter: I brought my burgeoning backroom smarts and succinct sense of the acerbic to American politics. Once I got my bearings, little pearls of dark invention began to roll out of my camera. I interviewed President Johnson and Vice-President Hubert Humphrey and both, under my instruction, said: "Cut the crap, vote Shapp." Things went swimmingly until the none-too-swift Shapp told a reporter that he, and he alone, had given JFK the idea to create the Peace Corps. The hostile Philadelphia press jumped all over Shapp: they beat him about the ears; they said he was too stupid to have ideas.

Their attacks stalled the campaign. I suggested that the only way out was to interview Senator Bobby Kennedy and have him tell the camera that the idea had been Shapp's. "It'll never happen," cried the Big Cigars and the wise guys who, tied up in their own knots, were committed to conventional wisdom. I flew to New York to talk to Bobby in his office.

I found him to be a fairly short fellow who suffered from wet palms.

On his desk, several yellow message slips were skewered on a spike. He was on the phone. "Sister Eloise, it's Senator Kennedy here. She set fire to her dormitory? I see. I'm terribly sorry. I'll talk to her at Christmas. In the meantime, would a cheque for $5,000 be of any help? Thank you, Sister Eloise."

His second call was equally intriguing. "Father Flaherty, it's Senator Kennedy here. He did what? Locked up a whole dormitory and wouldn't let the children out? I'm terribly sorry! Would a cheque for $5,000 towards the improvement of the school library be of any use?"

The third call was also fascinating: "Father Daniels, Senator Kennedy here. He led a panty raid on the neighbouring girls' college and some of the girls are still in shock? I see. Would a cheque for $3,000 help pay for psychiatric counselling?"

My hopes rose. Here, before me, was Senator Kennedy performing as Bobby the bountiful family man. We began to discuss my interview. Trying to finesse him, I asked if he, a rich man, didn't have something in common with Shapp, also a rich man: both were often envied and resented for their money. Bobby refused that idea, and, with a series of snorts, refused several more. I decided to lay my cards directly on the table (simple directness, I was learning, is close cousin to the acerbic): "Senator, Mr. Shapp gave your brother one million dollars in 1960. And here, in this moment, there is no more devoted Bobby-For-President man in the country than Milton Shapp. Mr. Shapp will give you two million dollars for your campaign, Senator Kennedy. Why spend your own money?"

Kennedy laughed heartily at my *chutzpah* and said: "Let's play this by ear."

And so we did: we played together; we sang together. Pretty soon, he made wonderful music on camera: "I remember President Kennedy calling me into the Oval Office to meet Milton Shapp. Mr. President said, 'Milton, here, has a wonderful idea for a Peace Corps.'"

Bobby Kennedy, with his little tea-for-two-and-two-for-tea *shtick*, put the Shapp campaign back on everybody's dance card. Shapp became governor for two terms. My reputation as a fixer soared; it went stratospheric.

"Somewhere there's music," insists that popular jazz standard. *"How high the moon?"*

Bobby became the one – the only – McCarthyite that I have ever liked.

I watched his California campaign on television, and the shocking news of his assassination. I also watched his funeral procession. As the cortege passed through America's heartland, rural people lined up along the railroad tracks and sung "Battle Hymn of the Republic." The outpouring of public sorrow devastated me in the privacy of my own mind. I, too, felt anguish at the loss of this man, this politician; I, who had been inclined to abhor. Not only had I liked Senator Kennedy, I'd cherished him. In particular, I'd cherished that moment of real music we had made together: he, a hardball-playing pro, had shown me more than simple consideration; he'd respected me as a pro in my own right.

—No;—I cannot stop a moment to give you the character of the people—their genius—their manners—their customs—their laws—their religion—their government—their manufactures—their commerce—their finances, with all the resources and hidden springs which sustain them: qualified as I may be, by spending three days and two nights amongst them, and during all that time making these things the entire subject of my enquiries and reflections—

Still—still I must away—the roads are paved—the posts are short—the days are long—'tis no more than noon—

— *STERNE*

DOWN IN MISSISSIPPI

It was five o'clock in the morning on the Sunday after Labour Day, 1969. The phone rang. It was my wild Irish colleague, Peter Reilly.

Reilly and I were the only reporters allowed to work for both the news and current affairs units on CBC's *Weekend*, a television program which boasted both Saturday and Sunday editions. Reilly was more than a colleague; he was a friend, and I never wanted to let Reilly down, never wanted to say no.

Reilly's voice was whisky hoarse. "I can't go to Mississippi. I want you to take my place. There's a flight to Washington at seven o'clock this morning; the connecting flight to Jackson is at ten." The voice suggested a weakness – a weakness in the knees that had sexual implications, but I heard also the wheeze of ill heath.

I'd be a liar if I said that I had been chomping at the bit to go to Mississippi. After all, ever since the first Freedom Bus Ride of '61, journalists and civil rights activists had been known to die involuntarily in the backwoods and swamps of the Deep South. But I was still young and frisky, still some-what guileless. In some respects, I was too dumb to know danger, malevolence, when it was staring me in the face. To an extent, my head was still back in the old movie images of the Ku Klux Klan and the deadly but doddering white trash of Old Miss.

"You've been in Mississippi, Peter, and you've been in Vietnam – what's the worst place?"

He laughed and said, "Mississippi by a mile. Everyone in Mississippi wants to kill you, even the liberals."

I assured Patsy that somehow I would manage to roam the land of men loopy enough to wear pointy white hoods and return – perhaps bent, but unscathed. She worried that my being Jewish would be an added danger, given the Klan's hatred of Jews. "Just be sure I get a full CBC funeral," I said, but she didn't like my mordant humour. She didn't laugh; she was upset.

I reflected on my wife's warning. I was going to Jackson as part of the media, and the media was the single most hated institution in Mississippi. Being Jewish put me in the same (body) bag as Andrew Goodman and Michael Schwerner, the young civil rights workers from New York City who, just five years prior, had been murdered by the down-home Klan.

Being Jewish also put me in the same (body) bag as Leo Frank, a northern Jew who had moved to Atlanta, Georgia, to manage a pencil factory and, five years later, found himself accused and convicted of slaying thirteen-year-old factory girl Mary Phagan. The prosecution's star witness had been Jim Conley, a black janitor who, under police pressure, revised his story numerous times before taking the stand to testify against Frank.

Not long after Frank's conviction, potentially exonerating evidence emerged and as a result, on June 21, 1915, Governor John H. Slaton commuted Frank's sentence – from execution to life imprisonment – with the expectation that Frank would eventually be cleared and released (in response to the commutation, a mob of two thousand descended upon the governor's home; the Georgia National Guard and local police staved off the attack). On August 16, however, a posse removed Frank from his cell and lynched him. I swallowed hard as I remembered Frank and his fate: I saw myself swinging from a gibbet down in Old Miss.

I landed in Jackson on Sunday afternoon. The airport was swarming with CBS, ABC and NBC trucks and technicians; the tarmac was a sea of television cables and remote equipment. Alas, I was the only member of the Hebrew persuasion in Jackson that day, or, to put it differently, I was the only Hebrew with a *schnozz* and frizzy head of hair. The other Hebrews looked like Mike Wallace and Morley Safer.

Moreover, I was the only Hebrew saddled with the world's worst film crew. My cameraman was known as the Flying Dutchman. He had the attention span of a newt. He shot cutaways that were only a second long – useless. And when he shot interviews, the centre of the frame was always in soft focus (if he'd shot the crucifixion, Christ the Master would have been a total blur, but at the corner of the frame you would see, crystal clear, a midget pickpocket working the crowd).

In 1969, the desegregation of public schools was a hotly contested issue in the South. Though various court rulings between 1954–1968 were in favour of integration, they were riddled with loopholes, which allowed schools to avoid implementation. In September, however, pressure was mounting (on October 29, a landmark Supreme Court decision would finally quash school segregation once and for all). The Klan responded in kind. They raised the spectre of miscegenation, and said that integration was a communist plot intended to weaken the South so that the Soviet Union could overcome the people and occupy the land. They took to the streets, parading openly in daylight in their white sheets, hoods off; whole virulent crowds waved Confederate flags and photos of old lynchings.

With my technicians in tow, I met with a liberal professor from the University of Southern Mississippi. He had a crew cut. His two little boys had crew cuts. I asked him what he was up to, intellectually, and he replied: "I am doing a phrenological study of the Negro skull. I'm trying to see what propensity for violence lies therein." I asked him to talk to me about this project on camera. He did, earnestly, dropping the names of his friends: C. Vann Woodward, the dean of Southern historians, and Thomas P. Abernethy, author of a multi-volume history of Mississippi.

I hoped my audience would understand and forgive the fact that erudition, erudition of any kind, can nurture idiocy.

Then, in the local paper, I read that the Klan had opened its own high school in attempts to resist the impending integration. The Klan school was going to teach their students the true ways of the Old South. I had a vision of a Mississippi chicken farmer in denim overalls teaching high-school children Euclidean geometry; I thought that a visit to the school might be enlightening, if not a hoot.

The Klan school was outside Hattiesburg. The place was patrolled by an ominous-looking security guard. There was something familiar about him. I had seen him before – but where? Then it hit me. He was the sheriff who had attempted to cover up the murders of Schwerner and Goodman, the sheriff who, of course, had been acquitted of all charges (Sheriff Rainey left office in 1968, shortly after his 1967 acquittal).

He looked murderous enough to me on that September afternoon in Old Mississippi.

And he was staring hard at me, a baleful, quizzical look.

I concluded that he had never seen such a Hebrew face.

I needed a tactic to get into the Klan school.

I walked up to him and said, "Sir, I know you don't trust me and I know why. You think I'm one of those nigger-loving commie Jew bastards from New York who have invaded Mississippi and are shoving the commie line down people's throats.

"I'm no commie, sir. I hate commies, especially Jewish ones. I'm a Canadian and we don't have niggers or commies back where I come from – and we've got very few Jews, thank God.

"Sir, I'd like your permission to film the Klan school."

He looked at me, at my nasal protuberance. He was leery. Never in his entire life had he heard a pitch like mine.

I was granted access to the school.

Inside, there were twelve students. Teaching them was a ham-handed farmer in blue denim overalls. On the walls were framed photographs of grass-skirted Zulus, Soviet tanks in Czechoslovakia, a Soviet firing squad... those dire consequences that were to follow hard on the heels of integration.

At the blackboard, the farmer, his lilting Mississippi drawl sounding so comforting, was trying to explain a grade ten algebra equation.

While I was filming, a white mob beat up a lone black stills photographer from the *New York Times* in the schoolyard. This was appalling, such beatings, they were like ugly boils bursting around the countryside. The best I can say is that over my few days in Mississippi I saw no lynchings, no burning crosses. But yes, bullying and beatings and baseless hatred. And I had looked into the Evil Eye, that old Calvinist eye of the justified sinner: I had heard, too, the seductive soft drawl of an ex-lawman who had been an accomplice to a murder. But I had also learned how to talk to power – not yield or give in to power but how to jokingly ingratiate myself to get what I needed to see and needed to hear, so that I could see and hear. And I had done this by being suave with the stiletto, astute but not arrogant, brazen but self-effacing, by making magic with my nose, my probative nose, the *schnozz*. I had shown, if only to myself, that I could read not only the bumps and lumps on my own head but actual situations – in this case, the situation in a small town in Mississippi.

I liked that.

I liked the idea of having become a reader of situations not as an *eilu* but a bona fide, if slightly jaded, observer – though admittedly, he of the false eyeglasses and false nose. As this Jaded Observer, as a working journalist – I was a strange apparition. Physically, I was now of Hitchcockian pro-portions, though my accomplishments, it would be fair even for my enemies to have said, were far less ambitious, far less spectacular than Alfred's. Still, like Hitchcock, I was in the film business in a loose sort of sense and like Hitchcock, I often tried to hide myself – like some kind of chicken-hearted Trotsky – in countless cross-referenced fables and anecdotes, monologues and mortifications of my own concoction. I had to admit, however, that there was a certain tension within me – a not entirely resolved tension – about my being not just the Jaded Observer but Larry Zolf, too. As Zolf, I was either blessed or cursed: the false eyeglasses and false nose worn by the Jaded Observer could come off at will, but my own *schnozz*, could not. Nevertheless, I was coming into my own, my own several selves, which meant, if only in my own eyes, that I was becoming who I was meant to be: my own man.

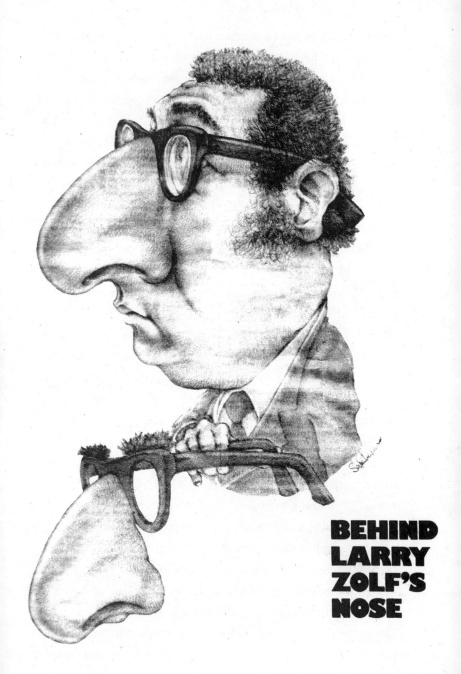

BEHIND LARRY ZOLF'S NOSE

LOSHN KOYDESH

On the morning of my mother's funeral, the North End streets were lined with Ukrainians, Poles and Germans waiting to see the cortege of gleaming black cars pass, funeral flags flying. Many had heard of her, and many had known her well; they all mourned her. Meyer and I, along with eight distinguished Winnipeggers, carried the coffin into the synagogue. The prime minister and the premier of Manitoba had both sent telegrams of condolence; these were read during the service. The *Hespet* was performed. *Kol Nidre* was sung: "*Kol nidre v'esare vaharame v'koname v'esare v'kinuse.*" *Kaddish* was recited. "*Yehay shmay raba mevarach l'aylah ulalmay almayah yitbarach.*" A Talmudic scholar, Rabbi Kravetz, gave the eulogy.

After the service, the few of her close friends still alive – old men and women wearing round black hats and shawls respectively – dispersed and went home. My brother and sisters went to their hotel rooms, to take a breather, to find a moment of stillness. I went to our family home for a last look around the rooms. As I sat in the kitchen, I decided I needed a cup of tea. I boiled the water. As I reached for the sugar bowl in the cupboard, I found a cue card on which was written, in very clear Yiddish: "I, Freda Rachel Pasternak Zholf, being of sound mind and body, leave all my earthly possessions equally to my four children, who are, in order of birth:

317

Reisele, Meyer, Yehudith, and Leibele." Signed, "Freda Rachel Pasternak Zholf, Jewish Wife and Mother."

I let the tea bag steep in my mother's old cup.

I found a second cue card with the same wording in the laundry chute, a third behind the furnace, a fourth, fifth and sixth in the three tiny bedrooms upstairs, a seventh in the china set and an eighth in the refrigerator.

I sat down and drank a cup of cold tea.

∞

The bank manager phoned and asked that we, the family, witness the opening of my mother's safety deposit box. We gathered. Inside the box were 17,000 one-dollar bills. The family lawyer noted that, with the sale of the house, the estate would approximate $40,000.

At the hotel where Judith, Meyer and I were staying, my brother said, "I don't need the $10,000 that's coming to me. Let Rose have my share."

Rose, still married to her jeweller, was the least prosperous of the four Zholf children. Her husband had never made more than a modest living.

Judith, who was alive and well on wealth that, unbeknownst to her, was precarious, chimed in: "Give Rose my $10,000, too."

I was infuriated. Mother had defended our innate dignity all our lives.

"Excuse me, Mr. and Mrs. Showoff, but I didn't see either of you giving Rose money while Mother was still alive to witness and enjoy such an act of family generosity. Mother worded her will very carefully – no doubt she got the language from watching *Perry Mason* – and she left eight copies.

318

Why? So that this very thing would not happen: the shaming of Rose, her oldest daughter and best friend. I'll take my $10,000, thank you, and spend it on my family. Rose has survived so far. She never needed your charity before. She does not need it now."

My mother's estate was divided as she wished. The memory of my mother, however, cannot be divided.

Freda Rachel Zholf died of a heart attack. Her death broke my heart: my world came crashing down on me, and the pain of loss led me to despair. Incessantly, I heard her voice. I hear her voice in mine now. And it is Freda Rachel Zholf who I see in my dreams. She comes to me on television, in books, and even on the street. These dreams remind me that I am no longer able to visit Winnipeg and take my mother, the most beautiful woman in the city, out on a date. There will be no more movie-house popcorn, no more visits to the Starland Theatre to see Paul Muni and John Garfield, Esther Williams, Larry Parks playing Al Jolson, Gregory Peck playing Captain Ahab ("Vat kind of a death is dat," my mother would say, "tied on his back to a fish?"); no more fiddlers on any roofs (she loved the *shtetl* in that film as if it were her own Zastavia – it was more real to her than the streets of Winnipeg, which she loved, but loved as if it were Winnipeg that was a dream); no more Bob Hope and Bing Crosby on the road; no Lana Turner ("This woman is a *shiksa* for sure"); no Lauren Bacall ("This woman, no question, is Jewish"); and no more singing along with Frankie Laine, our hearts going wherever the wild goose went while our hands mimicked the snapping of the *Mule Train* whip – Laine, a drover of all things, who my mother (and nearly all other Jews at the time) thought was Jewish, though he was Italian.

My mother's love for me was extraordinary.

I was her baby.

As a baby, I had not been able to stop eating and my mother had been unable to stop feeding me. So, tempered by her milk, I had grown and lengthened, grown and lengthened (she was six feet tall – three inches taller than my father – a dusky, fine-boned woman, and though we'd had no money, she made sure that I (like my siblings) had everything I wanted and needed. She'd wanted me plump, she'd wanted me to be a good eater, but she knew that she was not a good cook. And so one of the bizarre things she used to do was read me stories of Nazis chasing skinny little boys and sending them to concentration camps. I'd eaten and eaten but these tales gave me nightmares, so eventually she stopped reading them to me.

For the entirety of her life, however, she was a woman famous for her pessimism and her caution. She was always on the lookout for disaster, for the Evil Eye, and she believed until the last that Nazis were just around the corner (and if not our corner, then the next corner). "We are blessed," she would say, "but they are here. Things will get worse. There is no end to Nazis, you will see."

And though she was an Orthodox believer, she was never didactic; she never told me that I had to believe what she believed. I have always loved her for letting me grow up, not as a *wunderkind*, but as a real child. She was the mother who wiped my tears when Bambi was shot, the mother who said to me, "That was done by a white man, my son. Never trust a white man." She was the mother who warned me about snakes and Sabu, the jungles of India, as well as escalators, communists, socialists, women who favoured free love, Mounties (she feared deportation until the day she died), pool-rooms, *gonnifs*, Wonder Bread, glad-handers, overzealous and judgemental Jews, hot baths (I will never forget my father's attempts to abort me, and my mother's refusal), and all hunters, white or black, of wild animals – save for the *shochet*, and of course, the *rebbe* who pronounced the innards of animals kosher or not (whenever she saw me, my mother wanted that I should eat well and eat right).

During my visits back home, my mother and I would go for slow walks down Main Street, dropping in at Oscar's Deli-catessen for pastrami sandwiches and knishes, before moving on to People's Book Store. We'd talk about Sholem Aleichem, Isaac Loeb Peretz, Abraham Reisen (her favourite poet), and of course, my father ("He was a wonderful man, the only man in my life, but he did take *choisek machen*" – a satirical tone – "a bit too much. Never be a satirist, my son, it's not a lasting pro-fession." We also reminisced about our good times at the movies. One incident in particular stands out. My mother and I were watching Hitchcock's *The 39 Steps*. There is a sequence in the film, wherein a memory expert called Mr. Memory is answering questions from an audience. A British gentleman gets up and asks Mr. Memory a real tough one: "What's the capital of the province of Manitoba in the Dominion of Canada?" Mr. Memory answers instantly "Winnipeg." Then, the hero of the movie, played by Robert Donat, yells out: "What are the thirty-nine Steps?" Mr. Memory states that it is a network of spies engaged in a secret plot, but before he's able to divulge the details, he is shot to death. "And so why did they kill Mr. Memory?" my mother asked, *tsk*ing away. "Did they kill him just for mentioning Winnipeg?" We also talked and laughed about my madcap television encounters, especially if the *schnozz* had come under public attack – attack from Jews. She would reassure me, calling out (loud enough for everyone standing on the sidewalk to hear) in my defence (perhaps because she had begun life with me defending against my father's wrath, his prescription for abortion): I had in no way turned against my own people; I had certainly not turned against them by marrying a gentile (to whom she had shown only respect): and (here she always got a little angry, a little riled) I had in no way become an apologist for anti-Semites, nor was I (her proboscis-proud son) a self-hating Jew.

"*Nein, nein, nein.*" And more *nein.*

I loved these talks, my mother's Yiddish rich in a vernacular – the *loshn koydesh,* the holy tongue that, I liked to think wryly, no Hebrew-speaking Israeli would ever know. No, through Mama, I had managed to keep alive, if only in myself, an old authenticity, an old music, even while I stepped out of her ghetto to seek in somnolent environs my own singularity. I had tried to speak in my voice with her voice, which I now heard: "*Genug schoen.*"

Yes. Enough already.

I hold her in memory pure and white.

She had formed him of the best and kindliest clay—had tempered it with her own milk, and breathed into it the sweetest spirit—she had made him generous, and humane—

Accordingly *　　*　　*　　*　　*　　*　　*
*　　*　　*　　*　　*　　*　　*　　*　　*
*　　*　　*　　*　　*　　*　　*　　*　　*

— STERNE

GENUG

During the 1970 October Crisis, I, Larry Zolf, the Jaded Observer, was CBC *Weekend*'s man on Parliament Hill (the Jaded Observer: a compulsively committed member of the cult of political personality who, though compulsively indecisive, had a firm liking for politicians as a breed and didn't care a hoot about ideological consistency). Often, during those troubled days, Pierre Trudeau would stop me in the halls of parliament and ask how I thought the crisis had been sparked by the FLQ's kidnapping of two government officials was moving along. Without fail, I would furrow my brow, and urge Prime Minister Trudeau to build more detention camps and prison camps, and give the police more power to make more.

Trudeau would smile ruefully and say: "Zolf, are we getting too soft?"

I would say, "Yessir," and mention two despicable Press Gallery members whom he might personally round up for the sake of the country.

"But I always liked those guys," Trudeau would say with a twinkle in his eye. He, too, was kidding.

During the early days of the crisis, and as unlikely as it may seem, the head honchos of the Liberal Party held a policy convention and Trudeau addressed them in an open session, fielding questions from his Liberal delegates – tough questions that he had previously refused to take from the Press Gallery.

Afterwards, I, as a dutiful member of the fifth estate, asked him for an interview, Trudeau, however, came up with a dazzling post-session prohibition: "You're to confine your questions to the Party and its policies."

"Sure," I said, surprising Trudeau with my affability, my easy acceptance of his castrating diktat.

We sat down, not *schnozz* to nose, but certainly knee to knee. The interview was to be a full half-hour. To Trudeau, my first question was: "If I were a delegate to the Liberal Party and I had a chance to ask you a question from the floor as delegates did here today, I would, if that were the situation, ask you this question –" I then fired off a plain, simple, direct War Measures question, about battle-ready, fully armed soldiers strolling about the streets of the capital.

Trudeau held me with his best flinty eye and answered in his best oblique manner. Then he narrowed his eyes. He wanted to see how far I would dare to go. (I should explain that ever since our shared Hot Seat cross-examination of René Lévesque in the early sixties, we had – to a degree – developed a bond: we had toured Montreal in his sports car, eaten at fancy restaurants. I hadn't liked all the beautiful people who had flocked to him in 1968 and I'd told him so. He'd laughed and said: "Larry, what's the alternative?")

I repeated my circumloquacious preamble to the next War Measures question, a question about the government's suspension of individual civil liberties all across the country.

Trudeau was furious. He knew that he had been had – by me, for God's sake. He tapped me on the shoulder with a hint of menace. "You can drop the preamble. Just ask your question."

"Are you sure, Prime Minister? I don't mind doing the preamble at all."

"But I do," said Trudeau tartly. "The preamble is so long it makes me forget how to answer the question."

I dropped the preamble and he dropped the menace.

The interview went so well that the *Toronto Star* declared it a success, saying the Jaded Observer had been "deft but refreshingly undeferential."

I liked that.

To be deft, to be undeferential!

◎◎

In 1973, before my book *Dance of the Dialectic* came out, *Saturday Night* devoted an issue to what it described as: "The Big Circus on the Rideau, a stupendous twenty-page section composed of brilliant jokes, deep insights, witty anecdotes, jaded observances, deft ripostes, profound history lessons, perfervid puns and lovable reminiscing. Starring Pierre Trudeau as Philosopher King by Larry Zolf."

In time, I received a note from the Philosopher King:

Dear Larry,

Thanks for the Saturday Night article which I read with delight and I look forward to receiving a copy of your upcoming book in which I will read at least the lines about me.

I will do my best to be at the launching on October 2... If your launching lasts late enough I will make it; otherwise lunch the next day would be fine.

It will be nice to see you again.

Sincerely,

Pierre Elliott Trudeau

Think of it. As I thought of it.

Leibele Zholf (a.k.a. Unwanted Child) had become not only Larry Zolf, Jaded Observer, but pen pal to and luncheon date for a prime minister.

Huzzah and a hip hip hooray!

☙❧

At this point, to make myself clearer, I have to draw an ideational distinction.

I have to quote myself about myself from my book, *Dance of the Dialectic*.

In my personna as the Jaded Observer, I had written (and here I paraphrase) that as I watched the daily manoeuvrings, posturings, pratfalls and tours de force of the fragile 29th Parliament, my mind frequently drifted back – as it so often does – to childhood days in Winnipeg. Sometime in the early forties, while bouncing on my father's knee, I heard one Leibel Basman, the Bolshevik philosopher-king of our neighbourhood, inform my father (Mr. Basman's best friend as well as his bitterest political opponent) that one Karl Marx and one G.W.F. Hegel were just one more carnival act I could look forward to seeing at the Conklin Brothers or the Royal American Shows that visited Winnipeg each summer.

Years later, however, while attending Winnipeg's United College, I learned the true meaning of Mr. Basman's one-liner. Mr. Hegel believed that ideas ultimately shaped the social, economic and political condition of man, while Mr. Marx, standing Hegel on his head, believed that social, economic and political realities shaped the ideas of man.

There it was, the dance of the dialectic: Hegel had stood Marx on his head, and Marx had stood Hegel on his head.

They had been two head cases.

And for me, they brought to mind the Right Honourable Pierre Elliott Trudeau.

"In the late sixties," the Jaded Observer had written, "it was a well-known fact that Mr. Trudeau was a devout practitioner of yoga. As part of that system's demanding regimen, he had frequently stood upright on his head. The process, I'm told, relaxes the limbs and torso and brings the blood rushing to the brain. As a consequence, one achieves tranquility, a sense of inner purpose and a clue to the meaning of life."

Trudeau, who had proven to be a man of amiable manner and casual attire but stern intellectual disciplines, had indeed tried – as prime minister – to impose meaning on our political life. In so doing, he had disdained the hapless opposition parties as if they were floundering in Plato's Cave. He had ignored his backbenchers as if they were the Men of Brass – and he had operated out of the East Block of Parliament Hill as if it were the Lyceum Theatre. Within those walls, Thesis had clashed with the Antithesis – as a breathless nation had watched and waited for a final solution.

As the Jaded Observer, however, no matter my admiration for the clarity of Trudeau's reasoned arguments, his backbone as he sought to impose several final solutions on his fractious fellow citizens, I was neither Hegelian nor Marxist. True, I had grown up with those two head cases, but all final solutions were anathema to me. In my bones, I had become, plain and simple, a humble historical materialist. No matter the idea that was working from the top down or the idea that was working from the bottom up, all those head cases, those *a priori* guys – in so far as I could make out – were like long-tailed cats at a rocking chair convention, and they got it in the end every time, *a posteriori*.

The Jaded Observer, who had heard the suicidal clarion call from professors, producers, politicians and just plain poor folk, had learned how to keep his tail between his legs.

> But where am I going? these reflections crowd in upon
> me ten pages at least too soon, and take up that time,
> which I ought to bestow upon a certain conclusive fact.
> — *STERNE*

That conclusive fact is rooted in time, well before Trudeau wrote me that first letter. It is rooted in that time when I had begun to discover a possible accommodation with the world to which, to quote old Plato, my "nature was best adapted."

It all began with a Parliamentary Press Gallery Dinner, an annual event at which press and politicians, without shame, prepared to be *schmucks* and comedically roast each other.

From the first day of his tenure in power, Trudeau had let it be known that he despised the event, because he despised the press. Those times he had attended, he'd done so only under duress. Often, despite advice from his handlers, he had cancelled at the last minute.

The Gallery, irascible and thin-skinned, felt cheated. All year – almost every day – during his early tenure, Trudeau had insulted them, and that was because he took most of them for what they were: jockstrap journalists who had made their careers by finding bail-jumping labour leaders or bed-hopping courtesans, or by proving that the Mounties were terrorizing old cancer-ridden commies, journalists who thought Lord Acton was the first mayor of a small Ontario town.

The Gallery – my fellow scribblers – looked forward to laughing boisterously at any and all jokes that might belittle Trudeau. At past dinners, those that I had attended from 1968–1972, everyone agreed that the Opposition Leader, Robert Stanfield, had been funny and put Trudeau in his place. Trudeau, however, had not been funny and had put no one in place.

Of course, Trudeau had an advantage. His place was Prime Minister and he acted as if he had been born into office. But then came the election debacle of 1972. Trudeau had been skinned in English Canada by the Tories. David Lewis, the NDP ideologue, not only held the balance of power but held Trudeau the Philosopher King in contempt.

Scorn and the advantages to be gained by wit were in the air. Stanfield, upon hearing how a Trudeau-Lewis axis was going to operate, asked the House of Commons: "Who, in this dynamic duo, is the monkey, and who is the organ grinder?" Peals of laughter from Parliament's bell towers caused Trudeau – the organ grinder – a certain chagrin.

Trudeaucrats were not used to anyone laughing at their man.

They were not used to scorn.

They were not used to compromising power.

They didn't really know how to compromise power. Something had to be done; gears needed to be shifted.

Trudeau's handlers told the Press Gallery that he would gladly attend the Galley Dinner of 1973.

Pierre O'Neill, Trudeau's press secretary, called me into his office and said that Trudeau wanted me to write him a deft, satiric, self-deprecatory speech. There was to be, for this tone-changing speech, a censory committee of only three: O'Neill, Trudeau and me. Before I sat down to write the speech, I spoke with Trudeau; he confessed that the organ grinder line had hurt, not to the quick, but wincingly close.

I told him that the line could be turned to his favour.

At the Gallery Dinner, Trudeau – speech in hand – began by telling the press that because he was now a poor, starving minority prime minister, he could no longer hold press conferences; his new duties were too time-consuming.

Gallery members hissed and booed: *The nerve of that loser to demand less time with the press.*

Then Trudeau said: "After all, be reasonable, ladies and gentlemen. It's not easy being an organ grinder."

The line got a reluctant laugh.

"I have to take organ-grinder lessons five days a week."

That got an open but not quite fulsome laugh.

Trudeau continued: "It's not easy being an organ grinder. Have you people in the Gallery ever tried to feed a banana to a monkey while a hungry Stanfield is waiting in the wings?"

A huge laugh ensued. Stanfield, famous for eating bananas, had taken a pratfall on his own peel.

Trudeau, head down, continued to read his speech, but tonelessly and without timing. Unaccustomed to laughter, he was unnerved. He read rapidly, leaving no room for the laughs, so that this joke and that joke, this laugh and that laugh, collided midair. And on, and on. Collisions. Crashes. Confusion.

("O Dialectic! O Dialectic! Have you no sense of shame?"
"No, *schmuck* – and don't you ever forget it!")
— *Dance of the Dialectic*

I was at a table with Allan Gotlieb, mandarin of mandarins. My *pièce de résistance* lay at Trudeau's inept feet. His feet got bigger, they had to, as jokes lay heaped about his toe-caps. I told Gotlieb I wanted Trudeau's throat. Gotlieb tried to console me. I drank everything in sight and then headed to the National Press Club for more booze. There, I was surprised to hear approving Gallery members say that Trudeau had been funny.

Trudeau had been funny!

I saw Trudeau about five days later in the centre block of Parliament Hill.

Not his usual diffident self, he asked how he'd done at the dinner.

The horror show came back to me. "Prime Minister, do you want the truth?"

"Always, Larry, always."

"Well then, here it is. You, sir, couldn't deliver a joke in a Brink's armoured truck. You, sir, have absolutely no sense of timing." I turned on my heel.

Months passed. Then at a party in Rockcliffe, Trudeau way-laid me. "The last time we met you said that I had no sense of timing. What did you mean?"

"Prime Minister, a sense of timing means you wait for the laughs to come from a joke before going into another joke."

Trudeau looked at me quizzically. "How long do I wait for the laugh?"

"Three minutes," I said.

"That's an awfully long time," said Trudeau.

I told him that after three minutes the tension in the room would be enormous.

"Then what happens?" Trudeau asked.

"Then, Prime Minister, you say: 'And now, for my next joke...' The place will go wild; that'll be your biggest laugh of all."

Trudeau started waiting for laughs. He also started learning the difference between wit and humour, wit being directed at someone else's expense, humour at your own (the latter draws double the laughs – those of your own and those of your audience – which, in the long run, may double your votes). This new, eager-to-learn Trudeau was, wonder of wonders, getting it right, albeit awkwardly.

In 1974, in his preamble to the upcoming election, Robert Stanfield openly embraced, as policy, the idea of wage and price controls, saying that as prime minister, he intended to put such controls in place. This left the Tory caucus badly divided. Across the country, right-wing, pro-natural market force Tories balked at Stanfield's support for such a socialist idea. Pro-business Tories in the caucus were also about to balk.

I thought hard and came up with my own little sally: "Price and wage controls are the issue; finding Tories to support it, that is the problem."

Trudeau, suddenly sounding like the Sundance Kid, fired off that line up and down the campaign trail, to much laughter.

I was pleased. For him. For me. And especially for those moments of laughter.

Small, forgettable moments for some; in fact, forgettable for most.

But illuminating, unforgettable moments for me.

I, who had begun as Leibele Z(h)olf from nowhere, had at last become – in these many and marvellous moments of kinship between jokester and politician, this conspiracy between laughter and power – not only my own man, but a man openly adapted to his own nature, adapted to who I believed I was going to be for the rest of my life.

I felt buoyant, boastful.

I took off my false eyeglasses and false nose, and stroked my great proboscis with pleasure and satisfaction – on behalf of my mother, my father, Paul Muni and John Garfield, those stars of my father's minor epic, and in particular, on behalf of the Jaded Observer, the free-standing star (at least in my own mind) of my own minor epic that was now playing: *The Story of Larry Zolf.*

"*Genug iz genug!*" I heard my mother caution me.

Enough is enough!

I was ecstatic to hear from my beloved mother, but I was now on what I hoped would be a lifelong roll:

"*Genug iz genug ist nicht genug!*"

Enough is enough but not enough!

I would like to thank my intrepid,
devoted copy editors and proof readers,
Leigh Nash and Nina Callaghan,
and especially, Lisa Foad.

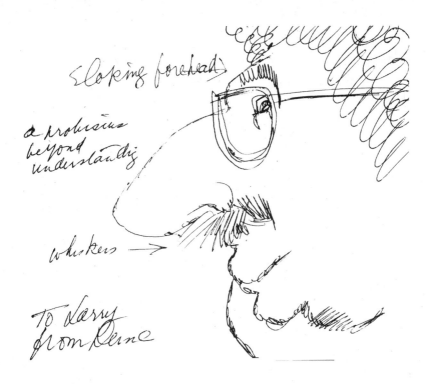

Sloping forehead

a profusion beyond understanding

whiskers →

To Larry from Derne

Original Drawings by: